ACKNOWLEDGEMENTS

A study of this kind is not possible without the assistance of many people. This is especially true in Japan, where no national freedom of information law exists, libraries and research centres are not known to be 'user-friendly', and the public's 'right to know' is not highly regarded by a bureaucracy that often treats even the most mundane research materials as secret. This is all very discouraging for aspiring scholars and when the subject is as sensitive as Japan's relationship with South Africa, researchers face even more insurmountable hurdles. For example, in 1987 materials on South Africa were suddenly removed from the JETRO (Japan External Trade Organisation) library for 'reorganisation' of an indefinite duration, and the Ministry of Finance refused even to reveal the exact amount of gold imported for minting gold coins to commemorate the sixtieth year of Emperor Hirohito's reign in 1986. A curtain of silence surrounds Japan's foreign policy decision-making that few citizens or scholars can penetrate.

Under such conditions, a book like this could never have materialised without the assistance and encouragement of many people. I owe a great debt of gratitude to Masudo Kinya, formerly of Keidanren (Federation of Economic Organisations), who agreed to be interviewed and provided much valuable information on the workings of that organisation as well as helping to arrange access for me to the Keidanren Library, which is not generally open to the public.

I must also thank the past and present members of the Japan Anti-Apartheid Committee (JAAC) who opened their files to me and untiringly responded to my inquiries and requests for additional data. Saso Hiroo, Suseki Tomoaki, Kambayashi Yoji, Ushijima Yasuo and Kusuhara Akira were especially helpful and without their assistance, Chapter 6 would certainly not have been possible. Tsuyama Naoko of the Japan International Volunteer Centre, Furukawa Tetsushi and Richard Bradshaw of Ohio University also kindly assisted in the search for information. Along with Yamanaka Kimiko, Richard

Bradshaw also assisted in the translation of some of the historical information in Chapter 2 and provided much valuable help and support.

Hayashi Koji of the Institute for Developing Economies, Tokyo, also offered encouragement and an introduction to my publisher. Yamada Hideo of Yachiyo University, Kanno Ryoko of Daito Bunka University, Takayama Iwao of Saitama University and Ago Shinichi of Kyushu University were also helpful.

I am grateful for the support of my colleagues Okakura Takashi, G.C. Mwangi, Yoshikuni Tsuneo, Tominaga Chizuko, Katsumata Makoto, Sadotomo Tetsu, Shitaba Tomoe, Watanabe Kozo (who first encouraged me to pursue a study of the relationship between Japan and Africa over a decade ago) and Peter Mayer of the University of Adelaide, who offered his support and kindly provided comments on the text of the manuscript.

I would also like to thank those teachers who inspired me early in my career, including Tanaka Naokichi, Miyake Tatsuru, Toda Misato, M.S. Rim of Denmark and Ola Oni and Bade Onimode of the University of Ibadan, Nigeria.

A 1982 dissertation grant from Tokai University allowed me to gather information firsthand in South Africa and Zimbabwe and I must also express my gratitude to Akiko Williamson of the University of Adelaide Library.

I would like to thank Michael Dwyer and Christopher Hurst of C. Hurst & Co. for their faith that a manuscript would indeed one day be forthcoming, despite numerous delays. Finally, I would like to thank my wife Kathy for her help with the translation of the text and my daughter Julie for her patience.

Although I am indebted to many people, it goes without saying that all responsibility for material translated from the original Japanese is entirely mine unless otherwise specified. Some data has been translated by the JAAC and a few Japanese publications are issued in English.

I hope this study of the relationship between Japan and Africa will also serve as a reflection of Japan's overall foreign policy.

Minami Aiki   JUN MORIKAWA
January 1996

CONTENTS

vii

PHOTOGRAPHS

FIGURES

JAPANESE TERMS AND ABBREVIATIONS

APIC	Association for the Promotion of International Co-operation
CCA	See KCCA
JAAC	Japan Anti-Apartheid Committee
JETRO	Japan External Trade Organisation
JICA	Japan International Co-operation Agency
JOCV	Japan Overseas Co-operation Volunteers
JODC	Japan Overseas Development Corporation
JSAPFL	Japan–South Africa Parliamentarians Friendship League
JSP	Japan Socialist Party (now officially called Democratic Socialist Party of Japan)
kanryo	bureaucracy
kanzai ittai shugi	government and business working in unison
KCCA	Keidaren Committee on Co-operation with Africa
Keidanren	Japan Federation of Economic Organisations
LDP	Liberal Democratic Party
minkan keizai	private business diplomacy
MITI	Ministry of International Trade & Industry
ODA	Official Development Assistance
PARC	Policy Affairs Research Council
SAA	Sasakawa Africa Association
SATA	Southern Africa Traders Association
senden gaiko	PR diplomacy
TICAD	Tokyo International Conference on African Development
zaikai	business world

1

INTRODUCTION

Since the early 1980s, Japan has emerged as an important foreign player in Africa's affairs, exerting influence on the states and peoples of the continent. Japan's growing interest in Africa was reflected in a speech by Matsuura Koichiro, Director General of the Economic Co-operation Bureau of the Japanese Ministry of Foreign Affairs, at London's Royal Institute of International Affairs in July 1989:

> Africa is remote from Japan. We have had few historical and cultural ties with Africa. Yet we are being urged to give more attention to that continent and we have been responsive. Since 1977, Japan has increased assistance to Sub-Saharan countries ten times over. Japan was a top bilateral donor in four African countries in 1987: Kenya, Zambia, Malawi and Nigeria. Right now, over 600 young Japanese volunteers, or 35 per cent of the total, are engaged in activities of technical assistance in ten African countries. This aid is not only bilateral. Many people may not know it, but Japan is the number two contributor to the African Development Bank from outside the region and the number one contributor to the African Development Fund.[1]

The Director General might also have noted that Japan, which now has the second largest GNP (gross national product) in the world, is among the top five trading partners of twentyfive African nations[2] and was the largest trading partner of the Pretoria regime in South Africa in 1986.

Japan's presence in Africa is larger and more significant than generally believed and is certain to grow in importance. As the 1989 Japanese *Diplomatic Blue Book* notes:

---

[1] Matsuura Koichiro, *Enjo Gaiko No Saizensen de Kangaeta Koto*, APIC, Tokyo: 1990, pp. 373N4.

[2] See Figure 1.2

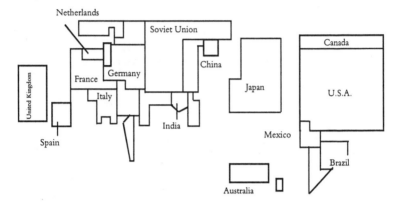

Fig.1.1 SCHEMATIC MAP OF G.N.P. SHARES WORLDWIDE, 1987

15 countries ranking high in GNP (unit: $1 billion)

1.	USA	4,486	9.	China	320
2.	Soviet Union	2,055	10.	Brazil	315
3.	Japan	1,926	11.	India	241
4.	Germany (Fed.Rep.)	880	12.	Spain	233
5.	France	715	13.	Australia	176
6.	Italy	597	14.	Netherlands	173
7.	United Kingdom	593	15.	Mexico	149
8.	Canada	390			

Source: Reprinted from *The Diplomatic Blue Book 1989 — Japan's Diplomatic Activities*, Ministry of Foreign Affairs, Tokyo, 1989, p. 2. (The original source was the World Bank Atlas; 1989 was the last year such a GNP map was included in the annual Diplomatic Blue Book.)

Japan is also considering playing a more active role in the solution of the southern African and other political problems. Japan has been striving to promote mutual understanding with African nations through personnel and cultural exchange in order to establish firmer economic and political relations between Japan and Africa.[3]

[3] Ministry of Foreign Affairs, *Diplomatic Blue Book 1989 — Japan's Diplomatic Activities*, Tokyo, 1989, p. 235.

More concrete involvement in African international relations is conducive to Japan's desire to become politically more powerful and influential on the world stage. Its decision in April 1993 to permit the despatch of a Self-Defence Forces unit to take part in UN peacekeeping operations in Mozambique and to host the Africa Development Conference in Tokyo in the autumn of 1993 are concrete examples of this intent.

The post Cold War and post-apartheid era have made African economic development problems and democratisation even more important issues, and African expectations of Japan (now the largest aid donor among all the countries of the world) have increased dramatically since the disintegration of the Soviet Union and the emergence of the 'aid fatigue' phenomenon in the United States and Western Europe. Japan has expanded its aid to Sub-Saharan African countries dramatically since the latter half of the 1970s.

Fig. 1.2. JAPAN'S RANKING AS A TRADING PARTNER WITH AFRICAN COUNTRIES (1987)

As an Export partner	*As an Import partner*
1. South Africa, Zambia, Mauritania	1. - - - - -
2. - - -	2. Kenya, Tanzania, Rwanda, South Africa
3. Ethiopia, Madagascar	3. Cameroon, Gabon, Benin, Seychelles, Mauritius (1988)
4. Ghana, Gabon, Tanzania	4. Ghana, Congo, Malawi, São Tomé & Principe, Nigeria, Niger, Burkina Faso
5. Zimbabwe, Malawi	5. Uganda, Ivory Coast, Liberia, Sierra Leone (1986-7)

Compiled by the author from data included in *Afurika Binran-Sahara Inan no Kuniguni*, ed. Ministry of Foreign Affairs Middle Eastern and African Affairs Bureau, Tokyo: 1990.

From the point of view of developing mutually beneficial relations between Japan and African countries, serious political and intellectual issues still exist. Despite the fact that the shadow of Japan's influence over Africa has spread rapidly, the implications of this influence have not been greeted with much interest or given much attention in Japan itself. Unfortunately, even many leading students of African international relations and Japanese studies regard Japan as an external actor of secondary importance in Africa and do not give much value or sense of urgency to the subject. This attitude has become deeply entrenched both within and outside of Japan. As a result, a large gap exists between perceptions and reality and little critical, analytical study of Japan's modern African diplomacy has been undertaken to date.[4]

This book is an attempt partly to fill this intellectual vacuum. It is not designed to be a chronological account of relations between the African continent and Japan in the post-war era but to offer an analytical framework for the further study of Japan-Africa relations. This framework may help to explain why Japan has acted (or failed to act) as it has in Africa, and to reveal the perceptions of Africa that have guided the behaviour of Japanese policy-makers. It is the present author's belief that this will be useful in understanding Japan's actions in other Third World countries as well.

The desire to elucidate the nature of Japan's policy in Africa does not derive solely from an academic motivation. It comes also from the hope of making a small contribution to the eventual realisation of more democratic control over Japan's African diplomacy. The current diplomacy has considerable

---

[4] Some analytical studies of particular areas (for example Southern Africa) and specific issues (trade, aid) related to Japan's policy in Africa did begin to appear in the latter half of the 1970s. See for example: Kitazawa Yoko, *From Tokyo to Johannesburg — A Study of Japan's Growing Economic Links with the Republic of South Africa*, New York: Interfaith Center for Corporate Responsibility, 1975; Hayashi Koji, 'A Halfhearted Anti-Apartheid Policy', *Japan Quarterly*, July-September 1989, XXXVI, 3, pp. 267; Richard J. Payne, 'Japan's South Africa Policy: Political Rhetoric and Economic Realities', *Journal of the Royal African Society, African Affairs*, 86, 343, April 1987, pp. 167.

Concerning Japan's trade and commerce policy, see Kitagawa Katsuhiko, 'Nihon Minami Afurika Kankei Shi' in Kawabata Masahisa and Ken Sasaki (eds), *Nanbu Afurika: Post Aparutoheito to Nihon*, Tokyo: Keiso Shobo 1992, pp. 182-204; Joanna Moss and John Ravenhill, *Emerging Japanese Economic Influence in Africa — Implications for the United States*, Berkeley: Institute of International Studies, 1985; Chiyoura Masamichi, 'Nihon Kigyo no Tai Afurika Toshi Katsudo', *Dokkyo Daigaku Keizai Gaku Kenkyu*, October 1979, pp. 83-138. For Japan's aid policy, see Khalil T. Darwish, 'Keizai Enjo to Nihon no Afurika Seisaku', *Kokusai Mondai*, May 1987.

influence, both positive and negative, on the peoples of Japan and Africa. More public interest in the subject would allow the public to perform a watch-dog function which could lead one day to the development of more reciprocal relations between Japan and African countries.

This framework will attempt to answer such essential questions as why the Japanese government continued for so long, and in certain case still continues, to extend a great deal of economic aid to the authoritarian regimes in Kenya, Zaire and Malawi, and why despite repeated requests for the introduction of economic sanctions, Japan maintained massive trade and commercial relations with the Pretoria government, which it continued to expand. Providing such an analytical framework may not merely have significance for the African states influenced by Japan's policy in Africa but also have a boomerang effect in impressing the importance of this relationship upon the Japanese people themselves.

Chapter 2 reveals the basic framework of Japan's African diplomacy by examining the priorities, guiding principles, policy goals and objectives that guide it and the methods used to achieve these goals. Chapter 3 looks at the post-Second World War historical development of Japan's African diplomacy, as well as the two separate sub-policies to which it gave birth: the White Africa and Black Africa policies.

Chapter 4 examines the main actors involved in Japan's African diplomacy: the Liberal Democratic Party (LDP), which held the reins of power continuously in Japan for almost forty years, the Ministry of Foreign Affairs and other elements of the bureaucracy and organised business known in Japan as 'zaikai'. Chapter 5 looks at the role played by big business in the implementation and execution of Japan's African diplomacy and examines several case-studies which reveal the full breadth of the co-operation and participation that exists between the Japanese government and big business in the areas of aid, personal exchanges, and public relations. Chapter 6 reexamines the connections between racist attitudes in Japanese society and Japan's African diplomacy, while the final chapter deals with the future prospects of Japan's relations with Africa.

The focus of the study is on Sub-Saharan Africa and not the African continent as a whole. In the perceptions of Japan's

Ministry of Foreign Affairs, the six countries of North Africa — Egypt, Sudan, Tunisia, Libya, Morocco and Algeria — are members of the Islamic world and are dealt with as part of Japan's Middle Eastern diplomacy.

Yet when speaking of the Sub-Saharan region of Africa, it is important to note that in the opinion of Japanese government officials it does not equal Black Africa. It is their general belief that the region is composed of two separate areas — Black Africa and White Africa — and these areas are dealt with accordingly.

To understand the government's particular view of Africa, it is enlightening to look at a statement made by the late Kono Fumihiko, the first chairman of the Japan Federation of Economic Organisations (Keidanren) Committee on Co-operation with Africa (CCA) and the head of an African economic mission sent to the continent in 1970:

> According to the Foreign Ministry, the area from the Sudan north is Islamic Africa and is classified as part of the Middle East. What we call Africa — Black Africa — includes all countries south of Sudan except the Republic of South Africa, Angola, Mozambique and other not yet independent areas.[5]

Therefore, when this book refers to Japan's Africa diplomacy, it refers in general to Sub-Saharan Africa. Since 1975 the victories of the African national liberation movements have caused a rapid shrinking of the area included in Japan's White Africa policy. In this study, White Africa refers to South Africa and the areas where it still maintains a dominant role and position and represents Japan's policy towards the Pretoria government. The Black Africa policy includes all other Sub-Saharan countries.

The time-frame emphasised here is the post-war period from 1945 to 1993, and especially the period from the establishment of the Foreign Ministry's Africa Division in 1961 till the beginning of the legal dismantling of apartheid in 1992. Over the course of those three decades, Japan's Africa diplomacy was structurally characterised by a policy of dual

[5] African Economic Mission (ed.), *Hirake Yuku Burakku Afurika*, Tokyo: 1970, p. 95 (not for public sale)

diplomacy that attempted to be both pro-White Africa and pro-Black Africa at the same time. In those three decades, dual diplomacy was formulated and established, then wavered, and finally disintegrated. Based as it was on the premise that White Africa was a self-contained political unit, dual diplomacy inevitably had to disintegrate as White Africa itself disappears.

What then will be the course of Japan's new diplomacy towards Africa? It is too early to make accurate predictions or to offer an objective assessement and evalution. Yet in order to provide alternative policy proposals and set a new course for the future, it is both necessary and beneficial to review Japan's past behaviour towards Africa.

2

JAPAN'S AFRICAN DIPLOMACY:
THE BASIC FRAMEWORK

What is Japan's Africa policy?
The government documents which explicitly state Japan's policy towards Sub-Saharan Africa are unfortunately not available to the general public. An alternative approach to determining the nature of this policy is to attempt to reveal the basic framework of Japan's policy towards Sub-Saharan Africa through an examination of the structural characteristics of Japan's post-war diplomacy generally.

Four major foreign policy tenets have evolved against the background of the nuclear arms race, the East-West confrontation and decades of successive conservative governments in Japan. These tenets were aimed at assuring Japan's security and prosperity. The first was maintenance and enhancement of friendly and co-operative relations with the United States under the umbrella of the US-Japan Security Treaty of 1951. This policy was clearly outlined in the 1983 *Diplomatic Blue Book* in which the relationship between the two powers was described as pivotal to Japan's diplomacy: 'In a wide sphere extending from politics and the economy to defence, America is Japan's most important partner.'[1] The Blue Book also posited that it was in Japan's own self interest to co-operate with the United States and make efforts to contribute actively to its security policy. In this role Japan has played an important part as a junior partner with the United States in the post-war anti-Communist military alliance.

The second pillar of Japan's foreign policy involves Japan's co-operation and solidarity with the industrialised Western countries, such as those in Western Europe, Canada, Aus-

[1] Ministry of Foreign Affairs, *Waga Gaiko no Kinkyo*, Tokyo: 1983, p. 3.

tralia and New Zealand. It is into this group that South
Africa also falls, as it was the Japanese government's view
that the Republic, despite having a black majority and a
policy of apartheid, could be regarded as an advanced free-
world country on a par with Australia or Canada.[2]

The third major element in Japan's overall foreign policy
strategy has been to establish and promote friendly and co—
operative relations with the Third World's anti-Communist
and non-aligned countries generally and with Asian countries in particular. The fourth tenet was to maintain a policy
of both confrontation and dialogue with the countries regarded as members of the Eastern camp, especially the former
Soviet Union. After the successful signing of a joint com-
munique normalising diplomatic relations between Japan
and China in 1972, the Soviet Union was perceived as the
biggest threat to Japan's security.

This four-faceted post-war diplomatic structure also defined Japan's policy towards Africa. In terms of priorities,
Sub-Saharan Africa has been of only secondary importance
to Japan's overall diplomacy. This is demonstrated by the
fact that no Japanese prime minister has yet visited an African country while in office.[3]

The place of South Africa in this overall picture is different. In general, it has been given rather high priority in
Japan's foreign policy. Pretoria has been regarded as important because it served as a self-proclaimed champion of the

[2] *Ibid.*, p. 607. The Japanese edition of the *Diplomatic Blue Book* notes: 'Developed
countries include the DAC (Developement Assistance Committe) member
nations, Greece, Luxembourg, Iceland (Faroe Islands), Portugal, Spain, Yugosla-
via, Israel and various other countries including the Republic of South Africa.' See
also Zai Puretoria Nihonkoku Soryojikan (ed.), *Minami Afurika Kyowakoku, Lesoto
Ookoku, Botsuwana Kyowakoku Suwajirando Ookoku, Nansei Afurika.* Tokyo: Nihon
Kokusai Mondai Kenkyusho, 1973, p. 62.
[3] The low priority given to Africa is reflected in the Ministry of Foreign Affairs
personnel policy. A study by Fukui Haruhiko found that Japan assigned the smallest
average number of officials per country (2.2) to Africa and noted: 'It would seem
from these statistics that, apart from its closest North-East Asian neighbours of
Taiwan (Republic of China) and South Korea (Republic of Korea), North
America, Oceania and Western Europe have been the most important, and Africa
the least important'. Fukui Haruhiku, 'Bureaucratic Power in Japan' in Peter
Drysdale and Hironobu Kitaoji (eds), *Japan and Australia*, Canberra: Australian
National University Press, 1981, pp. 281-2.

anti—Communist forces in the African region and maintained an intimate relationship with the United States.[4] For
Japan, it had grown into its largest export market in Africa
and by the later 1970s, it was a reliable supplier of strategically important minerals.

Guiding principles and policy objectives

What are the guiding principles of Japan's Africa policy?
Many people, especially Africans, assume that since Japan
itself is a non-white country, it should naturally support
anti-colonialism, national self-determination and anti-racism. But the position generally taken by Japan, as symbolised
by its pro-Pretoria policy, is one that emphasises anti-Communism and economic expansionism.

As Ishii Ryuichi, former Deputy Director of the Foreign
Ministry's Second Africa Division, has outlined:

> The basic policy when deciding which countries to help
> is to respond to specific requests . . . we try to help the
> poorest countries first. Also we look at the country's
> political relationship with Japan and we are a member of
> the Western bloc so the West's interests are important.[5]

The late Foreign Minister Abe Shintaro echoed this approach in a meeting with Japanese ambassadors to African
states in June 1984. He emphasised Africa's importance in
the East-West context and asserted that Japan 'should use its
economic influence to help entrench African countries in
the Western Camp'.[6]

In terms of economic expansion, the very first edition of
the government's *Diplomatic Blue Book*, published in 1957,
pointed out that the only way to improve the standard of
living of the 90 million residents of the small island nation
of Japan, develop the economy and cultivate national strength

[4] A good example of the close relationship between Pretoria, Tokyo and
Washington was their involvement in the Korean war (1950-3). Japan was deeply
involved in the conflict through its role as a rear supply base while the Union of
South Africa dispatched Air Force units
[5] Martin Roth, 'Japan and Africa', *Africa Economic Digest*, 3, 49 (December 1982),
p.12. Mr Ishii's statement here is misleading since Japan's African aid policy does
not necessarily give priority to the poorest nations.
'Kotani Toru, 'Rising Sun over Africa?', *Africa Report*, November—December
1985, p. 70.

was through peaceful economic advance overseas.[7]

It is important to note that economic expansion was seen by Japan not only as a means of giving concrete form to Japan's prosperity, but also as a means of increasing national power. In an address at the University of Witwatersrand in 1967 Martin Spring remarked: There is the view 'very strongly held in Japan — that economic and industrial strength is the real basis of political power in the world today, and that military strength is only an aspect of this, sometimes not even a major one'.[8]

Goals and objectives

In discussions of the goals of Japan's African policy, there is a general tendency to overemphasise the economic aspects, such as acquistion of natural resources and markets, but this standard explanation should not be accepted blindly. Rather, it is necessary to consider the issue in a wider perspective.

White Africa policy. To begin with, it is useful to look at the objectives of Japan's White Africa policy. The first objective involved support for the white minority regimes and confrontation with states and forces considered to be pro-Eastern, such as Angola, Mozambique, the South West Africa People's Organisation (SWAPO) and the African National Congress (ANC). The second goal was to secure a stable supply of rare metals, such as chrome, manganese, platinum and vanadium. These were necessary for the acceleration of the transformation of Japan's industrial structure from heavy chemical industries to internationally competitive knowledge—intensive, high-tech industries such as integrated circuits, computers and industrial robots.[9] Realising this goal was given high priority in the latter half of the 1970s after the oil crisis of 1973.[10]

---

[7] Ministry of Foreign Affairs, *Waga Gaiko No Kinkyo*, 1957, p. 9.

[8] 'Japan, China, and the Politics and Economics of the Far East', an address by Martin C. Spring, University of the Witwatersrand, Johannesburg, 25 October, 1967, p. 7.

[9] The necessity and urgency of knowledge-intensive industrialization was described in detail in the 1971 Ministry of International Trade and Industry MITI White Paper (Soron), pp. 387-405.

[10] Nakamura Takefusa descibes the serious damage suffered by Japan's leading export industries (iron and steel, shipbuilding, petrochemicals) during the first oil crisis in the book *The Postwar Japanese Economy — Its*

The two major producers of rare metals were South Africa and the former Soviet Union but although Japan made some purchases from the latter country, it was extremely reluctant to depend on it for strategic metals since Tokyo regarded the Soviet Union as hypothetically its principal enemy. Therefore, Japan chose to purchase most of its rare metals from South Africa (see Figure 2.1).

A matter of great concern for the Japanese government, especially during the later 1970s and early 1980s, was the possibility of a 'metals shock'. This was reflected in a statement by Hatano Yoshio, then Director General of the Middle Eastern and African Affairs Bureau of the Foreign Ministry, at a meeting on 4 March 1983 with members of the CCA. Hatano admitted that it was important for Japan to note the problem of the advance of Eastern forces into Africa. To date they had been concentrated in Ethiopia, Angola and Mozambique but the possibility of their penetrating further and taking a dominant position in areas with many rare metals caused Japan serious anxiety.[11]

The third goal of the pro-White Africa policy was to maintain and expand export markets. Trade statistics show that South Africa's share of Japan's overall foreign export market has remained constantly at about 1 per cent. Yet in

---

Development and Structure, trans. Jacqueline Kaminski, University of Tokyo Press, 1981, p. 257:

> The oil crisis came as a tremendous shock to the Japanese economy, which had developed primarily on the basis of the chemical and heavy industries. The expansion of Japanese industry primarily had revolved around the high-energy consuming steel industry, and the bulk of that energy was imported crude oil. The foundation upon which Japan's chemical and heavy industries grew, the low price of crude oil during the 1960s, made possible the growth of the high-volume energy-consumption industrial materials industries such as steel, aluminum refining, and petrochemicals. Most of these plants were located on the seacoast, where they used private harbor facilities for the off-loading of raw materials and the on-loading of finished products. After the oil crisis, while one could not go so far as to say that the profitability of the industries was completely destroyed, it was greatly impaired.

[11] Hatano Yoshio, 'Afurika to Nihon — Enjo, Kyoryoku no Mondaiten', *Gekkan Afurika* (Africa Monthly), 23, 5 (May 1983), p. 15. This article is based on the speech Hatano delivered at the Keidanren Committeee on Africa meeting of 4 March 1983.

relation to the great size of the Japanese economy, 1 per cent is far from being a small figure. The importance of the Republic of South Africa as an export market for Japan in Sub-Saharan Africa can be seen clearly in Figure 2.2. Almost half of Japan's exports to the region are with South Africa alone. (The figures for Liberia are excluded since Japan admits that most of these are shipping exports that make use of that nation's flag of convenience system.)

Black Africa policy. The goals of the Black Africa policy present a stark contrast. The first of these is the establishment and promotion of friendly and co-operative relations with pro-Western countries as well as the non-aligned nations and forces. The second goal is the maintenance of a policy of confrontation and dialogue with countries generally regarded as pro-Eastern. Third is to secure natural resources, both mineral resources such as copper, iron ore and uranium[12] and marine products such as squid, octopus, shrimp and tuna.[13] The fourth objective is to maintain and expand export markets in Africa. This goal rapidly decreased in importance after the mid-1970s, when the Black African economics in general (and non-oil-producing ones in particular) faced serious difficulties because of the oil crises and the relative decline in primary product prices, coupled with an increase in the prices of manufactured goods, natural disasters such as drought, polictical instability and civil wars. The debt question also became of graver importance. For example, Nigeria's exports to Japan declined drastically by the end of 1982 as a result of the oil glut. The decrease in Black Africa's share of Japan's overall world trade can be seen

[12] Japan's nuclear power plans accelerated after the oil shock of 1973 (see Figure 2.3). Niger was listed along with South Africa, Namibia, the USA, Canada and Australia as an important supplier of uranium. See *Keizai Kyoroku Kunibetsu Shiryo: Ministry of Foreign Affairs, Middle Eastern and African Affairs Bureau, Economic Co-operation Bureau, Senegal, Niger, Mali,* Tokyo, 1980, pp. 80-1.

[13] For example, Mauritania supplied 24 per cent of the octopus and 7 per cent of the cuttlefish that Japan imported in 1983. Ministry of Foreign Affairs, Public Information Bureau (ed.), *Afurika— Sahara no Muko no Sekai,* Tokyo, 1984, p. 309.

Fig. 2.1. SOUTH AFRICA'S SHARE OF JAPAN'S OVERALL MINERAL RESOURCE IMPORTS, 1977

	Overall import		SA's share		%	Main suppliers
Silico–chromium	5,497	t.	5,450	t.	99.1	(1) South Africa, (2) Taiwan, (3) —
Ferrochrome	104,098	t.	79,254	t.	76.1	(1) South Africa, (2) Brazil, (3) Sweden
Iridium	47,172	g.	26,498	g.	56.2	(1) South Africa, (2) UK, (3) Canada
Manganese ore	238,484	t.	121,476	t.	50.9	(1) South Africa, (2) Australia, (3) Mexico
Rhodium	50,197	g.	24,998	g.	49.8	(1) South Africa, (2) UK, (3) USSR
Ferromanganese	1,446,837	t.	704,078	t.	48.7	(1) South Africa, (2) India, (3) USSR
Chrome	899,934	t.	372,922	t.	41.4	(1) South Africa, (2) India, (3) Brazil
Platinum	23,636,622	g.	8,022,061	g.	33.9	(1) USSR, (2) South Africa, (3) UK
Palladium	2,728,675	g.	867,694	g.	31.8	(1) South Africa, (2) USA, (3) UK
Asbestos	298,333	t.	82,181	t.	27.5	(1) Canada, (2) South Africa, (3) USSR

Source: JETRO, *Africa Business Guide*, Tokyo, 1979, p. 305.

clearly in Figure 2.5.

The next objective was to secure the greatest number possible of the large mass of UN votes controlled by the Black African states. This grew increasingly important from the 1970s, when Japan began to nurse ambitions of entering the club of the world's politically powerful states.

The sixth and most important of the Black Africa policy goals was to deal with Black Africa in a way that would help to soften or lessen criticism within Africa of Japan's pro-White Africa policy and its cordial relations with the Pretoria regime. This goal was the most essential, for without neutralising criticism of the pro-White Africa policy, Japan's dual diplomacy could not continue to function. And as far as Japanese government officials were concerned, simultaneous implementaion of the White and Black Africa policies was considered both sound policy and logically consistent in the sense that the approach both maximised Japan's national interest in Africa and provided a direct contribution to Western security. The notion of consistency stemmed from the Japanese government's view that the biggest problem in African diplomacy was not racism or colonialism but the East-West confrontation, especially the efforts to deter Soviet penetration of Africa.[14] The maintenance of friendly and co-operative relations with White Africa's anti-Communist forces was thought to be consistent with this.

Needless to say, it was unlikely these Japanese policies and the subordination of human rights to national and Western bloc interests would be tolerated in Africa.

How policy objectives are achieved

The ways in which Japan has attempted to achieve these policy objectives in Africa can be classified into four main categories. These are: co-operation with the United States and Western Europe; the 'key countries' approach; *kanzai*

---

[14] The tendency for Japanese leaders to regard Third World national liberation movements as being composed of Communists or Communist sympathisers has its historical roots in the policy applied to China during the inter-war years. In the post-war period, it is symbolised by Japan's involvement in the Vietnam war.

Fig. 2.2 JAPAN'S LEADING TRADING PARTNERS, 1986-1988[a]

A. *Export Destinations*

	1986	1987	1988	1986	1987	1988
	US$m.	US$m	US$m	%	%	%
USA	80,456	83,580	89,634	38.5	36.5	33.8
EC[b]	30,675	37,693	46,873	14.7	16.4	17.7
Korea, Rep. of	10,475	13,229	15,441	5.0	5.8	5.8
Germany (Fed. Rep.)	10,477	12,833	15,793	5.0	5.6	6.0
Taiwan	7,852	11,346	14,354	3.8	4.9	5.4
China	9,856	8,250	9,476	4.7	3.6	3.6
Australia	5,227	5,146	6,680	2.5	2.2	2.5
Canada	5,526	5,611	6,424	2.6	2.4	2.4
UK	6,647	8,400	10,632	3.2	3.7	4.0
Indonesia	2,662	2,990	3,054	1.3	1.3	1.2
Saudi Arabia	2,762	3,239	3,142	1.3	1.4	1.2
Hong Kong	7,161	8,872	11,706	3.4	3.9	4.4
Singapore	4,577	6,008	8,311	2.2	2.6	3.1
Malaysia	1,708	2,168	3,060	0.8	0.9	1.2
France	3,152	4,014	4,987	1.5	1.8	1.9
UAE	1,033	1,118	1,286	0.5	0.5	0.5
Switzerland	1,887	2,266	2,775	0.9	1.0	1.0
USSR	3,150	2,563	3,130	1.5	1.1	1.2
Netherlands	3,261	4,071	5,054	1.6	1.8	1.9
Thailand	2,030	2,953	5,162	1.0	1.3	1.9
Italy	1,723	2,103	2,787	0.8	0.9	1.1
South Africa	1,355	1,863	2,047	0.6	0.8	0.8
Belgium	2,198	2,697	3,390	1.1	1.2	1.3
India	2,099	1,957	2,082	1.0	0.9	0.8
Mexico	1,032	1,389	1,772	0.5	0.6	0.7
Brazil	973	878	998	0.5	0.4	0.4
Philippines	1,088	1,415	1,740	0.5	0.6	0.7
Kuwait	1,220	857	730	0.6	0.4	0.3
Sweden	1,438	1,931	2,319	0.7	0.8	0.9
World total	209,151	229,221	264,917	100.0	100.0	100.0

(a) Listed in order of total value of exports plus imports in 1987.
(b) 1985, 10 countries; 1986, 12 countries.

Source: Keizai Koho Center, Japan Institute for Social and Economic Affairs,
Japan 1990: An International Comparison, Tokyo, 1989, pp. 40-1.

JUN MORIKAWA

Japan and Africa

Big Business and Diplomacy

Africa World Press, Inc.

P.O. Box 1892

Trenton, NJ 08607

P.O. Box 48

Asmara, ERITREA

Africa World Press, Inc.

P.O. Box 1892   P.O. Box 48
Trenton, NJ 08607   Asmara, ERITREA

Library of Congress Cataloging-in-Publication Data

Morikawa, Jun, 1949-
    Japan and Africa : big business and diplomacy / Jun Morikawa.
       p.   cm.
    Includes bibliographical references and index.
    ISBN 0-86543-576-6. -- ISBN 0-86543-577-4 (pbk.)
    1. Africa--Foreign relations--Japan. 2. Japan--Foreign relations-
-Africa. 3. Africa Foreign relations--1960- 4. Japan--Foreign
relations--20th century. 5. Africa--Foreign economic relations-
-Japan. 6. Japan--Foreign economic relations--Africa. I. Title.
DT38.9.J3M67 1996
327.5206--DC21
                                  96-47286
                                       CIP

Published in the United Kingdom by
C. Hurst & Co. (Publishers) Ltd.
38 King Street, London WC2E 8JZ

B. *Import Sources*

	1986	1987	1988	1986	1987	1988
	US$m.	US$m	US$m	%	%	%
USA	29,054	31,490	42,037	23.0	21.1	22.4
EC[b]	13,989	17,670	24,071	11.1	11.8	12.8
Korea, Rep. of	5,292	8,075	11,811	4.2	5.4	6.3
Germany (Fed. Rep.)	4,298	6,150	8,101	3.4	4.1	4.3
Taiwan	4,691	7,128	8,743	3.7	4.8	4.7
China	5,652	7,401	9,859	4.5	5.0	5.3
Australia	6,980	7,869	10,285	5.5	5.3	5.5
Canada	4,895	6,073	8,308	3.9	4.1	4.4
UK	3,573	3,057	4,193	2.8	2.0	2.2
Indonesia	7,311	8,427	9,497	5.8	5.6	5.1
Saudi Arabia	5,205	7,311	6,348	4.1	4.9	3.4
Hong Kong	1,073	1,561	2,109	0.8	1.0	1.1
Singapore	1,463	2,048	2,339	1.2	1.4	1.2
Malaysia	3,846	4,772	4,710	3.0	3.2	2.5
France	1,855	2,871	4,315	1.5	1.9	2.3
UAE	5,947	5,408	5,324	4.7	3.6	2.8
Switzerland	2,571	3,101	3,565	2.0	2.1	1.9
USSR	1,972	2,352	2,766	1.6	1.6	1.5
Netherlands	577	757	996	0.5	0.5	0.5
Thailand	1,391	1,759	2,751	1.1	1.2	1.5
Italy	1,459	2,135	2,895	1.2	1.4	1.5
South Africa	2,229	2,259	1,933	1.8	1.5	1.0
Belgium	677	859	1,125	0.5	0.6	0.6
India	1,297	1,530	1,804	1.0	1.0	1.0
Mexico	1,439	1,625	1,591	1.1	1.1	0.8
Brazil	1,875	2,032	2,950	1.5	1.4	1.6
Philippines	1,221	1,353	2,044	1.0	0.9	1.1
Kuwait	1,157	1,796	1,590	0.9	1.2	0.8
Sweden	575	682	977	0.5	0.5	0.5
World total	126,408	149,515	187,354	100.0	100.0	100.0

ittai (government and big business working in unison), a concept that is examined in detail in Chapters 4 and 5; and '*senden gaiko*' (PR diplomacy).

Co-operation with the United States and Western Europe. Even before the Second World War, one of the major characteristics of Japan's African policy was the pursuit of its national interests while respecting the position of the Western colonial powers which had vital interests in the African continent. After the war, America entered the picutre as a major player in this area. Consequently, Japan's post-war African diplomacy developed around the adoption of a policy of political and strategic co-operation with the United States and economic co-operation with the West European countries.

The June 1972 government economic mission to Africa reflected this view. It reported that while the countries were politically independent, it was clear that they belonged economically within the greater European sphere of influence.[15]

With this perception in mind, the report went on to propose methods for Japan to achieve economic penetration:

> Japanese companies that want to advance into Black African nations must take into consideration the presence of the former colonial powers, especially in Francophone Africa. It became very clear during this visit that Japan must make efforts not to directly compete now or in the future with the interests of the former colonial powers. The best policy is to co-operate and co-exist with them for our mutual self-interests.[16]

Japanese co-operation with the United States in Africa grew from the dicta of the US-Japan Mutual Security Treaty. Because of the restraints of Japan's 'Peace' constitution, its contribution to the anti-Communist world strategy of the United States has been made primarily through the economic means of aid and trade. This also suited the post-war domestic political situation in Japan and the concerns of the

---

[15] Africa Economic Mission, *Akaruku Nobiyuku Afurika*, Tokyo, 1972, p. 33 (not for public sale).
[16] *Ibid.*, p. 33.

Fig. 2.3. (A) ELECTRICITY GENERATED, 1988

			Thermal				Hydro geo-
		Electricity generated (GW-h)[a]	*Total (%)*	*Solid fuels (%)*	*Petro products (%)*	*Gas (%)*	*Nuclear power (%)*	*thermal solar (%)*
Japan	1978	562,372	76.1	7.3	59.2	9.6	10.5	13.4
	1985	671,952	62.9	14.9	28.9	19.1	23.7	13.3
	1986	676,360	62.2	14.7	28.2	19.3	24.9	12.9
	1987	719,069	62.4	15.2	27.7	19.5	26.1	11.4
	1988	753,728	63.4	14.9	29.1	19.4	23.7	12.9
USA		2,871,988	72.3	57.4	5.5	9.4	19.5	8.2
Canada		504,285	22.7	18.9	2.4	1.4	16.4	60.8
Germany (FR)		431,164	16.6	52.2	2.6	6.8	33.7	4.8
France		391,926	9.6	7.5	1.5	0.6	70.3	20.1
UK		308,231	77.2	67.1	9.5	0.6	20.6	2.3
Italy		203,561	76.3	17.1	44.1	15.1	–	22.9
OECD	*total*	6,478,429	58.3	40.9	8.7	8.7	23.4	18.3

(a) 1 GW (gigawatt) = 1 billion watts.

Source (A) OECD, Energy Balance of OECD Countries, 1970/85, 1987/8.

(B) NUCLEAR POWER GENERATION, END 1989

	In operation		Under construction and planned	
	Reactors	*1,000 kW*	*Reactors*	*1000 kW*
USA	109	102,637	12	14,278
France	54	53,648	13	18,560
USSR	50	37,551	38	37,800
Japan	38	29,445	17	16,908
Germany (FR)	21	23,584	3	3,162
UK	40	15,090	4	4,728
Canada	18	12,919	4	3,740
Swedan	12	10,172	–	–
Spain	10	7,852	5	4,850
Korea	9	7615	5	4,678
Belgium	7	5700	–	–
World total	425	335,681	177	166,368

Source: Japan Atomic Industrial Forum Inc. Both reprinted in Keizai Koho Center, Japan Institute for Social and Economic Affairs, *Japan 1991: An International Comparison*, Tokyo, 1990, p. 61.

international community that Japan should never again play a military role.

The idea that Japan should contribute to Western security through economic means was institutionalised in Article II of the revised treaty, signed in January 1961. This article, the so-called 'economic clause', reads:

> The Parties will contribute toward the further developement of peaceful and friendly international relations by strengthening their free institutions, by bringing about a better understanding of the principles upon which these institutions are founded and by promoting conditions of stability and wellbeing. They will seek to eliminate conflict in their international policies and will encourage economic collaboration between them.[17]

Although the statement appears vague, Yamamoto Tsuyoshi notes that Prime Minister Kishi took this to mean that third countries, especially those in South-East Asia, would in future be included in consultative discussions between Japan and the United States on economic co-operation matters.[18]

In the latter half of the 1960s, Japan's strategic aid focused on the anti-Communist countries in Asia, particularly South Korea, Taiwan, South Vietnam, Thailand, the Philippines and Indonesia. This aid was actively pursued, and in the 1970s it was gradually extended into the Middle East, Latin America and Africa against the background of the intensification of the US-Soviet confrontation, Japan's increasing economic power, and the relative weakening of American influence because of its commitment to the Vietnam war.

The American anti-Communist strategy in Africa required that Japan should make a contribution in Egypt, Sudan, Somalia, Kenya, Zaire and Malawi; these countries were given preferential treatment in the allocation of Japanese Official Development Assistance (ODA). At the same time, *de facto* economic sanctions were imposed on Angola and Mozambique and a policy of trade expansion was applied to South Africa. Opinion on aid strategy at that time strongly supported the idea that economic difficulties and social disorder cause political

[17] Tada Minoru, *Nichibei Ampo Joyaku*, Mikasa Shobo, Tokyo, 1982, p. 154.
[18] Yamamoto Tsuyoshi, *Nihon no Keizai Enjo*, Tokyo: Shakai Shiso Sha Publishers 1988, p. 77.

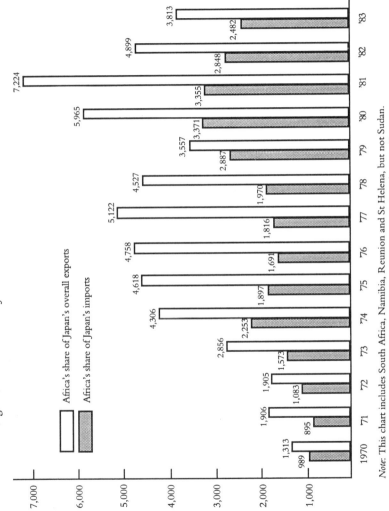

Fig. 2.4 CHANGES IN JAPAN'S TRADE WITH SUB-SAHARAN AFRICA

Africa's share of Japan's overall exports

Africa's share of Japan's imports

Note: This chart includes South Africa, Namibia, Reunion and St Helena, but not Sudan.
Source: APIC, *Kokusai Kyoryoku Tokubetsu Joho* 11 (15 January 1985), Tokyo, p. 45.

instability which can lead to Communist penetration. In other words, by offering development aid and strengthening the material base of anti-Communist regimes, a stable economic and social climate could be created that led to both stability in the long term and the prevention of conflict.[19]

The key countries approach. The key countries approach — giving special priority status to certain countries — was also an effective means of implementing Japan's African policy objectives. The Japanese government has never publicly disclosed either the reasons for the adoption of this system or the countries involved. However, LDP documents provide a valuable clue to understanding the concept:

> There are forty-four developing countries in Africa. As aid to African countries has increased, it has grown more difficult to give aid equally to all these nations. Thus it is necessary to give aid to those nations which meet certain criteria: for instance, nations with which we share a degree of interdependence nations which are important because we obtain resources from them, such as Zaire, Zimbabwe, Zambia and Niger, or influential Black African nations such as Kenya, Nigeria and Tanzania, that can play an important role in helping to maintain amicable relations in Africa. Also included are those nations which are important for the maintenance of stability in mineral-rich Southern Africa, such as Zimbabwe and Zambia.[20]

Apart from the countries listed here, other important ones included francophone Senegal, Ivory Coast and Gabon; Ethiopia, especially when it was ruled by Haile Selassie; and of course South Africa. Though geographically part of Arab Africa, Egypt and Algeria were also viewed as having political weight in the conduct of African international relations in general and in problems concerning Southern Africa in particular.

According to the Ministry of Foreign Affairs, Kenya has

[19] See, for example, Ministry of Foreign Affairs, *Waga Gaiko no Kinkyo*, Tokyo, 1983, p. 8.
[20] Democratic Party, Policy Affairs Economic Co-operation (ed.), Research Council Special Committee on External *Waga To no Keizai Kyoryoku Seisaku ni Tsuite*, Tokyo: 1982, pp. 186-7.

been also considered important because it is Japan's gateway to East Africa. Since its independence, it has maintained a stable political climate and sound economic and social development as well as maintaining a firm, pro-Western free economic system that actively invited foreign capital. Because of this, Japan has striven to promote friendly relations with Kenya and assist in its economic development as much as possible.[21]

Kenya has also been considered important to Japan for other reasons. Diplomatically, Kenya has been a leader of the moderate faction within the Organisation of African Unity (OAU) and the UN on questions such as colonialism and apartheid. Militarily and strategically, it has been of vital importance to the Western world's security and prosperity, providing a bridgehead in the securing of a maritime route to the oil-producing regions of the Middle East and allowing the United States the use of the port facilities at Mombasa for its Rapid Deployment Force.

Among these key states, Tanzania has been considered especially important.[22] Although it only has a small export market and is poorly endowed with mineral resources—its attraction lay in the influence that the country's President Nyerere possessed both in African international relations and in the North South axis, and also as an outspoken critic of Japan's pro-White Africa policy. As previously noted, Japan's dualistic African diplomacy could only be maintained by softening criticism of its pro-White Africa policy. Neutralising such criticism was considered vital. The LDP phrase 'influential Black African nations that can play an important role in helping maintain amicable relations in Africa' takes on a much deeper meaning in the context of Japan's dualistic policy towards Africa. For example, the government's readiness to use economic assistance as a means of appeasement in Africa becomes clear from remarks made by the Japanese Consul General in Pretoria, Nishizawa Kenichiro:

---

[21] Ministry of Foreign Affairs, Middle Eastern and African Affairs Bureau, Economic Co-operation Bureau (ed.), *Keizai Kyoryoku Kunibetsu Shiryo. Kenya*, Tokyo: 1981, p. 43.

[22] See also Ministry of Foreign Affairs, Middle Eastern and African Affairs Bureau, Economic Co-operation Bureau, *Keizai Kyoryoku Kunibetsu Shiryo. Tanzania*, Tokyo: 1980, p. 44.

'In order to avoid unjust criticism of a reported expansion of trade with South Africa, Japan should clarify its position in the UN and extend economic aid to Black Africa.'[23] Malawi and Zaire provide two clear examples of how the key countries were analysed. According to a Ministry of Foreign Affairs study done in 1980, Malawi was seen as a country that seemed to have adopted a non-alignment policy but in reality was undertaking neutral diplomacy. The analysis goes on to suggest that over Southern African issues, Malawi had responded with a moderate, careful posture; further it noted that in 1967, Malawi became the only Black African state to establish diplomatic relations with South Africa, send an ambassador and normalise and maintain trade relations. Malawi also maintained very close connections with Britain and other countries in Western Europe.[24]

The Japanese Ministry of Foreign Affairs study, *Economic Co-operation—Country by Country*, reported that Zaire had no direct effect on Japan's national security, but it occupied a position of strategic importance politically to Western interests in Africa; also, its importance in UN diplomacy cannot be underestimated. The report went on to note that economically, Zaire's copper and cobalt were important resources for Japan, and direct investment in its copper and oil ranked Zaire right behind Kenya and Nigeria in importance to Japan.[25]

Overall, fourteen countries are given a special place in Japan's 'key country approach': the Black African states of Zaire, Zimbabwe, Zambia, Niger, Kenya, Nigeria, Tanzania, Senegal, Ivory Coast and Gabon, the Arab African states of Egypt and Algeria, Ethiopia and South Africa. While these countries receive constant attention, there are also more than a dozen other countries in Africa which do not host Japanese embassies and have never been visited by Japanese government leaders or official economic missions. These include

---

[23] Springbok Club of Japan, *Springbok Nan-a Nihonjin Kai Gekkan Shimbun - 100 go Kinen Soshu,* 22 January 1974 edn, Johannesburg: Nippon Club of South Africa, 1981, p.76.

[24] Ministry of Foreign Affairs, Middle Eastern and African Affairs Bureau, Second Africa Division, *Malawi Kyowakoku Gaiyo,* Tokyo: 1980, p. 6.

[25] Ministry of Foreign Affairs, Middle Eastern and African Affairs Bureau, Economic Co-operation Bureau, *Keizai Kyoryoku Kunibetsu Shiryo. Zaire, Djibouti,* Tokyo, 1982, p. 59.

the Gambia, Botswana, Lesotho, Mauritius, Swaziland, Equitorial Guinea, Guinea-Bissau, Mozambique, Cape Verde, the Comoros, São Tomé and Principe, Angola, the Seychelles, Djibouti and Namibia.

Kanzai ittaishugi (government and big business working in unison). The government uses the term '*kanmin ittai*' to describe the efforts of government and people working together in the conduct of foreign policy. But in fact, participation by the people (*min*) is very limited, because what the government (*kan*) expects of such participation is the people's support and understanding of the government's decisions rather than that they will actually participate in the decision—making or subsequent implementation.

A term more precisely reflecting the reality of the situation would be '*kanzai ittaishugi*'. The word '*kan*' is a shortened form of '*kanryo* (the bureaucracy or, as here, government) and '*zai*' refers to '*minkan keizai kai*' (the world of private big business, known as the *zaikai).* The phrase '*ittaishugi*' means to act in unison.

The *zaikai* is allowed access to information, the free expression of its opinions, and participation in the decision—making process. Its involvement in the formulation and implementation of government policy takes place through both public and private channels. Examples of the former include presenting official requests and opinion papers to government ministries and serving as members of various consultative councils. Private channels include a wide variety of 'informal' actions such as donations of huge amounts of money to party political funds. By providing '*amakudari*' (lucrative post—retirement positions for bureaucrats) the *zaikai* is able to strengthen its network of contracts with bureaucratic organisations and use them to its own advantage. And of course there are private contacts with influential politicians and government officials at exclusive teahouses and hotels. These 'informal' channels may often be said to play a more important role in exerting influence on the government than any formal channels.

With the LDP and bureaucracy, the *zaikai* has been one of the three governing elites of post war Japan that, like a tripod,[26] supported the formulation of Japan's diplomacy from 1955 until the Liberal Democratic Party lost power in 1993 (it regained power in 1994 by forming a coalition with the Socialist Party). Their joint efforts have often led to *minkan keizai gaiko* (private business diplomacy),[27] which are examined in detail in Chapters 4 and 5.

There are four main reasons why the business community exerts such a potent influence on Japan's policy towards Africa. First, there is the general lack of interest in African affairs (with the obvious exception of Southern African affairs) displayed by the ruling LDP. Secondly, Japan has relied mostly upon economic means (trade and aid) to display its commitment to Cold War strategy; as the Foreign Ministry is limited in the amount of manpower and money it can allocate to the implementation of its dual diplomacy, the business community can thus be of additional and important assistance. It has long years of experience in the conduct of private economic diplomacy, and can compensate somewhat for the shortcomings of the Foreign Office.

Thirdly, the business community has the know-how needed to develop trade relations with Black African countries interested in working with Japan, and it has the necessary capital and skills to provide technical aid and assistance. Finally, in the case of South Africa, there is a clear advantage in having the business community take the lead in implementing policy since in this area the Japanese government has been the target of ever more serious international criticism of its position.

The following excerpt from an internal Foreign Ministry document entitled 'Preparation for the African Economic Attaches Conference' indicates the way in which the Foreign

---

[26] For more on the tripod system see Hosoya Chihiro, 'Taigai Kettei Katei ni Okeru Nichi bei no Tokushitsu ' in Hosoya Chihiro and Watanuki Joji (eds) , *Taigaiseisaku Kettei Katei no Nichi Bei Hikaku,* University of Tokyo, 1977, p. 6.

[27] For more on this topic see Misawa Shigeo 'Taigai Seisaku to Nihon Zaikai', Hosoya and Watanuki (eds), op. cit, pp. 179-211; 'The Role of Private Economic Diplomacy', *Keidanren Review,* 8 (March 1968), pp. 26-35; William E. Bryant, *Japanese Private Economic Diplomacy: An Analysis of Business Government Linkages,* New York: Praeger, 1975; and Ogata Sadako 'Nihon no Taigai Seisaku Kettei Katei to Zaikai', Hosoya and Watanuki (eds), op. cit., pp. 213-41.

Ministry and business community have co-ordinated their efforts.

The Foreign Minsitry will hold its eighth annual African economic attaches conference this 28-30 June 1967 in Nairobi. In attendence will be eleven Japanese diplomats, stationed in Africa (nine ambassadors and two consul-generals) and three Japanese economic attachés serving in the United Kingdom, France and Belgium, countries with close connections to Africa. [...]

Topics for discussion will include: economic relations between our country and African nations, the effect of the confrontation between Black and White Africa, trade balance, problems associated with the purchase of primary products, the expansion of trade and the issue of economic and technical co-operation. Representatives of private Japanese companies in Africa are also invited to attend this sixth joint trade meeting in order to exchange opinions with Foreign Ministry officials. The East Africa joint trade meeting will precede the Foreign Ministry economic attachs meeting and will be held in Nairobi on the 27th [of June]. The Southern Africa meeting will be on 3 July in Johannesburg and the Western Africa meeting will be held on 7 July in Lagos.[28]

This excerpt illustrates how meetings have been systematically organised to maximise the exchange of information and the co-ordination of activities between the government and business community.

Senden gaiko (PR diplomacy). Supporting the racist colonialist regimes on the one hand and making claims of friendship to Black Africa on the other is a balancing act that has certainly not been limited to Japan. It has also been carried out by the United States, Britain, France and other Western powers. However, Black African expectations of Japan, which it perceives as a coloured advanced industrialised country,

---

[28] Ministry of Foreign Affairs, Public Information Bureau, *Gaimusho Kohyoshu 1967 Kami Hanki* (a collection of official materials released to the general public by the Foreign Ministry for the first half of 1967), Tokyo, pp. 99-100.

have been higher; thus Japan's dualistic policy has been the source of strong criticism and disappointment in Black African countries and in the Black community in South Africa.

Clearly, Japan's African policy decision-makers understand that they must handle carefully any issue related to racism in general and apartheid policy in particular. For example, at an informal meeting of Keidanren's Committee on Cooperation with Africa, held on 4 March 1983, the then Director General of the Foreign Ministry's Middle Eastern and African Affairs Bureau, Hatano Yoshio, stressed: "The most important element of Japan's political relations with Black Africa is the policy that Japan adopts toward the Republic of South Africa. It is considered extremely important in connection with winning the trust of Black African nations.' [29]

Yet at the same time as expressing this policy the government had no intention of changing its driving principles of anti-Communism and economic expansionism. This left the sole option of somehow softening and neutralising criticism of Japan. One way of accomplishing this was the preferential distribution of aid to key countries with influence on the South African issue. Another was a systematic public relations effort, internationally and within Japan itself, to influence public opinion and project the view of Japan as strongly pro-Black African. This diplomatic rhetoric takes two chief forms. The first stresses Japan's historical relationship with Africa, arguing that Japan, never having possessed African colonies and in fact having attempted to get an anti-racist clause introduced into the League of Nations charter at the Versailles Peace Conference in 1919, has 'clean hands' in the continent and is a pioneer of anti-racism.[30] The second course is to publicise Japan's anti-apartheid stance and its claim to have enacted tough sanctions against

[29] Hatano, *Gekkan Afurika,* p. 15.

[30] For example, in the Africa guide *Afurika no Kuni Guni* issued in October 1974 by the Ministry of Foreign Affairs-affiliated organisation Sekai no Ugoki Sha, it is stated: 'in our country's political relations with Africa, there are no stains or blemishes The relations are clean'. For a more detailed account of Japan's relations with Africa in the inter-war period, see Jun Morikawa, 'The Myth and Reality of Japan's Relations with Colonial Africa, 1885-1960', *Journal of African Studies* (UCLA) 12, 1 (Spring 1985), pp. 39-46 and *Minami Afurika to Nihon.*

South Africa. Both of these ideas have been emphasised to reflect its innocence and reliability as a partner in Africa. But do these arguments stand up under closer scrutiny?

We should first look at Japan's historical relations with Africa in the period up to 1945 in relation to its links with South Africa, Namibia (then the mandated territory of South West Africa) and Ethiopia, and its actions during the Second World War.

From the time when its contacts with Africa began in the late nineteenth century,[31] Japan paid special attention to both South Africa and Egypt as gateways to Europe and as potential trading partners in the region. However, the development of mutual relations centring on trade relations did not progress significantly till the time of the First World War. This delay was caused by the political situation in both African countries and in Japan. The peace and unity between South Africa's White colonial populations (Boers and those of British stock),[32] symbolised by the formation of the Union of South Africa, did not materialise till 31 May 1910, followed by the bestowal of self-governing status on 1 July the same year. In Japan[33] it was not till after the

---

[31] The roots of Japan's historical contact with Africa can be traced back to the latter part of the sixteenth century. For more on this subject, see Fujita Midori, 'Edo Jidai ni Okeru Nihonjin no Afurika Kan', *Nihon Chuto Gakkai Nenpo*, 2 (1987) and Richard A. Bradshaw, 'Japan and European Colonialism in Africa, 1800-1937', unpublished Ph.D. thesis, University of Ohio, 1992, pp. 46-79.

[32] The South African or so-called Boer war began in earnest in the thirty-second year of Meiji (1899). At that time, Japanese army staff headquarters sent Hiraoka Heihachiro to the country to observe the war and report on military tactics. Nishino Terutaro, 'Meiji Ki ni Okeru Nihonjin no Afurika Kan (Japanese Views of Africa in the Early Meiji Period)', *Toyo Bunka Kenkyusho Kiyo*, 33 (March 1964), pp. 165-6.

[33] For pioneering works on Japan's relations with Africa in the pre-war period, see Nishino, note 32 as well as the same author's 'Ryo taisen kan ni okeru Afurika keizai chosa', *Afurika Kenkyu*, 1:1 (December 1963); 1:2 (March 1964). See also Okakura Takashi and Kitagawa Katsuhiko, *Nihon Afurika Koryushi*, Tokyo: Dobunkan, 1993.

Japan's interest in South Africa was also stimulated by the question of immigration. In this regard, Shiraishi Kenji notes that 'one of the main reasons for designating an honorary consul in 1910 was because Japanese immigration to Brazil had begun two years before and Japanese ships needed ports to call at.' *Zanjibaru no Joshigun*, Tokyo Tokisha, 1971, p. 70.

Fig. 2.5. TRADE WITH AFRICA, 1896–1962

(unit: ¥ 1,000)

		African continent Exports	Imports	South Africa Exports	Imports
Meiji period	29 (1896)	—	—	—	—
	30 (1897)	—	—	—	—
	31 (1898)	116	356	—	—
	32 (1899)	661	939	—	—
	33 (1900)	278	1,468	—	—
	34 (1901)	308	1,890	—	—
	35 (1902)	449	2,418	—	—
	36 (1903)	323	2,402	—	—
	37 (1904)	419	2,476	—	—
	38 (1905)	284	2,999	—	—
	39 (1906)	379	1,670	—	—
	40 (1907)	386	3,457	—	—
	41 (1908)	616	5,073	—	—
	42 (1909)	841	5,464	—	—
	43 (1910)	807	4,192	—	—
	44 (1911)	688	5,502	—	—
Taisho period	1 (1912)	1,338	6,391	454	0
	2 (1913)	1,846	7,189	475	46
	3 (1914)	2,315	6,829	493	0
	4 (1915)	2,199	6,162	1,000	0
	5 (1916)	10,147	8,566	4,276	7
	6 (1917)	20,809	39,796	6,788	18,852

		African continent Exports	Imports	South Africa Exports	Imports
	7 (1918)	48,202	39,285	18,343	29,449
	8 (1919)	24,782	54,578	8,195	37,164
	9 (1920)	39,621	88,449	8,206	73,895
	10 (1921)	9,057	16,998	3,851	2,862
	11 (1922)	11,644	17,020	4,820	3,778
	12 (1923)	25,240	22,716	4,749	665
	13 (1924)	41,202	22,072	4,764	991
	14 (1925)	42,951	41,477	9,539	1,325
Showa period	1 (1926)	43,155	41,286	10,741	917
	2 (1927)	51,235	36,402	11,640	1,082
	3 (1928)	43,924	32,209	11,695	1,341
	4 (1929)	60,534	42,537	13,179	1,448
	5 (1930)	57,040	23,977	14,196	1,618
	6 (1931)	58,868	16,227	19,283	1,333
	7 (1932)	85,695	27,450	16,418	2,636
	8 (1933)	137,239	48,407	26,741	4,313
	9 (1934)	182,397	79,574	29,540	8,234
	10 (1935)	183,528	69,186	32,769	4,762
	11 (1936)	197,703	108,143	41,534	22,561
	12 (1937)	242,735	206,330	53,749	88,852
	13 (1938)	137,336	60,621	35,291	1,810
	14 (1939)	152,909	92,788	16,802	9,486

(unit: ¥ million)

16	(1941)	46,818	42,291	24,545	13,915
17	(1942)	15	72	—	0
18	(1943)	—	80	—	44
19	(1944)	141	3	—	—
20	(1945)	—	1,328	—	—
21	(1946)	337	119	—	—
22	(1947)	2,714	435	0	0
23	(1948)	19,793	1,730	245	274
24	(1949)	26,555	12,264	751	1,405
25	(1950)	40,302	9,454	10,710	1,248
26	(1951)	34,003	28,850	10,679	2,158
27	(1952)	46,361	19,091	6,489	4,742
28	(1953)	49,857	20,113	10,168	7,048
29	(1954)	74,009	18,462	10,904	3,810
30	(1955)		22,664	10,405	6,302
31	(1956)	141,300	36,519	12,465	9,492
32	(1957)	179,623	37,364	17,985	12,275
33	(1958)	149,584	30,145	14,039	5,747
34	(1959)	147,561	46,186	18,634	12,451
35	(1960)	126,638	59,002	12,543	20,470
36	(1961)	137,460	68,513	17,661	29,297
37	(1962)	120,659	78,522	21,611	40,708

Source: Nihon no Keizai; Tokei, Jijo (Economic Statistics of Japan), prepared under the supervision of the Research Bureau of the Economic Planning Agency, Statistics Division, and published by Shiseido in 1986, pp. 302–5. This data first appeared in Jun Morikawa, 'The Myth and Reality', p. 41.

Russo-Japanese war (1904–5) and the regaining of full tariff autonomy in 1911 that basic political and economic changes both at home and in the international arena permitted Japan to turn its attention to Africa in the years before the First World War. The following passage from a 1917 report illustrates the nature of relations between the two countries before the war.

On reflection, there is nothing much to report regarding the historical relations between Japan and South Africa. South Africa lies in a distant location about 10,000 nautical miles away by sea, so there is first of all the difficulty of communication. A Japanese battleship, the *Ikoma*, did stop by the Cape of Good Hope and anchor at Cape Town during an official trip to the South American Republic of Argentina and to Britain in 1910, but apart from this, calls by Japanese ships at South African ports have been almost unheard of. There are only about ten Japanese in the whole of South Africa. As for Japanese stores, Komahei Furuya's 'Mikado' in Cape Town is about all there is.[34]

The limited relations between the two countries during this initial period also reflected in the trade figures for the years 1912–14 (see Figure 2.5).

With the development of trade which accompanied the outbreak of the First World War, direct and regular contacts of various kinds were established between the two countries. As this further excerpt from the same 1917 report shows, international, political and economic factors caused the expansion of this trade:

When the First World War broke out, imports from Europe (from Germany in particular) were interrupted and goods shipped to the South African market became scarce. The cost of living in South Africa, which even in normal circumstances was 30 to 50 per cent higher than in England, began to riser even higher. Demand became so great that people competed for goods of whatever quality and make. The European war, moreover, continued month after month without pause, so that imports from Europe gradually declined.

[34] Noshomusho, Shokokyoku (Ministry of Agriculture and Commerce, Department of Commerce and Industry), 'Minami Afurika Boeki Jijo', *Shoko Isan*, 48 (1917), pp. 25-6.

Attention finally turned to Japan as the supply of goods became minimal. In order to conduct business directly, about ten South African businessmen travelled by ship to Japan. From January 1916, in order to avoid the dangers of passing through the Mediterranean sea on their European voyages, the Nihon Yusen Kaisha (NYK) ships made detours via the Cape of Good Hope. Japan's trade with South Africa thus became more prosperous than ever before.

Except for a small amount of direct importing by companies such as the aforementioned 'Mikado', Japanese goods had until that time gone first to London or India and were then re-exported via these countries to the South African market. Because direct exports from Japan to South Africa were very few, the number of Japanese who were attentive to [the potential of] South Africa as a market was naturally small as well. Thus to say that documents and other written materials regarding South Africa are practically non-existent at this time is hardly an over-statement. Even so it is disturbing to find how inadequate the general public's knowledge of South Africa is.

Trade between the Union of South Africa and Japan is still in a state of infancy. Japanese exports to the Union are definitely large in comparison to the small quantity of Union exports to Japan; thus the trade is unbalanced in our favour. Among the European and American exporters to South Africa, Japan ranks between thirteenth and seventeenth.[35]

The rapid entry of Japanese goods into the South African market was made easier by an active foreign trade policy. Japan had already appointed a White South African, Jeppe Julius, as honorary consul in 1910, and in 1916 Japan sent its first official trade mission to South Africa. A Japanese consulate[36] was then established in Cape Town on 14 August

---

[35] *Ibid.*, p. 26.

[36] See also Kitagawa Katsuhiko, 'Senzenki Nihon no Ryoji Hokoku ni Mirareru Afurika Keizai Jijo Chosa no Kenkyu', *Kansai Gaikokugo Daigaku Kenkyu Ronshu, Dai 50 60* (Review of Inquiry and Research), 50 (July 1989), pp. 303-20 and 'Japan's Economic Relations with Africa Between the Wars: A Study of Japanese Consular Reports', *African Study Monographs*, 11, 3 (December 1990), pp. 125-41.

1916 and in 1926 the OSK (Osaka Commercial Shipping Company) inaugurated a regular steamship line linking the South African port of Durban with the Japanese port of Kobe via Mombasa.

As a result, Southern Africa became an important foothold for the penetration of the African market.[37] However, the rapid increase in trade which accompanied the First World War was prevented from fully developing after the war primarily by the following three impediments: the predominant position of British capital in South Africa, the re-establishment of trade with South Africa's traditional partners (the Netherlands, Germany, France, Belgium, Italy etc.) after the war ended, and the existence of anti-Japanese sentiment.[38]

An examination of the most immediate and important of these problems, the presence of anti-Japanese sentiments, requires the discussion of two distinct phenomena: the intense flooding of the South African market by dumping Japanese goods, together with the extreme trade imbalance, and the Union's Immigration Act of 1913.[39] Oyama Ujiro, who served as Consul-General in San Francisco from 1923

[37] With regard to the particular attention paid to Blacks in South Africa as a potential market, see *Minami Afurika Boeki Jijo, Shoko Isan*, p. 12: 'The focus of this native demand is for low-priced cotton cloth and wool blankets, ornamental trinkets, bamboo baskets, musical instruments and the like. In terms of trade, we can't afford to overlook the importance of the fact that these natives make up most of the population.'

[38] According to 'Afurika Keizai Jijo Tenbo', a report issued by the Japanese Foreign Ministry's Commerce Bureau, Second Section, in 1932: 'Right after the outbreak of the Great European [*sic*] War, it was cotton blankets that were introduced into South Africa . . . However, as soon as Belgian and Dutch cotton blankets reappeared, the Japanese products were gradually pushed out of the market and importation of Japanese blankets was stopped completely around 1924. Then in 1926, due to the falling price of cotton yarn as well as the favourable exchange rate, Japanese cotton blankets re-appeared on the South African market but unfortunately have not recovered their former position' (p. 703).

[39] Moreover, South African businessmen and others are advocating a boycott of Japanese goods by shouting the slogan that South Africa should only buy from countries that import lots of South African goods. In light of this, it is regrettable that Japan only imported ¥1.6 million worth of goods from South Africa in 1930 while we exported ¥14.2 million worth. For our own sake, we ought to purchase more from this region in order not to give rise to such arguments. If not, we may end up in a deadlock.' *Ibid.*, p. 1120.

to 1924, and as head of the East African fact-finding mission
of 1927-8 described the problems associated with the law in
this way:

Although the White population [of the Union] is by no
means small, if compared to the Black population in any
of the provinces, Whites are approximately one-third or
less their number. The Whites are deeply disturbed by
the necessity of somehow preserving their privileged
position *vis-a-vis* these races in the future. For this reason
racial prejudice is much stronger in South Africa than it
is elsewhere. They have erected high 'colour-line' barriers
everywhere and coloured people are given no opportunities for either social or occupational advancement.[...]

Thus, this immigration law which was aimed at the
exclusion of Indians did not appear to be directed specifically at Indians. It could, in a broader sense, be applied
to all Asians and as a natural consequence could be applied to Japanese as well. After the enactment of the law
Japanese were treated by the Union of South Africa as
persons who were not permitted to immigrate. In keeping with further provisions regarding the enforcement of
this same law, Japanese travelling to South Africa had to
give two weeks' advance notice to receive temporary entry
permits from the Minister of the Interior. But even if
they did receive such temporary permits, unless they were
classified in one of the non-immigrant categories of the
law (as crew members of foreign ships, as foreign government officials or employees in their service, as persons
born within the Union or current residents and their
households etc.), they still had to face various restrictions
on entering the country as prohibited immigrants.[40]

The primary objective of Japan's South Africa policy at
that time was to resolve the above two problems as quickly
as possible. Of the two, the Immigration Law question[41]

[40] Oyama Ujiro, 'Nan-A Yushoku jin haiseki to Nihonjin Nyukoku Mondai',
Gaiko Jiho, 56-4, 623 (1930), pp. 24-6.
[41] For more on the Indian problem in South Africa, see Paul F. Power, 'Gandhi
in South Africa', *Journal of Modern African Studies*, 7, 3 (1969); and Hilda Kuper,
'Strangers in Plural Societies: Asians in South Africa and Uganda', *Pluralism in Africa*,
Berkeley: University of California, 1969, pp. 247-82.

was particularly important to the Japanese authorities, for in order to adjust the existing one-sided trade and to balance the future growing trade more equitably, it was essential that Japanese merchants and businessmen should be able to move about freely and to reside where they wished in the same way as Whites.

Furthermore, the immigration question also had various political, diplomatic and psychological ramifications which could not be ignored by Japanese policy-makers. Japan had become one of the Five Great Powers after the First World War; thus the question of obtaining the freedom for Japanese people to enter the Union of South Africa and to conduct economic activity there on an equal footing with Whites could not be ignored if Japan was going to maintain the honour of its Empire. The Japanese policy of asking Pretoria to allow the Japanese, though members of a 'yellow race', to be treated legally as Whites in South Africa finally achieved its end when, in November 1930, the status of 'honorary White' was granted. Ujiro Oyama had the following to say about this:

> According to recent reports, an understanding has been reached by South Africa's Acting Vice-Minister of External Affairs and in Cape Town our acting Consul, Mr Yamazaki, concerning the long-pending issue of Japanese nationals entry into the Union. As a result, the application of the Immigration Law in the case of Japanese has been rescinded and our merchants, clerks and others such as travellers can enter the country freely. With regard to residence, Japanese will be also treated in the same way as Europeans and Americans. This difficult problem, pending since 1913, has been resolved in a manner satisfactory to us. In recent years, our people have gradually begun to notice the prospects for Japan's trade with Africa. In fact, there is today even an African Exhibition in Osaka which opened last year on 1 November and continues to attract large crowds. For these regulations regarding entry and housing which have constituted such a difficult problem for Japanese travellers to be rescinded now when relations between our countries look as if they might finally start prospering is certainly most timely and appropriate.

It is difficult to restrain the joy we feel at this development of our mutual commerce and amicable relations and we must also express our appreciation to the Japanese officials at Cape Town for the efforts they have made.[42]

It is generally claimed that the Japanese first gained the right to be treated as 'honorary Whites' in South Africa in April 1961 when, in response to questions in the National Assembly during a debate on how the Groups Areas Act should be applied to the Japanese, the Minister of the Interior replied that Japanese were to be treated on a par with Europeans.[43] But such claims overlook what this same Minister of the Interior added afterwards by way of explanation: 'that this had become common practice under successive prior administrations'.[44] This is an important acknowledgement of a practice that started during the second Hertzog government (1929-33) and lasted for well over half a century.

Quite apart from the pressure from the Japanese government, we should also note here not only the timing but also that what lay behind the decision to have Japanese treated as 'honorary Whites' was the shock to the South African economy, especially to the White agricultural sector, brought about by the Great Depression; this combination of forces brought about the change in status.

In 1930 the total value of South Africa's main agricultural exports of wool, mohair, maize, skins, sugar, wattle-bark etc. fell to £17 million. Compared to £23,760,000 the previous year before and a total of 29.4 million in 1928, this was a remarkably large decrease. Quite unimaginable distress in farm households accompanied this sharp decline

[42] Oyama, p. 22.

[43] This has had unfortunate consequences. People's awareness of the relationship between South Africa and Japan (and of Japan's current actions in regard to South Africa) have been limited by the tendency of researchers, critics and journalists to misinform the public with regard to this point. People thus have the mistaken impression that the relationship between the two countries began in the 1960s. See Noma Kanjiro, *Sabetsu to Hangyaku no Genten: Aparutoheito no Kuni*, Rironsha, 1969, p. 236; Kusuhara Akira. *Afurika no ue to aparutoheito*, Aki Shobo, 1984, pp. 54-5; Kitazawa Yoko, *Kuroi Afurika*, Seibun Bukkusu, 1981, pp. 177, 211; Shinoda Yutaka, *Kumon Suru Afurika.*, Iwanami Shoten, 1985, p. 41.

[44] Zai Puretoria Nihonkoku Soryojikan (ed.), p. 113.

in the value of exports. Given agricultural commodity prices at present, the vast majority of farm households are losing money but continue to produce anyway.[45]

South Africa's change of policy towards Japan at the time of the Great Depression first appeared in the form of permission for Japanese wool purchasers to enter the country. On 2 September 1930, the Union of South Africa's Minister of Agriculture decided to permit the entrance of Japanese buyers into the Union to trade on the wool market, on the condition that they respected fair competition.[46] But this did not immediately correct the trade imbalance as the South African authorities had hoped it would. There was thus a fresh outburst of anti-Japanese feeling within South Africa:

> . . . South Africa's policy to promote the buying of wool was far less successful than expected. The South African market was flooded by Japanese products. In contrast, imports of European goods, especially British goods, were declining sharply and pro-British elements in South Africa thus strongly attacked the failure of the 'Gentleman's Agreement' with Japan and the fact that Japan purchased such a small quantity of South African wool. In addition, since all the newspapers have joined in running articles about Japanese insincerity and the unfair competition of Japanese traders, anti-Japanese sentiment is increasing dramatically and it has reached the point that the people are filled with antagonism toward Japan and her products.[47]

After November 1930, the severe imbalance in trade between the two countries was the key issue which Japanese policy towards South Africa had to face, but its importance subsided after trade friction between Japan and Australia erupted in 1936:

> At the beginning of 1936, a trade dispute broke out between Japan and Australia. Aiming at a boycott of Australian wool, the Japanese government enacted pro-

[45] 'Afurika Keizai Jijo Tenbo', p. 640.
[46] Yagi Nagato, 'Minami Afurika no okeru hai-nichi no shinso', *Gaiko Jiho*, 56-61, 620 (1930), p. 264.
[47] Nihon Gomu Seihin Yushutsu Kumiai, *Minami Afurika Renpo*, Chosa Kenkyu 8 (1937), p. 3.

tectionist legislation against Australia on 25 June. As a result, the quantity of wool which was usually imported from Australia was of necessity being supplied by the Union of South Africa. The former trade imbalance between Japan and South Africa, greatly favouring Japan, was thus suddenly reversed. Between January and May of this year, an excess of imports from South Africa over exports totalled ¥18,071,570, with imports valued at ¥33,917,087 and exports valued at ¥15,845,517. Last year's exports during the same period amounted to ¥12,477,768 and imports ¥3,596,640, with exports exceeding imports by ¥8,881,128. As this indicates, imports will very likely exceed exports by some ¥30 million by the end of this year [in 1930 there were roughly ¥10 to £1 sterling].

In short, introduction of protectionist trade legislation against Australia has brought about a revolutionary change in trade and commerce relations between Japan and the Union of South Africa. Consequently, the anti-Japanese sentiment and hostility to Japan and her products which resulted from our excessive exports have, at this juncture, begun to fade. Although the influx of Japanese products is not necessarily welcomed in South Africa, if, after this, it is judged that trade is going smoothly, I feel keenly that this will afford a good chance to strengthen exports to South Africa and develop an external market based on orderly exports.[48]

A closer examination of this dramatic invasion of the

---

[48] *Ibid.*, p. 15. E.M. Andrews describes the causes and effects of the trade diversion policy which was introduced by the Australian government in May 1936: 'The motives behind the policy remain unclear. Australian manufacturers resented Japanese competition with its lower prices, but probably the main interest group at work was the British textile industry. As early as 1934, Japan had displaced Britain as the largest supplier of textiles to Australia, and Joe Lyons, the Australian prime minister, in explaining his government's policy against the torrent of criticism it received, laid much stress on "unfair" Japanese competition. This was a disastrous policy. In effect, Australia was embarking on a trade war with both Japan and America at the same time. The policy was soon modified and later abandoned, but the shock to Japan had been great. From that time, Japanese industrialists began to look elsewhere for wool supplies and to toy with synthetic materials.' *A History of Australian Foreign Policy*, 2nd edn, Melbourne: Longman Cheshire, 1988, pp. 72-3.

South African market by Japanese goods in the 1930s is warranted here. Compared to that of other leading exporters to South Africa, Japan's position was as follows:

In 1934, the leading exporters to South Africa were Great Britain, the United States, Germany, Japan and Canada, with Japan in fifth position. But in 1935, Canada's share of exports dropped from 3.9 to 3.2 per cent and Japan advanced to fourth place. It was at this time that the other previously oblivious countries of the world woke up to the fact that this Japanese activity was not limited to South Africa but was happening Africa-wide as well as in every corner of the world still considered to be new markets.

In terms of the position of each importing country, Britain was first in 1936. Of total imports valued at £111,173,000 Britain imported £93,008,000 worth. In second place was France whose imports were worth £2,843,000, leaving a gap of £90,165,000 between France and Britain. Due to trade adjustments, the value of exports to our country has recently shown an increase. They were £428,000 in 1935, indicating the situation was still one of severe trade imbalance compared with the import figures. In 1936, however, the figure rose to £2,335,000, raising Japan to third place behind France. Then in 1937, wool exports to Japan increased rapidly. By as early as the end of May, the value of exports was almost double the value of imports from Japan.[49]

Trade between Japan and South Africa continued to develop in 1937 and reached its pre-Second World War era peak. What is noteworthy about this period is the evolution of close relations between the two countries, both personally and economically, which led to the establishment of formal diplomatic relations in 1937. In the same year, Japan set up an Imperial legation in Pretoria.[50]

[49] *Ibid.*, pp. 7, 11.

[50] In reference to the activities of the Union of South Africa with regard to the establishment of diplomatic relations between the two countries, see Yoshida Kenichi, *Nan-A Renpo Shi,* Tokyo: Fuzanbo, 1944, p. 568: 'The Union of South Africa included the expenses for establishing a legation in Japan in its budget but because of Japan's invasion of China etc., its plan to send a minister there could never be realised.'

This investigation has demonstrated that, in contrast to common belief, the development of relations between Japan and South Africa is not a relatively recent phenomenon, dating from the 1960s. The roots of these relations are much older and deeper. However, intimate relations between the countries were to cool soon after their development as Japan moved towards its alliance with Germany and Italy and embarked on a path of confrontation with Britain.

Having considered Japanese-African relations up to the Second World War, we should now look at those relations in terms of the events of the Versailles Peace Conference of 1919. More specifically we look at the pre-1945 historical relationship between Japan and South West Africa (now Namibia), particularly Japan's actions during the Versailles conference.

South West Africa came into the orbit of colonial powers in the latter part of the nineteenth century. First, Walvis Bay and the adjacent territory was brought under the control of the British Empire in 1878, and this enclave was incorporated into Cape Colony in 1884. The rest of South West Africa came under the control of Germany and so remained from 1884 till 1915, when White South Africans invaded the territory and took charge of it.

The difficulty of the South West African problem arose in large part from Pretoria's ability to take advantage of the First World War by occupying this territory and then annexing it under the pretext of administering it as a mandate for the League of Nations. The combination of these two factors was largely responsible for the delay in this problem being resolved.

Other countries too, besides Britain, Germany and South Africa, contributed to the problem. These countries were involved in decisions taken during both the Congress of Berlin (1884-5), when the powers made agreements concerning the partition of Africa, and at Versailles in 1919-20, when certain countries agreed on a re-partition.

In Berlin the country which is now Namibia became the German colony of South West Africa with the agreement of Britain, France, Italy, Belgium, Spain and Portugal. At Versailles South West Africa became a Class C mandate of the League of Nations by agreement of the five major powers of the time — Britain, the United States, France, Italy and Japan — as well as South Africa, Australia, New Zealand and Canada. Thus Japan in its way contributed to — and should accept some responsibility for — the Namibian problem. As will be made clear below, the important role which Japan played at Versailles in influencing the decisions taken on the mandated territories, especially the political and legal matters relating to Class C mandates (in which Japan had a clear interest and acted accordingly), underlines its special responsibility for decisions taken on South West Africa.

To understand these actions it is necessary to examine the actual proceedings at Versailles. The settlement of the former German colonies in the aftermath of the First World War was one of the central concerns of those attempting to create a framework for the promotion of international peace. However, the leading powers were also interested in using the Paris Peace Conference to ensure their predominance in the post-war international arena. As one Japanese scholar has noted:

> During the Paris [Versailles] Peace Conference which began in January 1919, only a few general assembly sessions were held. All important matters and decisions were handled by the Supreme Council, which was composed of the representatives of the five major powers — Japan, England, France, Italy and the United States.[51]

The following excerpts illustrate the process of deliberation concerning the former German colonies in the Highest Council of the League and Japan's reaction. Following unanimous agreement not to return the colonies to Germany there were three concrete proposals regarding the disposal of these territories: (1) internationalisation, pure and simple; (2) a mandate given to one of the Powers of the League of Nations; and (3) annexation pure and simple by a sovereign power.[52] Annexation was an option favoured by many. South

---

[51] Sato Shintaro, 'Inin Tochi to Nihon' in *Nihon Gaiko Shi*, vol. 14, Tokyo: Kajima Kenkyusho, 1972, p. 213.
[52] US Department of State, Papers Relating to the Foreign Relations of the United States, *The Paris Peace Conference, 1919*, vol. 3, House Document no. 874, Washington, DC, 1943, p. 760.

Africa's Minister of Defence General Smuts put forward a claim to the former German territory of South West Africa. It was noted that

> ... he would press very strongly that, whatever might be decided in respect to the valuable African Colonies in other parts of the Continent, this desert country, so closely connected with South Africa, should be included in the Union. The community to which he belonged had been in South Africa since 1650. They had established a white civilization in a savage continent and had become a great cultural agency all over South Africa. Their wish was that one of the effects of the great settlement now to be made should be to strengthen their position and to consolidate the union of the white races in South Africa. The Boer pastoralists were always looking for uninhabited country in which to settle. He was quite sure that if German South West Africa were given by the Conference to the Union, its work in this respect would be good.[53]

On 27 January 1919, Japan also disclosed its demands when its representative, Baron Makino, declared:

> The Japanese Government feels justified in claiming from the German Government the unconditional cession of: (a) the leased territory of Kiaochow together with the railways, and other rights possessed by Germany in respect of Shantung province, and (b) all of the Islands in German possession in the Pacific Ocean North of the Equator, together with the rights and properties in connection therewith.[54]

On the same day, the US President, Woodrow Wilson, argued the case against outright annexation and for the application of a mandate system:

> President Wilson said that in order that the field of discussion should be defined as clearly as possible, perhaps it would be better to begin with a clear statement of what was the mind of those who proposed a trusteeship by the League of Nations through the appointment of mandatories. The basis of this idea was the feeling which had

[53] *Ibid.*, p. 723.
[54] *Ibid.*, p. 738.

sprung up all over the world against further annexation. Yet, if the Colonies were not to be returned to Germany (as all were agreed), some other basis must be found to develop them and to take care of the inhabitants of these backward territories. It was with this object that the idea of administration through mandatories acting on behalf of the League of Nations arose.[55]

South West Africa was cited as an example of how such a system could work. In response to the Wilson formula, the British offered a compromise plan that was discussed on 30 January 1919. The most important points at issue were included in paragraphs 5 and 8:

(5) The Allied and Associated Powers are of the opinion that the character of the mandate must differ according to the stage of development of the people, the geographical situation of the territory, its economic conditions and other similar circumstances.
(8) Finally they consider that there are territories, such as South West Africa and certain of the Islands in the South Pacific, which, owing to the sparseness of their population, or their small size, or their remoteness from the centres of civilization, or their geographical contiguity to the mandatory state, and other circumstances, can be best administered under the laws of the mandatory state as integral portions thereof, subject to the safeguards abovementioned in the interests of the indigenous population.[56]

The compromise plan in effect classifed South West Africa and the South Pacific islands as Class C territories and allowed their *de facto* annexation. The promoters of annexation had won but President Wilson and Baron Makino confronted each other on 8 February 1919 in a last ditch effort. Wilson argued that the wording of the compromise plan should read 'as *if* integral portions' not 'as integral portions' and that this point should be clearly defined. By doing so, he tried to block the *de facto* annexation of C Class mandate territories by mandatory states. Baron Makino countered that they should respect the compromise reached at the

[55] Ibid., p. 740.
[56] Ibid., p. 796.

meeting of the five major powers and British Dominions on 30 January and strongly resisted Wilson's demand. Wilson eventually conceded and the C Class mandate territories were administered 'as integral portions' of the mandatory states.[57]

Japan's behaviour here was clearly motivated by self-interest, for the former German colonies in the South Pacific were classified as C Class mandate territories and Japan thus won their annexation. Although Tokyo may not have directly intended it, this type of self-serving behaviour also contributed favourably to the colonial nations re-scramble for Africa, reflected in South Africa's *de facto* annexation and integration of South West Africa, thus giving birth to the complicated and protracted Namibia problem.[58] In this context, Japan's historical influence is far from insignificant in South West Africa's annexation by Pretoria.

Two other issues related to the Versailles Peace Conference and its aftermath should also be mentioned briefly here. The first is the Japanese government's assertion that Baron Makino attempted to have an anti-racial discriminatiuon clause included in the Covenant of the League of Nations. As demonstrated in this chapter and further detailed in Chapter 6, Japan's claim to have championed the cause of anti-discrimination contrasts sharply with actual historical practices and in fact appears rather spurious.

Nevertheless, the Japanese government's statement has been accepted by some African and Japanese researchers.[59] Because of this, what was once no more than a political myth

---

[57] Japanese Ministry of Foreign Affairs, *1919 Pari Kowakaigi Keika ni Kan Suru Chosho* No. 3, (15 March 1919), Tokyo, p. 199.

[58] See the letters from the Portuguese government and the government of the Union of South Africa to the Secretary-General of the League of Nations and the agreement between the two governments in relation to the boundary between the mandated territory of South West Africa and Angola in the *League of Nations Official Journal*, November 1926, p. 1533.

[59] In UN Information Center, *Aparutoheito — Nihon ni Totte no Imi*, Tokyo, 1983, p. 4, it is noted that at a symposium titled 'South Africa's Racial Discrimination Policy and Japan's Role' held in Tokyo on 20 January 1983, the Chairman of the UN Special Committee Against Apartheid, Alhaji Yusuff Maitama-Sule, sent a message noting that almost sixty years earlier Japan had taken the lead in attempting to get the principle of racial equality included in the Covenant of the League of Nations. He recalled the fact that international action was a forerunner of the latter-day movement against racism.

has taken on a real life of its own, and recently its propagation has spread with increasing speed. For instance, in a presentation at the thirteenth autumn symposium of the Japan Peace Research Association (10 December 1984), it was reported that there had been talk of including references to Japan's attempt to introduce such a clause into the League of Nations Covenant within primary and middle school textbooks in order to make more people aware of it. Some might consider it irresponsible for researchers not to study the actual nature of these relationships and attitudes before pronouncing such dicta.

The second point deserving mention is Japan's participation in the San Remo conference of 1920 where decisions were made on the Middle East. Itagaki Yuzo has analysed Japan's role at that conference:

> It is frequently stated that the Japanese have not dirtied their hands when it comes to the Palestinian issue . . . The Palestinians probably wouldn't agree. After the First World War, there was a meeting of the League of Nations at San Remo in 1920. Here decisions were reached regarding the partition of the Middle East in accordance with claims staked out mostly by Britain and France. . . this partition of territory was related from the start to the proposal reality soon to be, to 'establish a national home for the Jewish people' in the midst of these spheres of influence.

> It was at this San Remo conference that decisions regarding the division of the surrounding areas into [the mandates of] Syria, Jordan Transjordan, Iraq etc. were taken. It was here that the system was established by which the Arab territories or the Ottoman empire would be partitioned and the Middle East would be divided up by the Allied victors after the First World War. As one of the Allied powers who sent a representative to the San Remo conference, Japan shoulders some responsibility for the decisions taken at this conference.

Japan's attitude during the conference was a very ambivalent one. It is clear that, in order to protect the interests and rights acquired in Asia and the South Pacific, Japan's position at the San Remo conference was to leave the Middle East to Britain and France. She said in effect, please do whatever you like. [60]

In fact, how well does the Japanese government's 'clean hands' argument hold up in an analysis of Japan's behaviour just before and during the Second World War? One may begin to answer this by looking at the relationship between Japan and Ethiopia.[61]

During the late 1920s and early 1930s Japan pursued an active pro-Ethiopian diplomacy based on a kind of 'imperial court' diplomacy. On 21 June 1927 and again on 15 November 1930, Imperial Japan signed a treaty of friendship and commerce with the Ethiopian empire; it later established a legation at Addis Ababa on 1 January 1936. However, Japan's active African diplomacy collapsed when it became known that it was siding with Fascist Italy in its African expansion rather than with the African countries.[62]

Fascist Italy's invasion of Ethiopia began on 2 October 1935 and the official annexation was announced the following year on 9 May 1936. One of the most important international factors enabling Italy's aggression in Ethiopia to succeed was the tacit support of the major colonial powers in Africa (notably Britain and France) out of fear that if Ethiopia should repel the Italians it might encourage anticolonial movements in other areas.[63] It is interesting to note that while Italy prepared its invasion of Ethiopia from the spring to the autumn of 1935, the movement within Japan to support Ethiopia, with ultra-nationalist groups at its centre, was very active. However, once the war with China

---

[60] Itagaki Yuzo, 'Paresuchina Mondai to Nihon' in Shinji Kojima *et al.*, *Ima Ajia o Kangaeru*, Tokyo: Sanseido 1985, pp. 255-6.

[61] See Morikawa, 'The Myth and Reality.' See also Okakura Takashi, 'Japan and Ethiopia', in Okakura & Kitagura, pp. 29-61; Unno Yoshio, 'Dainji Itaria-Ethiopia Senso to Nihon', *Niigata Dai Hosei Riron*, 2 (January 1984), pp. 188-240: Bradshaw, unpublished Ph.D. dissertation, pp. 320-62; Furukawa Tetsushi, 'Japanese Ethiopian Relations in the 1920-30s: The Rise and Fall of "Sentimental" Relations', paper presented at the Thirty-fourth Annual Meeting of the African Studies Association, St Louis, Missouri, November 1991.

[62] See Okakura, 'Japan and Ethiopia', pp. 38-46.

[63] See Takashi Saito, *Senkanki Kokusai Seiji Shi,* Tokyo: Iwanami Shoten, 1979, p. 186.

broke out, the pro-Ethiopia movement lost momentum, since criticism of Italy's military action was indirect criticism of Japan's own behaviour in Manchuria.

With Japan's aggression against China and establishment of Manchukuo, Mussolini had been given an impressive precedent to follow. It had thus been made plain that international public opinion could be ignored; that withdrawal from the League of Nations did not necesarily bring international isolation (Japan withdrew from it on 27 March, 1933); and finally that aggression could pay off . . . Furthermore, Japan gave more than tacit approval to Italy's Ethiopian campaign, because after it had succeeded, Tokyo refused to recognise the Ethiopian government-in-exile, and closed its legation in Addis Ababa on 3 December 1936. It concluded the Tripartite Pact with Italy and Germany in September 1940.[64]

During the Second World War Japan maintained its African presence, this time in a military form. The Japanese Navy's submarines and support ships conducted significant activities off the coast of Africa from around the middle of 1942. They made search and reconnaisance missions over a wide area and in May 1942, the I-30 submarine was sent to East Africa to search out the enemy. It passed Aden on 6 May, Djibouti on 7 May, Zanzibar and Dar es Salaam on 19 May, and Mombasa on 25 May.[65]

Reconnaissance planes operating from the I-10 submarine made observations of Durban in South Africa on 20 May, but this mission produced no concrete results.[66] However, on 31 May a submarine reconnaissance mission sighted the British fleet in Diego Suarez Bay, which led to Japan's decision to attack. On that day two midget submarines sank a merchant ship, the *British Loyality*, and inflicted heavy damage on the British battleship *Ramillies*. This attack, taking place as it did

[64] Japan feared that criticism of Italy's aggression in Ethiopia would also lead to criticism of its occupation of Manchuria. See also Okakura, 'Japan and Ethiopia', pp. 45–6; Unno, p. 225; Bradshaw, pp. 358–61.

[65] *Sensuikan Shi* in Boei Kenkyujo Senshibu (ed.), *Dai Toa Senso Senshi Sosho* (The History of the Greater East Asian War), Defence Agency, National Institute for Defence Studies, Military History Department, Asagumo Shimbunsha, 1979, pp. 344–5.

[66] *Ibid.*, p. 240.

soon after the British occupation of Madagascar and almost simultaneously with the Japanese attack on Sydney harbour, was a serious political and psychological shock to the Allied forces.[67]

The Mozambique campaign took place from June to July 1942 and caused great losses to Allied convoys. Between 4 and 12 June the first operation alone sank twelve ships totalling 52,840 tons.[68] This action was seen as a supportive gesture for the German offensive in North Africa and the Soviet Union, as Takeuchi Kenichi, a crew member of the I-30, testified:

> Since Germany and Italy controlled the Mediterranean, Allied nations depended on remote supply routes round the southern tip of Africa for their Middle East and Asian supplies. The Germans wanted to destroy these supplies and after repeated requests from them, the headquarters of the Eighth Submarine Fleet undertook the mission as ordered. [69]

Submarines travelling via the Cape of Good Hope were utilised in various co-operative activities with the German military, such as the exchange of weapons, material, personnel and technology. Though sporadic, these activities were not insignificant for Japan for since the outbreak of the war between Germany and the Soviet Union, the African route was almost the only one left that linked Germany and Japan. Indeed, the importance of these connections is clear from the fact that the transfer of military technology by this route enabled Japan to develop jet fighters just before the end of the war.[70]

The Cape route was also used to bring the anti-British Indian independence movement leader, Subhas Chandra Bose, to Asia. On 27 April 1943, the I-29 submarine met a German U-boat south-east of Madagascar and Bose, who

[67] For more on this point, see East Indies Station War Diary for the Period 1 May to 18 June 1942 in Peggy Warner and Seno Sadao's *Tokushu Senkotei Senshi*, Tokyo: Jiji Tsushinsha, 1985, p. 195. English edition *The Coffin Boat* also available.
[68] Yoshimura Akira, *Shinkai no Shisha,* Tokyo: Bungei Shunju, 1990, pp. 15-16.
[69] See *Sensuikan Shi* in Boei Kenkyujo Senshibu (ed.), p. 344.
[70] See Maema Takanori, *Jetto Enjin ni Toritsukareta Otoko*, Tokyo: Kodansha, 1992, pp. 110-59.

had been in exile in Germany, came on board.[71] With the full backing of the Japanese military, he then went to Singapore and set up the Free India provisional government-in-exile on 21 October 1943. Bose's Indian National Army fought in Burma with Japan in a joint operation during the Imphal campaign,[72] but was soundly defeated. By contrast, among the victorious Allied forces there were many African soldiers, such as those of the 81st and 82nd West Africa Divisions and the 11th East Africa Division.

Africa's contribution to the defeat of Japanese militarism may have been of only secondary importance, but it was uranium mined in the Belgian Congo that was used in the atomic bombs dropped on Hiroshima and Nagasaki.[73] The dropping of the bombs and the Soviet Union's entry into the war against Japan in its final stage were decisive in finally forcing the Japanese government to concede defeat. There were also political and diplomatic elements: the Ethiopian government-in-exile declared war on Japan on 14 December 1942, Liberia did so on 27 January 1944 and Egypt on 26 February 1945. South Africa declared war on Japan on 8 December 1941, immediately after the attack on Pearl Harbor.[74]

Thus historically Japan's relationship with Africa has not been as non-political and 'clean' as has sometimes been suggested. This becomes even clearer if one considers that Japan's significant economic penetration of Africa was made possible by taking advantage of the European colonial structure in place in Africa.[75] In any case, the judgement on whether Japan has had 'clean hands' in Africa should be left to the African side to decide. The Japanese government cannot

[71] Yoshimura, pp. 90-7.

[72] *Inpaal Sakusen—Biruma no Boei* (The Imphal Campaign — The Defence of Burma) in Boei Kenkyujo Senshibu (ed.), *Dai Toa Senso Senshi Sosho*, pp. 170-6; 272-5, 613-5.

[73] John Gunther, *Inside Africa*, London: Hamish Hamilton, 1955, pp. 657; 665-6.

[74] See Morikawa, 'The Myth and Reality' p. 44.

[75] *Ibid.*, pp. 40-2. See also Kweku Ampiah, 'British Commercial Policies against Japanese Expansionism in East and West Africa, 1932-1935', paper presented at the African Studies Association Conference in Atlanta, November 1989; Bradshaw, unpublished Ph.D. dissertation, pp. 363-415.

profess such a view unilaterally without providing objective and comprehensive evidence to support it—and without laying itself open to the charge of political myth-making.

3

JAPAN'S AFRICAN DIPLOMACY: POST-WAR DEVELOPMENT

The post-war development of Japan's African diplomacy will be discussed here in relation to three continually fluctuating factors: the development of international politics in general and in the African region in particular, and Japan's evolving role and position in the world.

Japan's post-war policy can be divided into three main periods: 1951-60, the decade in which the dual diplomacy was formulated; the years from 1960 to 1975, when the policy was consolidated and flourished; and the post-1975 period, when serious cracks began to appear and the structure began to disintegrate.

The first phase, 1951-60

After defeat in the Second World War and the subsequent Allied Occupation, Japan regained its independence on 28 April 1952. But its post-war African diplomacy began somewhat earlier, in September 1951, when it signed a peace treaty in San Francisco with the Allied nations of the Western bloc (including Ethiopia, Liberia, Egypt and South Africa) and concluded a security treaty with the United States.[1] The explicit and implicit support of South Africa through these treaties was strengthened during the Korean war (1950-3), for it was in the context of the pro-American, anti-Communist climate of the early 1950s that Japan's dual diplomacy with White and Black Africa was formulated. This discussion looks first at the White Africa policy.

In November 1952, Tokyo opened a consulate-general in

[1] Although the former Soviet Union, Poland and Czechoslovakia participated in the San Francisco conference, they expressed their dissatisfaction with the peace treaty and did not sign it. See Ministry of Foreign Affairs (comp.), *Nihon Gaiko Hyakunen Shoshi,* Tokyo: Yamada Shoin, 1959, pp. 266-85.

Pretoria and a consulate in Salisbury, Rhodesia. Relations with Portugal were resumed in 1953 and an embassy was opened in Lisbon in 1959. Thus Japan had re-established friendly relations with the countries that controlled the 'White Triangle' area of Africa well before 1960. With this diplomatic groundwork in place, its economic presence in Southern Africa expanded rapidly after 1960.

Economic relations with South Africa had resumed in 1948 while Japan was still under Occupation rule. This was the same year that the National Party took power in South Africa and introduced apartheid as an official policy. On 20 November 1959, Tokyo tentatively agreed to and formally concluded on 15 Feburary 1960 a trade agreement with the Federation of Rhodesia and Nyasaland (1953-63), which was virtually controlled by the White settler forces of Southern Rhodesia. This agreement allowed Japan to establish an economic foothold in the mineral rich Copperbelt region and was described in the 1960 Japanese Diplomatic Blue Book as being of special significance since it was the first international agreement concluded with a Sub-Saharan country.[2] This agreement also contributed to the strengthening of the material base of the White racist power. For example, Japan's exports to the Federation in 1959 increased by 82 per cent and imports increased eightfold compared to 1958.[3] In 1960, Japan's exports to the Federation increased 13 per cent and imports doubled over the previous year.[4]

For the most part, Black Africa in the 1950s was still under the domination of European colonialism. Thus Japan placed emphasis on economic re-entry into areas with which it had maintained relations before the Second World War, such as British East and West Africa. By the latter half of the 1950s, Black Africa had already recovered its position as an important export market for Japanese textile products.[5]

---

[2] Ministry of Foreign Affairs, *Waga Gaiko no Kinkyo*, Tokyo, 1960, pp.164-5.
[3] MITI, *Tsusho Hakusho: Kakuron*, Tokyo, 1960, p. 444.
[4] MITI, Tsusho Hakusho: Kakuron, Tokyo, 1961, p. 504.
[5] In 1957, 66.9 per cent of Japan's total exports to Africa (excluding ship exports to Liberia) was textile products, and Japanese textile products held an overall 15.1 per cent share of the African market. See MITI, *Tsusho Hakusho Kakuron*, Tokyo, 1958, p. 378.

In this same decade, Japan also took an especially active
diplomatic approach to Ghana and Ethiopia, the new and old
leaders of African politics. Japan immediately extended diplomatic recognition to Nkrumah's Ghana and established an
embassy in Accra in March 1959. The Japanese government
was eager to improve the bilateral relations with Ethiopia that
had been seriously damaged by its predecessor's acceptance of
the annexation of Ethiopia by Fascist Italy in 1936. Court
diplomacy was seen as one way of assisting restoration of the
relationship.[6] It was not surprising then that in 1957 Haile
Selassie became Japan's first post-war state guest and a welcom-
ing reception was held for him with Emperor Hirohito in
attendance. A veteran member of the Imperial Household
Agency Press Club described the Emperor as very nervous
about the visit and much relieved at its successful completion.[7]
The Emperor, Crown Prince and other members of the
Imperial Family even made a rare trip to Haneda airport to
give an official welcome to Haile Selassie. Throughout his
visit, every effort was made to avoid anything that could be
considered embarrassing to Haile Selassie, so as to portray the
Japanese Emperor as an impeccable host and demonstrate that
Japan could provide the same first-class treatment Haile Selassie
had received in American and European countries.[8]

---

[6] In Japan's diplomacy, especially towards Africa, important supplemental roles have
been delegated to the *zaikai* (i.e. business diplomacy) and the Emperor and his
family (the so-called *Koshitsu Gaiko* or Court Diplomacy). However, it is generally
difficult to obtain relevant information on the latter and Japanese scholars have
been reluctant to pursue a critical and analytical examination of the subject. As
result, there is no real democratic control of court diplomacy. For more on this
subject, see Jun Morikawa, 'Japan's African Diplomacy and the Hirohito Factor:
A Case Study of Japan's Post-WWII Court Diplomacy', paper presented at the US
African Studies Association, Seattle, November 1992.
[7] Takahashi Hiroshi, *Shocho Tenno*, Tokyo: Iwanami Shoten, 1987, p. 110. It is not
difficult to understand why the Emperor was so nervous. As previously mentioned,
friendly relations between the two nations had been established through Imperial
court diplomacy in the middle of the 1930s. When Mussolini invaded Ethiopia,
the Addis Ababa government repeatedly requested support from Tokyo but the
requests were ignored, and it is easy to imagine the disillusionment that flowed
from this. Twenty years later, Hailie Selassie, one of the heroes of the anti-Fascist
forces, and Hirohito, the defeated leader of Japanese imperialism, were meeting
face-to-face for the first time.
[8] *Ibid.*, p. 110.

No record is available of the formal meeting between Hirohito and Haile Selassie, but it is clear that relations between Tokyo and Ethiopia improved dramatically after this visit. In April 1958 embassies were opened simultaneously in Tokyo and Addis Ababa, and in December 1959 the Japan Ethiopian Friendship Treaty was concluded. Crown Prince Akihito paid a return visit to Ethiopia in November 1960.[9]

These early post-war contacts with both White and Black Africa established the base on which Japan's dual diplomacy was to be built. Although Japan's presence in Africa was still limited by European colonial domination of the Sub-Saharan area and Japan's own preoccupation with post-war reconstruction and re-establishing its presence in Asia, the overtures of the 1950s allowed the full-fledged development of Japan's dual diplomacy to take clear shape in the 1960s.

The second phase, 1960-75: the White Africa policy

During this period, Japan actualised its dual diplomacy towards White and Black Africa in the context of the intensification of the East-West confrontation in Africa and the rapid economic growth of Japan. The increase in Japan's economic power was confirmed on 28 April 1964, when Japan achieved membership in the 'advanced nations club' when it was admitted as a full member to the Organisation for Economic Co-operation and Development (OECD).[10] Only four years later, Japan's gross national product had reached a level surpassed only by the United States and the Soviet Union.

The White Africa policy in this period was characterised by a broadening of relations and an increase in the economic support that helped prevent the diplomatic, social and psychological isolation of the White minority regimes. Japan's support was reciprocated on 14 April 1961 with the acknowledgement, noted earlier, by the South African Min-

---

[9] Ministry of Foreign Affairs, Middle Eastern and African Affairs Bureau, *Afurika Bin Ran*, p. 25.

[10] In 1964, Japan joined the OECD, and with this action, became a member of the advanced group of nations in both name and reality. Gaimusho Sengo Gaikoshi Kenkyukai (ed.) *Nihon Gaiko Sanjunen—Sengo no Kiseki to Tenbo*, Tokyo: Sekai no Ugokisha, 1982, p. 122.

ister of the Interior of Japan's treatment by South Africa as
equal to that of White.[11] This was an active affirmation of
the honorary White status that Japan had had, in essence, since
the 1930s. This reconfirmation paved the way for even broader
business, sports, educational and cultural exchanges and was to
set an important precedent for South Africa's new Asian trading partners, Taiwan and South Korea.[12]

A major step towards expanded exchanges was the establishment of the Nippon Club of South Africa by the Japanese
business community in Johannesburg in 1961. This club,
created to assist the growing number of Japanese companies
in Johannesburg, was also responsible for the promotion and
early development of the Japanese School of Johannesburg. The
racist behaviour of these 'honorary Whites'[13]—doing business
with South Africa and residing in White residential areas—soon
brought criticism at home and abroad.

The government of Japan reached an agreement and offically
announced its intention to resume diplomatic relations with
Pretoria, which had been disrupted by the Second World War,
on 1 March 1961. The 1961 *Diplomatic Blue Book* described
the situation this way:

> While economic relations have been the main link between
> the two countries in recent years, exchange has increased
> significantly. Hence government discussions between the two
> nations on the resumption of diplomatic relations are un-
> derway. Since both sides are in agreement on this, embas-

[11] Zai Puretoria Nihonkoku Soryojikan (ed.), p. 113.

[12] For more on Taiwan and the Republic of Korea's relations with Pretoria, see
Kusuhara Akira, 'Apartoheito to Ajia—Nihon, Taiwan, Kankoku wa Do
Kakawatsute Iru ka', *Sekai*, January 1988, pp. 305-6. See also *Far Eastern Economic
Review*, 7 August 1986, pp. 14-15, and Geoffrey Roger Woods, 'Taiwanese
Investment in the Homelands of South Africa', unpublished Ph.D. thesis, Univer-
sity of Ohio, November 1991.

[13] 'In South Africa, it is not good to excessively emphasise that one is
Japanese but sometimes it is necessary. Ambulances and hospitals are
designated "for whites" and "for non-whites" and there is a big difference
between them. In the case of a traffic accident or sudden illness, it is
necessary to be sure to shout "Japanese".' JETRO, *Africa Business Guide*,
p. 277.

sies will be established in Tokyo and Pretoria as soon as the necessary internal procedures of both countries can be completed.[14]

It should be noted that this agreement was reached a year after the Sharpeville massacre, when over sixty Black African demonstrators were killed by White South African police, and two weeks before South Africa's withdrawal from the Commonwealth. There is no doubt that Japan's decision provided major support to South Africa since it faced grave diplomatic isolation abroad.

Of course, the Japanese government did indeed fear that its pro-Pretoria behaviour would invite severe criticism from Black Africa and the international community in general. To cope with this possibility in June 1961, the government made a tactical decision to keep the existing consulate-general in Pretoria and not upgrade it to the status of an embassy. However, it did not cancel or abrogate the original accord.[15] Although not officially admitted, the Japanese Foreign Ministry classified South Africa as a state with which diplomatic relations existed, and ambassadors were exchanged.[16]

This *modus operandi* satisfied Pretoria and had the added benefit of avoiding direct criticism from international public

---

[14] Ministry of Foreign Affairs, *Waga Gaiko no Kinkyo*, 1961, p. 136.

[15] This information was obtained in an interview with an official of the Japanese Foreign Ministry's United Nations Bureau on 24 March 1983. The official agreed to discuss the matter on the condition of anonymity.

[16] See Ueno Takao, 'Nihon to no Kankei — Mada Toi Afurika', *Shinko Afurika*, a report published by the Asahi Newspaper Investigative Research Bureau for internal use, 92, Z, p. 67, December 1962. Ueno cites Foreign Ministry data showing Japan had embassies in eight African states as of June 1961: Egypt, Sudan, Morocco, Ethiopia, South Africa, Ghana, Congo (Leopoldville) and Nigeria. See also the book *Gaimusho*, Tokyo: Kyoikusha Publishing Co., 1979, p. 140, in which it is noted that the Republic of South Africa is one of nine nations where embassies have legally been established but are not yet in actual operation. Julian R. Friedman, 'Basic Facts on the Republic of South Africa and the Policy of Apartheid', Unit on Apartheid, Department of Political and Security Council Affairs, Notes and Documents, no. 20/74 (August 1974), p. 57, in which Japan is listed as one of the thirty-seven nations that 'maintain diplomatic relations' with South Africa.

opinion in Black Africa. The dispatch of an ambassador-level representative to a consulate was not precedented. In the United States, for example, Japan maintains a consulate-general in New York but it is customarily headed by a senior ambassador because of New York's importance both on the American economic, political, cultrual and educational scene and as the site of the UN headquarters.[18] While Japan's official stance *vis-à-vis* the media was to deny any exchange of ambassadors with Pretoria, off-the-record comments by officials substantiate the view that this was just diplomatic rhetoric. At an informal meeting with members of Keidanren's Committee on Co-operation with Africa on 30 January 1979, Chiba Kazuo, Director-General of the Middle Eastern and African Affairs Bureau of the Foreign Ministry clearly admitted that Japan maintains diplomatic and trade relations with South Africa because it is dependent upon her abundant mineral resources.[19] Equally revealing is the statement made on 1 April 1984 by the late LDP Dietman, Hasegawa Takashi, a member of the Japan-South Africa Parliamentarians' Friendship League, who answered an open letter from the Japan Anti-Apartheid Committee by noting: South Africa has an ambassador in Japan and exchange visits by parliamentarians are OK . . .[20] A final example of this attitude is found in a special supplement on Japan in the *Financial Mail* of Johannesburg for 19 November 1982. J.S.F. Botha, then South African Consul-General in Tokyo, who had first been appointed in 1976, was described as one 'of our most senior ambassadors.' [21]

Soon after the decision was made to downplay diplomatic representation in favour of strong consular relations, the Japanese government also opened a consulate in Cape Town in

---

[18] For example, in 1988 the influential diplomat Hanabusa Masamichi, Director-General of the Foreign Ministry's Economic Co-operation Bureau, was dispatched to serve as Japan's top representative in the New York consulate-general. Subsequently, he became Director-General for Public Information and Cultural Affairs, and on 28 October 1993 he was appointed Ambassador to Italy. *Asahi Shimbun*, 27 October 1993.

[19] *Keidanren Shuho*, 15 February 1979, p. 5.

[20] *Nanbu Afurika Nenpo*, Nanbu Afurika Mondai Kenkyujo, Tokyo, 1985, p. 35.

[21] 'Japan: A Survey' Supplement to the 19 November 1982 edition, *Financial Mail*, p. 16.

April 1964. By the 1980s it was very clear that in terms of personnel and activities these two consular offices in South Africa were much more important and influential than the Japanese embassies in either Nigeria or Kenya. In November 1982, according to the Foreign Ministry, eleven Japanese embassy officials were employed in Lagos and twelve in Nairobi. By way of contrast, the *Springbok Newsletter*, published by the Nippon Club of South Africa, reported that in 1979 Japanese officials and their families, totalling sixty-six people, were living in the Republic.[22]

Japan's decision officially to call its presence in South Africa a consulate rather than an embassy was a choice veiled in diplomatic rhetoric. However, its policy of trade enlargement and economic support for the Pretoria government was much more difficult to obscure. Economic support for the Pretoria regime was not limited to the expansion of trade relations alone. Japanese enterprises directly participated and co-operated in Pretoria's economic development projects such as the Iron and Steel Corporation of South Africa (ISCOR) expansion plan and the Sishen-Saldanha Plan for iron ore mine development (mentioned in detail in Chapter 4). First, we will look at matters related to the expansion of trade.

In the latter half of the 1950s, trade figures for Japan and South Africa were not significantly different from those for Japan's major Black African trading partners — Nigeria, Ghana and Kenya. In 1957 Japanese exports to South Africa were about $50 million and imports about $34 million,[23] while exports to British East Africa were $34 million and imports about $18 million.[24] In British West Africa, Nigerian exports were worth $55 million and imports $1 million.[25] Exports to newly independent Ghana were $24 million and imports about $1 million.[26]

However, in spite of repeated calls for economic sanctions against South Africa by both the OAU and the UN in the 1960s, Japan's trade there grew phenomenally. By 1967 exports

[22] *Springbok, Newsletter* 16 January 1980.
[23] MITI, *Tsusho Hakusho: Kakuron*, 1958, p. 401.
[24] *Ibid.*, p. 397.
[25] *Ibid.*, p. 388.
[26] *Ibid.*, p. 391.

were $157 million and imports $267 million,[27] a threefold and eightfold increase, respectively, over the 1957 figures.

This huge increase led the Japanese consulate-general in Pretoria to issue the following report:

> For South Africa, Japan is a very important trading partner with a high growth rate. Since 1961, imports from Japan have increased rapidly and in 1967, Japan became South Africa's second largest export market after Britain and fourth largest supplier of manufactured goods.
>
> South Africa represented one-third of Japan's entire African export market in 1967 and its importance as a supplier of maize, wool, sugar, iron ore, pig iron and other mineral resources has been increasing. Currently, South Africa is Japan's eighteenth largest export market and its eleventh largest supplier of raw materials.[28]

Japan's trade with South Africa continued to grow during the next decade. By 1975, exports were $872 million and imports $868 million.[29] Figure 3.1 vividly reflects Japan's position as one of South Africa's very important trading partners.

Why did this trade grow so rapidly? During the period of rapid economic growth beginning in the early 1960s — the so-called Japanese Miracle — huge amounts of natural resources were required. Japan had a desperate need for stable supplies, which South Africa was in a position to meet. This compatible bilateral trade structure[30] explains these trade figures but there is another important aspect of the relationship that has been neglected, namely the existence in Tokyo of a strong political will to expand support for

[27] Zai Puretoria Nihonkoku Soryojikan (ed.), p. 99.

[28] *Ibid.*, p. 99.

[29] MITI, *Tsusho Hakusho: Kakuron*, 1977, pp. 725-6.

[30] 'Most spectacular has been trade with Japan. Exports to Japan rose from R 1.3 million in 1950 to over R 84 million in 1964 — a sixty-five-fold increase. During this period, great economic expansion occurred in Japan and South Africa was able to supply many products that country required, notably pig iron, steel, sugar and maize. Imports from Japan also increased greatly, so that in 1964, there was approximately balanced two-way trade.' D. Hobart Houghton, *The South African Economy*, Cape Town: Oxford University Press, 1967, p. 171.

the White regimes through trade. This was symbolised by the opening of a JETRO trade promotion office in Johannesburg as well as by the support and expansion of trade with Rhodesia and Portuguese Africa. In 1964 trade with Portugal and its so-called overseas provinces of Mozambique and Angola stood at $36 million.[31] This had soared by 1973 to $392 million.[32] In the case of Rhodesia, Colin Legum notes:

> Japan has in the past held a notorious record in breaking sanctions against Rhodesia. It was not until May 1968 that Tokyo finally withdrew its two diplomats from Salisbury in response to a Security Council decision on mandatory sanctions . . . Despite previous UN decisions and British policies on sanctions, Japan exported about £4.5 million worth of supplies to Rhodesia in 1967, and admitted to importing £400,000 worth of Rhodesian goods. There is little doubt, however, that its imports were much higher but these were disguised under re-routed bills of consignment through South Africa and Mozambique.[33]

Fig. 3.1. SOUTH AFRICA'S EXPORT PATTERN BY MARKETS, 1975

	%
United Kingdom	23.10
EEC	21.08
Japan	12.36
Africa	11.53
USA	11.09
Rest	20.84

Source: Reprinted from *South Africa, 1976* (official yearbook), Johannesburg: Chris van Rensburg, p. 513.

The opening of a JETRO office in May 1961 was a significant move towards the promotion of trade. Currently claming thirty offices throughout Japan and seventy-seven overseas, JETRO offices identify what products Japan wants

[31] Japanese embassy in Portugal (ed.) under the supervision of the Foreign Ministry's European and Oceanic Affairs Bureau, *Porutogaru* (Portugal), Tokyo, 1974, p. 118.
[32] *Ibid.*
[33] Colin Legum, 'Japan and Africa 1968', in Colin Legum and John Drysdale (eds), *Africa Contemporary Record Annual Survey and Documents, 1968-69*, vol. 1, London: Africa Research, 1969, p. 44.

to import and assist foreign countries in learning how to export to the Japanese market. There are eight offices in Africa: Abidjan, Lagos, Douala, Nairobi, Kinshasa, Dar-es-Salaam, Harare and Johannesburg. JETRO's own English-language promotional brochure describes itself as:

A non-profit government-related organisation established in 1958. Its mission is to support trade between Japan and other countries, with the aim of achieving balanced global trade. To achieve this, JETRO promotes imports in Japan, industrial co-operation between Japan and other countries, the strengthening of trade and industry in developing countries and international exchange.[34]

The organisation also promotes the goal of becoming 'one of the world's leading databanks for economic information on Japan and other countries.'[35] Besides providing connections with the Japanese market, JETRO also sponsors overseas seminars and other activities aimed to 'maintain and strengthen harmonious trade relationships'.[36]

Since JETRO is a public corporation under the direct supervision of the Ministry of International Trade and Industries (MITI), the Japanese government's strong political will and determination to maintain and expand trade with the Pretoria regime could not be doubted.

The second phase, 1960-75: the Black Africa policy

Between 1960 and 1975 the Japanese government formulated

---

[34] *JETRO: Japan External Trade Organization* (in English), Tokyo, March 1991, p. 1.

[35] *Ibid.*

[36] *Ibid.*, p. 2. The importance of JETRO's presence and connections in the promotion of trade can be seen in the fact that Japan's first moves towards promotion of trade with Russia came with the opening of a JETRO office in Moscow in October 1992, along with a special exploratory mission to Khabarovsk, slated to became a special economic zone. See 'JETRO to Open Office in Moscow', *Daily Yomiuri*, 21 August 1992. From another view, 'During 1972, for example, the *Digest of Japanese Industry* carried a report by Hiroshi Toyama, Director-General of the Trade and Development Bureau of the Japanese Ministry of International Trade and Industry, in which he said he was aiming at both a qualitative and quantitative expansion of trade between Japan and South Africa.' Godfrey Morrison, 'Japan's Year in Africa', in Colin Legum (ed.), *Africa Contemporary Record Annual Survey and Documents, 1972-73*, London: Africa Research, p. A 89.

the organisation of its African diplomacy while establishing diplomatic relations and expanding economic relations with the newly-born states of Black Africa. Noting that 'it was important to establish immediately the basic principles that will define Japan's future policy towards Africa', the Foreign Ministry held its first conference of ambassadors to African states in London on 10-13 January 1960 to consider the situation in Africa.[37] The conference was attended by the Japanese Ambassadors to Ethiopia and Ghana, the Consul-General to the Union of South Africa the Consuls to Kenya, the Congo and Nigeria, and the Japanese representatives in charge of Africa at Japan's London, Paris and Brussels embassies. The Foreign Ministry sent the Parliamentary Vice-Minister for foreign affairs, the Director-General of the Economic Affairs Bureau and the deputy director of the European and Oceanic Affairs Bureau.[38]

As can be seen from Figure 3.2 overleaf, more and more new embassies were being opened in Africa. Systematic research and information gathering on African affairs was required, a task entrusted mainly to the National Diet Library, MITI's Institute of Developing Economies and JETRO. Yet the organisational structure of Japan's African diplomacy was still weak, and in order to supplement their efforts the government relied on support from the LDP and the *zaikai*.

As will be demonstrated below, the LDP became actively involved in natural resources diplomacy after the early 1970s with the formation of the Diet Association of African Economic Development in April 1970. During the 1960s *zaikai* support was filtered primarily through the Africa Society of Japan, but on 31 August 1970 Keidanren formed its own Committee on Co-operation with Africa (CCA). This group was soon at the centre of the constellation of organisations dealing with Africa, such as the Africa Society of Japan and the bilateral friendship associations that grew from 1965 onward (see Figure 3.3).

The central focus of Japan's economic diplomacy towards Black Africa in the period 1960-75 consisted of export promotion and securing a stable supply of mineral resources.

---

[37] Ministry of Foreign Affairs, *Waga Gaiko no Kinkyo*, 1960, p. 143.
[38] *Ibid.*

The export promotion policy. In the early 1960s, Japan faced two problems in its attempts to promote exports to Black Africa. One was the serious trade imbalance in its own favour with the main trading partners — the Anglophone countries such as Nigeria and Kenya. The second difficulty was the application of Article 35 (the so-called escape clause) of the General Agreement on Tariffs and Trade (GATT) that imposed tariffs on Japanese goods in Black Africa in general and in the Francophone countries in particular.[39]

In Figure 3.4 (p. 67) Nigeria's trade figures show clearly the seriousness of the trade imbalance. With Zambia, Japan was able to avoid problems because of the huge importation of copper from there, but elsewhere in Africa the trade imbalance was a serious issue. As a result, in April 1965 Kenya, Tanzania and Uganda, followed by Nigeria in August, imposed tough import restrictions on Japanese goods that shocked the Japanese government.[40] Japan responded with measures to calm the situation down. It hurriedly offered yen loans equivalent to £15 million to four countries: Nigeria (£10 million), Kenya and Tanzania (£2 million each) and Uganda (£1 million). In Feburary 1967, Keidanren, the Japan Productivity Council, Japan Chamber of Commerce and Industry, Japan Federation of Employers Association (Nikkeiren) and the Japan Association of Corporate Executives also sent a joint

---

[39] In addition to these problems, the Japanese government and business world at that time were also concerned about whether the strengthening of relations between the EEC and Africa would affect Japan's economic advancement. An example of this can be seen in the Japanese government's dispatch of a fact-finding mission to EEC member states, West Africa and Equatorial Africa from 19 January to 16 February 1966. See Ministry of Foreign Affairs, *Waga Gaiko no Kinkyo*, 1966, p. 272. The concern was also reflected in the government's desire to obtain the research reports from the embassies in London and Paris and have them translated and published in Japanese. 'Difficultés et Possibilités de l'Expansion Economique par les Pays Tiers dans les Etats Associés à la CEE'; 'The Impact on Trade with Japan of the Three East African Community Countries Associating with the European Economic Community', Tokyo Nihon Keizai Chosa Kyogikai, 1968 and 1969 respectively.

[40] Ministry of Foreign Affairs, *Waga Gaiko no Kinkyo*, 1966, p. 47. As Figure 3.4 reveals, Japan's exports to Nigeria in 1965 totalled $58,984,000 and Japan's imports from Nigeria in 1965 amounted to only $9,285,000.

Japan's African Diplomacy: Post-War Development

Fig. 3.2. JAPANESE EMBASSIES IN SUB-SAHARAN AFRICA

	Established	Other countries served[a]
Ethiopia	April 1958	
Ghana	12 March 1959	
Congo (Zaire)	30 June 1960	Congo (Brazzaville), Rwanda, Burundi
Nigeria	26 December 1960	
Senegal	6 January 1962	Mali, Mauritania, Gambia, Guinea-Bissau, Cape Verde
Ivory Coast	22 February 1964	Burkina Faso, Niger, Benin, Togo
Kenya	1 June 1964	Uganda, Seychelles, Somalia
Tanzania	18 February 1966	
Madagascar	February 1968	Comoros, Mauritius
Zambia	15 January 1970	Botswana, Lesotho, Swaziland
Gabon	21 November 1972	Cameroon, Chad, Equatorial Guinea, São Tomé & Principe
Liberia	January 1973	Sierra Leone
Central African Rep.	25 January 1974	
Guinea	20 January 1976	
Zimbabwe	2 May 1981	Angola, Mozambique, Namibia

[a]Without Japanese embassies, though Japan has diplomatic relations with them.

Source: Compiled by author from Japanese Ministry of Foreign Affairs, Middle Eastern and African Affairs Bureau, *Afurika Binran Sahara Inan no Kuniguni.*

Fig. 3.3. BILATERAL FRIENDSHIP ASSOCIATIONS WITH BLACK AFRICAN COUNTRIES

	Established
Japan-Nigeria	1 February 1965
Japan-Ethiopia (Ethiopian Assoc'n of Japan)	27 April 1971
Japan-Zaire	3 June 1971
Japan-Guinea	29 May 1974
Japan-Gabon	19 March 1975
Japan-Zambia	20 December 1975
Japan-Senegal	25 February 1978
Japan-Tanzania	28 September 1978
Japan-Malawi	26 February 1983
Japan-Somalia	27 September 1983
Japan-Liberia	1 July 1984
Japan-Mali	31 July 1985
Japan-Niger	31 July 1985
Japan-Mauritius	5 December 1985
Japan-Mozambique	1 April 1986
Japan-Ghana	2 September 1987

Source: Japanese Ministry of Foreign Affairs, Middle Eastern and African Affairs Bureau, *Afurika Binran,* pp. 130-1.

economic mission to Kenya, Uganda, Tanzania, Malawi, Zambia and Nigeria.[41]

As a long-term method for settling the problem, the importance of expanding imports from these four countries was advocated. The then Director of African Affairs division of the Ministry of Foreign Affairs, Yoshida Nagao, observed:

> In order for Japan to respond to the requests of these nations, it is necessary to further strengthen our efforts to purchase primary products from the African nations to improve the trade imbalance. The increase of our export of Japanese goods now depends on the ever greater purchase of imports from our trading partners.[42]

However, demand in Japan for tropical agricultural products was not large and its trump card (used to increase its imports from most of these countries), namely large-scale mineral development and importation projects, did not materialise. Consequently, Japan attempted to counter and eventually alleviate dissatisfaction towards Japan's expanding imports by providing them with preferential allocations of ODA, diversification of imports and encouragement and promotion of direct investment.

GATT Article 35 was a very serious issue for Japan. Discriminatory high tariffs and an import quota system were applied to Japanese goods chiefly by the Francophone countries. The Japanese Foreign Ministry concluded that these countries, though independent, had carried over the institutions and policies of their former colonial master. They imposed maximum custom rates on Japanese goods approximately three times higher than those to which GATT Article 35 was not applied. As a result, Japan's exports to Francophone Africa, except Zaire, remained insignificant.[43] One major method for expanding its exports to Black Africa was to have the application of Article 35 to Japan by the Franchophone countries stopped, and to achieve this the Japanese government

---

[41] *Teikaihatsukoku Keizai Kyoryoku: Afurika Keizai Shisetsudan Hokokusho*, Tokyo: Nihon Seisansei Honbu Japan Productivity Center, International Department, 1967 (not for public sale).

[42] Yoshida Nagao, 'Afurika Shokoku no Doko to Nihon', *Kokusai Mondai*, 54 (September 1964), pp. 44-5.

[43] Ministry of Foreign Affairs, Public Information Bureau (ed.), *Afurika Sahara no Muko no Sekai*, p. 253.

Fig. 3.4. TRADE WITH AFRICAN STATES 1955-78 (Unit: ¥ 1m.)

	Ghana		Nigeria		Zaire		Ethiopia		Kenya	
	Exports	Imports	Exports	Imports	Exports	Imports	Exports	Imports	Exports	Imports
1955	7,014	15	15,020	47	1,226	45	1,423	375	1,685	498
1960	10,384	1,320	27,077	2,936	587	1,399	4,040	1,366	7,985	3,209
1965	8,481	2,857	21,234	3,343	1,871	1,374	7,738	1,552	9,236	1,998
1970	10,257	11,607	22,641	4,623	15,548	13,539	9,164	3,280	14,958	1,679
1973	7,763	21,162	38,393	51,471	13,813	22,115	7,697	6,241	19,827	6,600
1974	12,592	22,452	83,482	130,879	19,646	31,659	10,746	7,719	30,291	7,842
1975	11,327	20,725	173,655	82,810	11,180	17,764	9,140	8,943	21,292	7,794
1976	12,795	23,709	169,872	32,675	9,962	25,632	16,860	6,526	29,975	7,026
1977	15,435	40,537	270,287	5,537	9,999	24,344	17,066	8,994	38,319	4,805
1978	8,615	22,149	203,900	1,559	4,966	17,486	10,757	4,446	31,994	3,424

	Uganda		Tanzania		Mozambique		South Africa		Zambia	
	Exports	Imports	Exports	Imports	Exports	Imports	Exports	Imports	Exports	Imports
1955	952	764	4,611	1,349	213	165	10,382	6,295	—	—
1960	1,908	1,895	3,332	3,436	663	1,394	20,463	20,470	—	—
1965	2,249	1,966	3,545	1,943	3,199	3,938	49,491	43,293	2,940	21,919
1970	4,018	11,969	7,767	6,504	13,282	8,130	118,423	112,951	11,425	106,077
1973	1,761	7,225	11,612	4,467	10,705	6,601	161,710	142,070	13,827	79,333
1974	2,186	7,976	20,351	5,047	10,679	24,262	279,980	223,767	31,768	93,314
1975	2,712	8,200	16,060	5,132	7,072	18,796	258,454	257,283	15,502	41,915
1976	1,863	7,252	22,395	3,752	3,960	10,633	210,239	223,372	5,875	49,887
1977	5,622	10,035	18,383	5,282	4,275	10,014	203,103	241,517	9,912	50,532
1978	3,391	6,995	23,301	2,455	6,565	9,004	206,654	219,322	5,560	34,408

Source: Bureau of Statistics, Office of the Prime Minister, Dai Sanju Kai Nihon Tokei Nenran, Tokyo, 1980, pp. 296-7. Reprinted from Morikawa, *Minami Afurika to Nihon*.

reached bilateral trade treaties with Black African countries and urged them not to apply Article 35 towards Japan when they became members of GATT.

The Foreign Ministry's first trade treaty with a Black African nation was agreed with Cameroon in September 1962; from 1962 to 1963, similar agreements were also reached with Niger, Dahomey (now Benin), Guinea, Togo, Rhodesia (now Zimbabwe), Nyasaland, Zambia, Malawi and Madagascar.[44]

However, policy did not move along the lines of Japan's proposed scenario. The Black African countries were not interested in rescinding Article 35 when they joined GATT, the exception being Madagascar which entered GATT in 1963 and repealed the use of Article 35 towards Japan the following year.[45] It was Japan's understanding that as long as Article 35 continued to be applied, the discriminatory policies of the immediate post-war era remained in force. It took more than a decade longer to settle the problem.[46] Cameroon informed Japan that it would rescind application of Article 35 in 1974 and other countries soon followed suit. Kenya was the last country in Africa to do so in 1977.

[44] *Ibid.*

[45] *Ibid.*, p. 254.

[46] *Ibid.*

[47] Greg Lanning with M. Mueller, *Africa Undermined: Mining Companies and the Underdevelopment of Africa*, London: Penguin Books, 1979, notes: 'During the 1960s, Japanese trading companies signed long-term contracts with major iron ore and copper mining companies throughout Africa, in order to secure metal supplies for Japan's rapid industrial expansion. Zaire and Zambia are already major sources of copper, and Liberia of iron ore, and African minerals will become increasingly important in the 1970s. Japanese companies have taken minority stakes in several large projects, with the aim of getting a share in as many mining consortia as possible, to overcome their disadvantage compared with established French, Belgian, British and American corporations. The Nippon Mining Co. operates the Musoshi mine in Zaire and a small copper mine in Ethiopia. Sumitomo Metal Co. and Mitsubishi have a 76 per cent stake in Tin and Associated Minerals of Nigeria. Japanese aluminum producers have a 20 per cent stake in the BASOL consortium in Ghana, and Japanese steel mills have investments in Liberian, Guinean and Sengalese iron ore projects and in a manganese mine in Upper Volta [Burkina Faso]. Japanese companies are searching for uranium in Gabon, Mauritania and Niger, and for chrome in Madagascar. Although investments in Africa account for only just over 2 per cent of Japan's world investments, it is the most profitable area of Japanese foreign investment after West Asia.' (p. 297)

Securing a stable supply of mineral resources. Natural resources diplomacy became the focus of Japan's attention in Black Africa from the latter half of the 1960s onwards. As the phenomenal growth of its capitalism took off, Japan became extremely worried about the possibility of a natural resources crisis.[47] Against this background, its natural resources diplomacy was born as it strove to secure a stable supply of base metals such as iron ore, copper ore and bauxite.

The first direct opportunity to promote natural resources diplomacy came in February 1970 when the government dispatched the Kono economic mission to nine countries: Ethiopia, Kenya, Tanzania, Zambia, Congo, Nigeria, Ghana, Ivory Coast and Senegal.[48] Headed by Keidanren vice-chairman and Mitsubishi Heavy Industries chairman Kono Fumihiko, it included top executives from companies such as Mitsui, Toyota and Nippon Mining.

The *Diplomatic Blue Book* for 1969 described it as the largest and most important economic mission Japan had thus far sent to Africa.[49] Kono himself described it as seeking to secure natural resources and paying courtesy calls and return visits.[50] The main emphasis was, of course, on the first goal; the mission spent 15 and 16 February at a copper mine on the outskirts of Lumumbashi in Zaire, where Japanese enterprises had engaged in a large-scale mineral development and importation project.[51]

---

[48] See *Hirake Yuku Burakku Afurika.*

[49] Ministry of Foreign Affaris, *Waga Gaiko no Kinkyo,* 1969, 14 (April 1969-March 1970), p. 178.

[50] Fumihiko Kono, 'Afurika Shokoku o Rekiho Shite', *Kokusai Jihyo,* 65 (September 1970), p. 9. See also Ministry of Foreign Affairs, *Waga Gaiko no Kinkyo,* 1969, p. 178. The third goal of the Japanese government in dispatching the Kono mission was to heighten the business community's interest in Black Africa. The *zaikai's* active participation was indispensable for improvement of the trade imbalance and natural resources development and importation projects.

[51] In 'Japan's Year in Africa', Colin Legum (ed.), *Africa Contemporary Record Annual Survey and Documents 1972-1973,* vol. 5 (1973), pp. A86-A87, Godfrey Morrison points out: 'Notable investment developments during 1972 included the ceremonial opening of the joint Japan-Zaire copper mine in the Musoshi area in October. The president of Nippon Mining, Takaharu Kawai, who heads the Japanese consortium involved (CODEMIZA), said it was the first really large-scale mining development ever undertaken by Japanese interests. Ore reserves are estimated at 110 m. tonnes and the mine's production capacity is 5,600 tonnes per day.'

Resource diplomacy accelerated further after the economic mission returned home. On 12 March 1970 the Kono mission members visited the Foreign Ministry; emphasising the importance of mineral development in Black Africa, they appealed for more support from the Japanese government.[52] The response was almost immediate. On 19 March, the Foreign Minsitry and companies with interests in Africa set up the Afurika Kaihatsu Kyokai (Association of African Economy and Development). And on 24 April, the Diet Association for African Economic Development was set up by LDP members with former prime minister Kishi Nobusuke as its chairman. This group's basic approach was to exert its political influence in Africa by applying the same aid methods that the Japanese government had up to then used in its approach towards Asia and Latin America. This was a joint approach in which Japanese industries would provide direct investment and related technology and help with natural resources developement projects. For the former, the government would offer Official Development Assistance (ODA), especially low-interest yen loans to developing countries to upgrade infrastructure such as transportation, communications and power plants. In 1969, Black Africa's share of Japan's bilateral ODA was only 1.1 per cent or $339.7 million. By 1975, it had rapidly grown to $850 million or 6.9 per cent of the total.[53] More than half of this bilateral ODA was allocated for infrastructure and related projects. The plan for the formation of the Keidanren Committee on Co-operation with Africa was also approved in the spring of 1970 and the committee began its work on 31 August 1970. On 25 October 1970, the Kono Mission Report, which emphasised the importance of resource development and increasing aid to Black Africa, especially for infrastructure, was submitted to the government and the LDP.[54]

From March to September 1970, the Osaka International Exposition was held. Algeria and Egypt as well as eleven Black

---

[52] Keidanren Africa Economic Mission (ed.), *Hirake Yuku Burakku Afurika*, p. 57.

[53] Ministry of Foreign Affairs, Economic Co-operation Bureau (ed.) *Wagakuni no Seifukaihatsu Enjo, Gekkan Kunibetsu Jisseki*. Tokyo: APIC, 1988, p. 281.

[54] Ministry of Foreign Affairs, *Hirake Yuku Burakku Afurika*, p. 58.

African countries (Ethiopia, Gabon, Tanzania, Ivory Coast, Sierra Leone, Nigeria, Uganda, Mauritius, Ghana, Madagascar and the Central African Republic) were invited to set up pavilions at the Expo as an expression of Japan's active interest in Africa.[55] This gathering could also be considered part of the promotion of amicable relations with the supplier countries necessary if the resources diplomacy was to produce results. The April 1971 visit to Japan of Zaire's President Mobutu as a state guest was yet another example of this policy's promotion. On 3 June 1971, the Japan-Zaire Association was formed.

Japan's interest in Africa's mineral resources, especially rare metals, greatly increased in the middle of the 1970s for several reasons. During the 1973 oil crisis, Japan learned the bitter lesson that its belief that sufficient cash could always obtain the resources desired at any time was no longer applicable. Secondly, with the birth of socialist regimes in Guinea-Bissau, Mozambique, Angola and Ethiopia and developments in the anti-colonialist and anti-racist movements in Rhodesia, Namibia and South Africa, Japan felt a critical situation had emerged in which the 'East wind prevailed over the West wind'.[56] Finally the acceleration of the Japanese economy's knowledge-intensive industrialisation ensured that a stable supply of rare metals became an important national security issue.

Within this context, the 1974 speech made by Foreign Minister Ohira Masayoshi to a conference of Japanese ambassadors stationed in Africa takes on deeper meaning:

It is widely recognised today that the African continent is rapidly gaining in importance in the international arena. It is also clearly evident the African nations are wielding a growing influence in the handling of important international problems, both political and economic. And we should acknowledge that Japan's existence and prosperity can no longer be viewed as something unrelated to the vast area

[55] 'Africa and the First World Exposition in Asia', *Africa-Japan*, August 1970, pp. 65-8.
[56] Together with the Oil Shock the establishment of Socialist regimes in the three Indochinese nations of Vietnam, Laos and Cambodia inflicted serious economic damage on the advanced capitalist nations as well as creating an increased sense of crisis.

that is Africa. I believe that those problems require in-depth assessment in light of the new situation, and that the problem of where to position Japan's relations with Africa in this country's diplomacy represent a task to be tackled from now on.[57]

Kimura Toshio replaced Ohira as Foreign Minister in July 1974; three months later, he visited Ghana, Nigeria, Zaire and Tanzania. He was the first Japanese foreign minister ever to visit Black Africa.[58] As can be seen in the choice of Zaire and Tanzania as destinations, his visit sought both to secure natural resources and to attempt to soften criticism in Black Africa for Japan's support of the White anti-Communist regimes in Africa.

As has been shown, dual diplomacy — the Black Africa and White Africa policies — in this second period (1960-75) were consolidated and advanced simultaneously. The establishment of this overall policy led inevitably to criticism of Japan's White Africa policy in the OAU and from the nations of Black Africa. In the autumn of 1965, the campaign for a non-permanent membership on the UN Security Council became a difficult battle for Japan because of severe opposition from the African nations. The Foreign Ministry claimed that some African countries persistently obstructed Japan's election campaign because of their dissatisfaction with Japan for not implementing the Seventeenth UN General Assembly resolution demanding trade boycotts against South Africa. They severely criticised Japan during the open discussions on apartheid and in General Assembly debates.[59]

It is true that Japan faced difficulties during the Security Council election. One reason for immediate criticism was Pretoria's rapid growth of trade with Japan during the seventeenth session of the UN General Assembly in 1962. Japan countered this criticism by arguing that it had long held an anti-racial discrimination policy; it felt that the best method to get South Africa to change its policy was by getting all the members of the UN to put moral pressure on South Africa

[57] Ministry of Foreign Affairs, *Japan and Africa South of Sahara — Expanding and Deepening Relations*, Tokyo, 1979, p. 4.

[58] Ministry of Foreign Affairs, *Waga Gaiko no Kinkyo*, 1975, pp. 36-70.

[59] Ministry of Foreign Affairs, *Waga Gaiko no Kinkyo*, 1966, pp. 11-12.

to encourage it to reflect on its policies and reconsider them. Japan regarded moves to cut off economic and diplomatic relations or to expel South Africa from the UN as being impossible realistically to implement. The Japanese position held that such measures could not be expected truly to solve the problem; thus they were not an appropriate course of action to take.[60]

However, such a passive posture towards the South Africa problem only served to invite more severe criticism from Black Africa. As a result, Japan was forced to change its stance somewhat from the latter half of the 1960s onward. In 1968 it prohibited direct investment in South Africa, and in 1974 introduced sports, educational and cultural exchange restrictions. Yet such measures were only superficial and eventually led to the intensification of criticism of Japan among Black countries in the OAU and the UN.

The third phase, 1975-89: the White Africa policy

In this third phase, especially the years 1975-85, Japan strengthened its support of the White minority regimes. The confrontation between the United States and the former Soviet Union intensified as the United States suffered defeat in Indochina, Portuguese colonialism fell in Africa and the Soviet Union invaded Afghanistan in 1979. At the same time, Japan became an economic superpower and it was expected by Washington that Japan should now make a much larger contribution to Western security.[61] It was against this background that Japan strengthened its support for the perceived

---

[60] Ministry of Foreign Affairs, *Waga Gaiko no Kinkyo*, 1963, p. 39.

[61] Japan's contribution (or burden-sharing) in relation to America's anti-Communist world strategy was outlined in the Nixon Doctrine of July 1969; enlarrgement of this role was spurred by the United States's retreat from Vietnam in 1973. From the middle of the 1970s on, this led Japanese decision-makers to think that the US-Japan relationship had become an equal partnership. See Kitamura Hiroshi, Murata Ryohei and Okazaki Hisahiko *Nichibei Kankei o Toitsumeru*, Tokyo: Sekai no Ugoki Sha, 1983, pp. 105-6. The authors were, respectively, Director-General of the American Affairs Bureau of the Foreign Ministry, Director-General of the Economic Affairs Bureau and Director-General of the Research and Planning Department.

anti-Communist forces in Pretoria. However, there were other factors which led to the eventual failure of this approach.

First, there was the rapid disintegration of White minority rule in countries and regions that had served as a buffer zone after the victories of the African national liberation movements in Mozambique and Angola in 1975 and in Zimbabwe in 1980. There was also the development of the anti-apartheid movement within South Africa itself. Secondly, Japan's pro-Pretoria behaviour elicited mounting international criticism which inflicted serious damage on Japan's policy of dual diplomacy by the mid- 1980s. Thirdly, after Gorbachev took power in 1985, Cold War tensions eased and the transition to the post-Cold War era began. This forced the Japanese government to restructure its African policy.

This section, then, will examine the development of dual diplomacy by focusing on the early 1980s, the so-called new Cold War era.

In April 1980, the Ministry of Foreign Affairs, Middle Eastern and African Affairs Bureau was reorganised and a new Second Africa Division was established to deal with the countries of Southern and Eastern Africa.[62] These included South Africa, Namibia, Botswana, Swaziland, Lesotho, Zimbabwe, Angola, Mozambique, Malawi, Zambia, Tanzania, the Seychelles, Kenya, Uganda, Ethiopia and Somalia. Although the Second Division encompasses a wide area, the main focus is South Africa.

The reasons for the establishment of the division have not been made public by the Ministry but the move came right after the Afghan crisis and reflected the necessity of formulating and implementing an effective anti-Communist African strategy. This was, in fact, a policy centering around Pretoria and extending in a fan-shaped fashion to Nairobi, Mogadishu and even Cairo, areas of Africa which were considered important for Western security.

In the early 1980s, two important organisations for support of the government's pro-Pretoria policy were created within the LDP and the business community. In June 1984, Ishihara Shintaro, an influential leader of the LDP who also had strong

---

[62] See Ministry of Foreign Affairs, *Waga Gaiko no Kinkyo*, 1980, p. 303, Figure 3.4.

connections with Israel,[63] led the initiative to form the Japan-South Africa Parliamentarians' Friendship League (JSAPFL), which openly advocated the strengthening of bilateral relations with South Africa. In August 1984 members of the league visited the Republic and met government leaders and Chief Buthelezi, leader of the Inkatha Freedom Party.

In April 1985, the main corporate members of the CCA secretly formed a new private economic organisation called the Southern Africa Traders Association (SATA). According to the Secretary-General's explanation,[64] the group's aim was to promote mutual understanding and smooth trade and commercial relations with Southern African nations. But although SATA used the word 'Southern' in its official title, in substance, the group focused on South Africa.

As we see in the trade statistics for 1985 (Figure 3.5), South

Fig. 3.5. JAPAN'S TRADE WITH SOUTHERN AFRICA, 1985
(Unit: US $ 1,000)

	Exports	Imports	Total
Namibia	17,926	543	18,469
Lesotho	211	33	244
Botswana	607	338	945
Swaziland	1,267	9,167	10,434
Malawi	16,788	11,727	28,515
Mozambique	11,996	14,818	26,814
Angola	45,838	1,301	47,139
Zimbabwe	24,676	55,883	80,559
Tanzania	75,695	16,680	92,375
Zambia	222,552	60,134	282,686
South Africa	1,019,915	1,843,883	2,863,798

Source: Compiled by the author with data from Ministry of Foreign Affairs, *Afurika Binran — Sahara Inanno Kuniguni, 1986.*

Africa clearly held the lion's share of trade and commerce in this area. Even so, a bilateral committee to deal with South Africa did not exist within the zaikai. South Africa was included in the overall activities of Keidanren's CCA.

The argument that SATA was necessary to promote trade

[63] Ishihara was selected to serve as chairman of the Japan - Israel Friendship Association on 17 October 1989. See *Israel Monthly*, published by the Japan-Israel Friendship Association, 22, 9 (December 1989), pp. 1, 6.
[64] *Springbok Club Kaiho*, 10 (1 November 1987), p. 42.

with all of Southern Africa is not convincing since that trade outside of South Africa was and remained minimal and Keidanren's CCA had for a long time adequately fulfilled that role in Black Africa. Other organisations also existed, such as the Japan-Zambia Friendship Association formed in December 1975. This group dealt with Japan's second most important trading partner in the region. Perhaps the most revealing evidence of SATA's central interest in South Africa can be seen in the selection of the man who was to become SATA's first Secretary-General, Makiura Toshio.[65] Makiura was also senior promotion officer for South African Airways, the Tokyo representative of the South Africa Foundation, and Secretary-General of the Springbok Club, the pro-Pretoria Tokyo club composed of businessmen and diplomats who had once served in South Africa.

Japan's determination to carry on its ties with the Republic despite international criticism became obvious in 1985-6 when a string of cabinet-level ministers from the White regime were invited to Japan for meetings with government officials and business leaders. In October 1985, Finance Minister Du Plessis and Dr Gerhard De Kock, Governor of the Reserve Bank, visited Tokyo. They were followed in June 1986 by the Minister of Environmental Affairs and Tourism and in August 1986 by the Minister of Trade and Industry, David De Villiers. In September 1986, Foreign Minister Pik Botha himself made a visit to Japan.

All of these visits took place at a time when the White minority regime was facing serious political and economic difficulties at home and abroad.[66] Pretoria had declared a state of emergency on 21 July 1985, and on 1 September, it had further ordered a four-month standstill on the repayment of foreign debt. On 15 August 1986, the United States Senate passed the South Africa Sanctions Bill, symbolising the seriousness of the crisis South Africa confronted. Pik Botha's well-publicised visit to Japan was conducted under these conditions

[65] See Kusuhara Akira, 'Nihon Sei-Zaikaito Aparutoheito Taisei no Fukai Yuchaku — Nan-A to Nihon o Tsunagu Kage no Fixer', *Nanbu Afurika Nempo*, JAAC, 1987 (January 1988), pp. 55-7.
[66] James Barber and John Barratt, *South Africa's Foreign Policy — The Search for Status and Security, 1945-1988*, Cambridge University, 1990. See 'Domestic and International Crisis and Pretoria's Response', pp. 299-326.

and it led to even more criticism of the Japanese government's stance. This international concern forced the cancellation of the following month's scheduled visit by the South African Minister of National Education, Frederik De Klerk.

Japan's determination to promote non-elite contacts with Pretoria despite criticism was also evident throughout the third phase of Japan's dual diplomacy. This was shown in the reluctance to restrict tourists to and from South Africa, the government's support of the Japanese School of Johannesburg and the establishment of the Springbok Club in Tokyo in 1977. The importance of this club (discussed more fully in Chapter 5) and the network of contacts it provided to South Africans in Japan and the business community in Tokyo can not be overlooked or underestimated.

South African tourism was also encouraged during this period. For the typical Japanese tourist, South Africa was geographically distant and due to the country's negative image as a land of apartheid, it was not a popular destination. But this situation began to change somewhat after the South Africa Tourist Corporation (SATOUR) was allowed to open its Tokyo office in April 1975; the previous month a South African Airways office also opened in Tokyo. The number of Japanese tourists travelling to South Africa increased from 3,500 in 1975 to 8,500 in 1981, and over 10,000 in 1983, partly because of the success of the South African tourist promotion campaign.[67] This again quite naturally invited criticism from Black Africa. At a symposium on 20 January 1983 titled 'Apartheid and its Meaning for Japan', the Tanzanian Ambassador to Japan, Ahmed Hassan Diria, broached the subject and noted that the number of Japanese visiting South Africa was increasing despite the opposition of Black African countries. He also pointed out that the best safari park tours were to be found in East and Central African countries, and that the profits generated from Japanese tourists visitng South Africa helped strengthen apartheid.[68]

The question of tourism raised several issues beyond for-

---

[67] Morikawa Jun, 'The Anatomy of Japan's South African Policy', *Journal of Modern African Studies*, 22, 1 (March 1984), p. 135.
[68] UN Information Center, Tokyo, 'Aparutoheito-Nihonni Totte no Imi', May 31, 1983, p.14.

eign exchange earnings. First was the expectation that Japanese would behave as honorary Whites in South Africa. Secondly, almost all of these Japanese tourists used first-class 'Whites only' transport and accommodation. Thirdly, most of them followed pre-arranged tourist routes to scenic spots which were almost entirely restricted to White areas. As a result, there was no meaningful contact with the non-White community, thus dulling the tourists' judgement of the apartheid system. With only a one-sided view, apartheid did not appear to many as bad as it was made out to be. From the comfort of the tour bus, South Africa could be considered a beautiful, peaceful, affluent country and this image enlarged the constituency of South African sympathisers on their return to Japan. In fact, the pro-Pretoria Springbok Club actively recruited returning tourists as members. According to the club's membership regulations, tourists could become members if they were sponsored by two members.[69]

Protests by anti-apartheid groups inside Japan finally led the government to introduce sanctions on tourism on 19 September 1986, but the vague wording ('to request Japanese people to refrain from touring South Africa') lacked force and could hardly be expected to have any significant effect.[70]

Next of concern here are the economic relations during this third period. While the international community repeatedly called on Japan to participate in economic sanctions against South Africa, Japan's trade links with Pretoria continued to grow. Total trade between the two nations in 1975 was valued at $1.74 billion; by 1988, it had doubled to $3.98 billion. The 1988 trade figures were thirty-six times greater than the $114 million figure registered in 1960.[71]

By 1982 Japan was South Africa's biggest customer, with 15.6 per cent of its total exports. The South African Institute of Race Relations described the situation this way:

Japan became South Africa's biggest export market for the first time in 1982, proving that efforts over the past decade

[69] By-Laws of the Springbok Club, Tokyo, p. 135.
[70] Morikawa, *Minami Afurika to Nihon*, p. 135.
[71] MITI, *Tsusho Hakusho: Kakuron*, 1961, pp. 501-2.
[72] South African Institute of Race Relations, *Survey of Race Relations in South Africa 1983*, Johannesburg, 1984, p.116.

to diversify South Africa's trade links beyond Europe and North America have proved succesful. The UK moved into second place in 1982, with the US, the prime export market in 1981, falling to third place. South Africa's sales to Japan consisted mainly of coal, maize, sugar, ferro alloys and iron ore.[72]

Japan's importance as a trade partner grew even greater thereafter; in 1986 and 1987, its total trade with Pretoria made it South Africa's largest trading partner for two consecutive years.[73] Or, put another way, Japan had become the biggest violator of the economic sanctions against South Africa.

Japan's desire to support Pretoria through trade and commerce was clearly reflected in the composition of trade mentioned above. Most of the items, such as coal, sugar and maize, could also have been obtained from other nations in Africa or Asia comparatively easily. Furthermore, many of the items can by no means be considered indispensible to the survival of the Japanese economy.

One good example of this non-essential trade is eggs. The *South Africa Digest*, published by Pretoria's Department of Foreign Affairs, reported in 1984 that a contract to export 47 million eggs had been signed by the South African Egg Board and the QP Corporation, Japan's largest egg processor. The story noted the export contract offered to the South African side a 'premium price of 3 million rands' for their eggs.[74] A similar example can be seen in the fishing industry. Japan bought $14,606,000 worth of shrimps, prawns and lobsters from South Africa in 1987. Japan's imports from Nigeria that year were only $5,260,000 and of this $4,625,000 was for the import of shrimps, prawns and lobsters.[75]

With the high valuation of the yen in the early 1980s,

[73] Japan's trade statistics with Pretoria do not always reflect the actual state of affairs, since many of the figures are distorted by third-country trade. For example, much of Japan's gold imports from South Africa come via Switzerland or Britain and thus does not show up in Japan's records of trade with South Africa.

[74] *South African Digest*, 30 November 1984, Department of Foreign Affairs, Pretoria, p. 4.

[75] MITI, *Tsusho Hakusho: Kakuron*, 1988. See appendix: Import Commodity by Country chart for 1987.

precious metals such as gold and platinum became major import items. Like eggs, this trade was a case of trying to widen imports from South Africa, since these metals were not for industrial use but mainly for accessories and speculation. For example, of the 87 tonnes of platinum produced world-wide in 1987, Japan imported 30 tonnes and used 23.4 tonnes for accessories.[76] As only 27 tonnes of platinum were used worldwide for accessories, Japan's consumption constituted 86 per cent of this total.[77]

Another matter that cannot be overlooked when examining Japan's import transactions with Pretoria was the illegal purchase of Namibian products by Japanese companies that ignored Decree No. 1 (Protection of the Natural Resources of Namibia), adopted in 1974 by the UN Council for Namibia.[78] In short, Decree No. 1 stated that until Namibia achieved independence, developments and transactions involving its natural resources should be prohibited. Despite this decree, the Japanese government gave tacit approval to a contract signed in 1970 by the Kansai Electric Power Company, Japan's second largest electric power company, and the Rossing Mining Company. The ten-year contract, running from 1976 to 1986, was for 8,200 short tons of uranium ore (see Figure 3.6).

UN reports noted the lack of safeguards to protect local inhabitants and the Black workers at the mine in question from radioactive contamination[79] and the UN Council for Namibia sent a delegation to Japan in May 1975 to ask that it cancel its contract for the purchase of Namibian uranium. The delegation warned Japan that if it continued to buy minerals it would be obliged to pay compensation when Namibia became independent. The Japanese government countered that the

[76] *Asahi Shimbun,* 5 October, 1987.

[77] In 1986, Japan's share of South Africa's main export items was: coking coal 18 per cent; gold 16.4 per cent; platinum 12 per cent and ordinary coal 10.4 per cent Ministry of Foreign Affairs, *Tsusho Hakusho: Kakuron,* 1988 pp. 650-1.

[78] Kitazawa Yoko, 'Japan's Namibian Connection: Illegal Japanese Uranium Deals Violate UN Resolution', *AMPO Japan - Asia Quarterly Review,* 12, 3 1980, pp. 34-7.

[79] UN Council for Namibia, 'Report on the Activities of Foreign Economic Interests', April 1987, p. 12.

Fig. 3.6. KNOWN AND POSSIBLE URANIUM CONTRACTS

	Country processing	Amount (tonnes)	Expiry of contract
British Nuclear Fuels	United Kingdom	7,500	1984
Comurhex, France	France	11,000	late 1980s
Veba, Germany	Netherlands		
Urangesellschaft, Germany	Netherlands	6,140	
Kansai Electric Power, Japan	USA/Canada	8,200	1986
Taiwan Power Corp., Taiwan	Netherlands	4,000	2005
Other Japanese corporations	USA/Canada	23,000	

Source: UN Council for Namibia.

Namibian imports were necessary since Japan had no natural resources of its own.[80] It further attempted to justify its behaviour in debates of the Diet (the Japanese parliament) by noting that, unlike a UN Security Council resolution, the degree was not legally binding.[81]

The third phase, 1975-89: the Black Africa policy
To activate the pro-Pretoria policy it was necessary that Japan strengthen its appeasement policy towards Black Africa. Black Africa's dissatisfaction had increased as Japan enlarged its trade with Pretoria in the 1980s at the same time as its trade with the rest of the continent rapidly decreased to a relatively insignificant level (see Fig. 3.7). Japan attempted to neutralise and soften the criticism of its pro-Pretoria policy and anti-Communist African diplomacy in a systematic way by projecting a pro-Black Africa image. In its attempt to assuage Black Africa, the Japanese government adopted the following four-point approach.

First, Japan began to show sympathy for the cause of the

[80] See Ahmed M. Khalifa, *Assistance to Racist Regimes in Southern Africa: Impact on the Enjoyment of Human Rights*, New York: UN, September 1979, p. 20.
[81] Kitazawa Yoko, 'Namibia Uran no Mitsuyu o Yameyo', *Sekai Kara*, August 1983, p. 30. See also Mine Yoichi, 'Kokujin no Chi o Suu Genpatsu', *Buraku Kaiho*, June 1989, pp. 55-8

Fig. 3.7. SUB-SAHARAN AFRICA'S SHARE OF JAPAN'S
OVERALL TRADE, EXCLUDING SOUTH AFRICA
(*Unit: US $ 1m.*)

	Exports			Imports		
	Total	*Africa*	*%*	*Total*	*Africa*	*%*
1981	152,030	7,223	4.8	143,290	3,330	2.3
1982	138,831	5,822	4.2	131,931	3,450	2.6
1983	146,927	3,813	2.6	126,393	2,482	2.0
1984	170,113	3,981	2.3	136,503	2,600	1.9
1985	175,638	2,100	1.2	129,538	839	0.6
1986	209,151	1,974	0.9	126,408	1,092	0.9
1987	229,221	1,956	0.9	149,515	801	0.5
1988	264,917	2,208	0.8	187,354	1,400	0.7

Source: Ministry of Foreign Affairs, *Afurika Binran*, 1990, p. 115.

African national liberation movements. One example of this
came in August 1974, when Japan recognised Guinea-Bissau
much earlier than Western countries did. However, it is also
interesting to note that when the Japan Anti-Apartheid Committee presented the Foreign Ministry with a petition on 19
October 1973 requesting diplomatic recognition to Guinea-
Bissau,[82] the government had refused by stating that more than
half of the UN member nations had not yet recognised
Guinea-Bissau. Further it was impossible to verify PAIGC
(Partido Africano da Independencia da Guiné e Cabo Verde)
claims that two-thirds of the territory had been liberated, and
the Japanese government was still collecting information and
studying the validity of these claims. The Foreign Ministry also
argued that, in international law Guinea-Bissau was currently
still represented by Portugal and that while the rebellious forces
(the PAIGC) were in principle fighting a just battle, it only
represented the aspirations of the inhabitants; it was thus
important to encourage the Portuguese to make efforts to alter
their rule of the area.[83]

Japan's recongnition of Guinea-Bissau less than a year later
and in advance of other Western countries was a diplomatic
coup designed to win support in Africa, as the government's
actions later demonstrated. Rather than send an ambassador to

[82] See Kusuhara Akira, 'The Attitude of the Japanese Government on the
Recognition of Guinea Bissau', *Africa: News and Reports*, 17 (February 1974), pp.
70-1.
[83] *Ibid.*, p. 72.

Guinea-Bissau, it was decided to have the ambassador in Senegal serve both countries. In addition Japan's cumulative ODA to Guinea-Bissau up to 1988 was only ¥24.2 million.[84]

The second method of appeasement was to show an interest in African international politics in general and the Southern African question in particular, as well as actively promoting personal exchange with pro-Western and non-aligned nations with influence on the Southern African question.

Following the epoch-making visit of Foreign Minister Kimura Toshio to Ghana, Nigeria, Zaire, Tanzania and Egypt in the autumn of 1974, two other top Ministry officials were dispatched. In July 1979, Foreign Minister Sonoda Sunao travelled to Nigeria, Ivory Coast, Senegal, Tanzania and Kenya, and in November 1984 Foreign Minister Abe Shintaro visited Zambia, Ethiopia and Egypt. However, these visits were not sufficient in themselves to convince Black African states, and court and business diplomacy were used to supplement this official exchange. In place of Emperor Hirohito, Crown Prince Akihito and Crown Princess Michiko visited Kenya, Tanzania and Zambia in March 1983; while from February to March 1984 they were sent to Senegal and Zaire. In Tokyo, the Emperor greeted state guests from Black African states in an attempt to assist in the enhancement of bilateral relations. However, since the invitation budget and the Emperor's schedule were both limited, state guests were basically restricted to one per continent per year. As we see in Figure 3.8, the invitation of state guests from Africa became routine from 1979, especially from nations with influence on Southern African issues.

Further support for the government's personal exchange programme came from powerful business leaders who took part in economic missions sent by the Japanese government to Black Africa in 1978 (Tanzania, Ivory Coast, Nigeria and Senegal), 1984 (Zambia, Zimbabwe, Nigeria and Zaire) and 1988 (Zimbawe, Cameroon and Nigeria).

The third method of softening Black Africa's criticisms of Japan was to provide it with aid for development and emergency relief. Japan's official bilateral development assistance to Black Africa at the time of the 1973 oil shock was only $765

---

[84] Ministry of Foreign Affairs, *Afurika Binran*, 1990, p. 122.

million, or just 2.4 per cent of the total disbursed worldwide.[85] As shown in Figure 3.9, it increased rapidly thereafter.

However, the effects of such bilateral assistance should not be overestimated. First, it was not being equally distributed or allocated among the countries of Black Africa. The lion's share went to the key countries, although there was no guarantee for Japan that providing large amounts of ODA would mute their criticism of its pro-Pretoria policy.[86]

Secondly, there was Japan's use of emergency relief aid for the purpose of appeasement (critically examined in Chapter 4). Two examples will suffice to illustrate the point. During 1984-5) a famine relief campaign and drive to send blankets and aid to Black Africa was carried out in Japan. This was followed in 1987 by an aid plan directed at South African Blacks. The 1989 *Diplomatic Blue Book* described the latter plan as follows: 'The Japanese government began in fiscal 1987 to make contributions to medical, educational and other projects to aid South African Blacks victimised by apartheid. It has also stepped up economic assistance to countries neighbouring South Africa.'[87]

Fig. 3.8. JAPANESE STATE GUESTS FROM BLACK AFRICA

November 1956	Ethiopia	Emperor Haile Selassie I
November 1965	Madagascar	President Tsiranana
April 1971	Congo (Zaire)	President Mobutu
April 1979	Senegal	President Senghor
September 1980	Zambia	President Kaunda
March 1981	Tanzania	President Nyerere
April 1982	Kenya	President Arap Moi
September 1984	Gabon	President Bongo
September 1986	Niger	President of Supreme Military Council Seyn Kountche
June-July 1988	Senegal	President Diouf
October 1989	Zimbabwe	President Mugabe
December 1989	Tanzania	President Mwinyi

Source: Ministry of Foreign Affairs, *Afurika Binran*, 1990, pp. 132-3.

[85] *Ibid.*, p. 120.

[86] From 1960 to 1980, Japan's ODA to Black Africa was $765 million. Of that amount approximately 60 per cent went to just five countries: Kenya ($107 million); Tanzania ($92 million); Zambia ($87 million); Nigeria ($76 million); and Zaire ($75 million). See Hatano, pp. 11-12.

[87] Ministry of Foreign Affairs, *Diplomatic Blue Book — Japan's Diplomatic Activities 1989*, p. 237.

Fig. 3.9. JAPAN'S BILATERAL OFFICIAL DEVELOPMENT
ASSISTANCE (ODA) TO AFRICA, 1969-88 (*Unit: US $1 m.*)

	ODA to Africa	*Africa's share of* Japan's ODA (%)	Total Japanese ODA
1969	3.77	1.10	339.67
1970	8.15	2.19	371.51
1971	12.38	2.86	432.02
1972	5.01	1.04	477.79
1973	18.49	2.41	765.18
1974	36.23	4.11	880.37
1975	58.82	6.91	850.40
1976	45.93	6.10	752.95
1977	56.25	6.25	899.25
1978	105.49	6.89	1,530.97
1979	186.72	9.71	1,921.22
1980	222.91	11.36	1,960.80
1981	210.53	9.31	2,260.41
1982	268.23	11.33	2,367.33
1983	261.41	10.77	2,425.22
1984	210.83	8.68	2,427.39
1985	252.22	9.86	2,556.92
1986	418.46	10.87	3,846.21
1987	515.72	9.82	5,247.64
1988	883.93	13.76	6,421.87

Note: There figures do not include Sudan.
Source: Ministry of Foreign Affairs, *Afurika Binran* 1990, p. 120.

Fig. 3.10. MAJOR RECIPIENTS OF JAPANESE AID IN AFRICA,
CUMULATIVE TO 1988 (*Unit: US $ 1 bn.*)

Kenya	140.2
Tanzania	94.2
Zambia	87.0
Nigeria	81.4
Ghana	75.9
Zaire	61.9
Madagascar	45.8
Senegal	37.1
Malawi	30.3
Niger	27.0

Source: Gaimusho, *Chukinto Afurika Kyoku, Afurika Binran*, Tokyo, 1990, p. 120.

Much has been written about the Japanese concepts of *tatemae* (the public face) and *honne* (true feelings), so often submerged below the surface. An excellent example of this concept in action can be seen in Japan's final form of appeasement of Black Africa — the public announcement of a series of sanctions and other measures directed against South Africa (see Fig. 3.11).[88] These measures were implemented in 1974 after criticism of Japan's policy had increased. The introduction of most of the sanctions was concentrated in the mid-1980s, when criticism of Japan became especially intense.

On closer examination, however, the sanctions were not highly effective. There was no way to gauge accurately whether

Fig. 3.11. JAPAN'S RESTRICTIVE MEASURES AGAINST
SOUTH AFRICA

(1) to keep its relations with South Africa down to a consular, not diplomatic level;

(2) to prohibit direct investment (in 1969) and to restrict financial loans;

(3) to limit sporting, cultural and educational exchanges (15 June, 1974);

(4) to prohibit the export of arms to South Africa (7 Aug. 1963);

(5) to refrain from importing arms from South Africa;

(6) to prohibit the export of computers which might assist the activities of apartheid-enforcing agencies, such as the armed forces and the police (1 Nov. 1985);

(7) to urge all those concerned to co-operate in the voluntary halting of imports of krugerrands and all other South African gold coins (9 October 1985);

(8) to call upon companies which have offices in South Africa to follow equal and fair employment practices (9 Oct. 1985);

(9) to prohibit imports of iron and steel (1 Oct. 1986);

(10) to suspend the issuing of tourist visas for South African nationals and to request Japanese people to refrain from touring in South Africa (19 Sept. 1986);

(11) to confirm suspension of air links with South Africa (19 September 1986);

(12) to prohibit government officials from using the international airlines of South African Airways (4 Oct. 1986).

---

[88] This list of sanctions compiled by the Foreign Ministry was obtained from the ministry and translated by the JAAC.

whether the sanctions were being enforced or what effect they were having on South Africa, if any. They were not geared to cause severe damage to Pretoria since they were not strictly applied and included no penalty clauses. In addition, the sanctions often included-loopholes. For example, the Japanese language version of the ninth sanction (prohibiting imports of iron and steel) notes that this did not include those companies that already had import contracts in place in 1986. It should be also stressed that in the Japanese-language version, many of the restrictive measures merely ask that self-restraint (*jishuku*) be shown; in Japanese, the nuance conveyed by this term is that almost anything is acceptable if done circumspectly.

As a result of the numerous problems involved with the sanctions, the gap between the government's assertions and its actions became even more obvious and the sanctions plan backfired, leading to an increase in criticism from abroad.

Black Africa's criticism of Japan's pro-Pretoria policy had already begun to inflict some serious damage in the latter half of the 1970s when Japan's candidacy for a seat on the UN Security Council suffered a totally unexpected defeat due to the support given by Black African states to the candidate from Bangladesh in 1978.[89] In the 1986 election Japan again failed to win the support of Black African states but was elected this time by a slim margin of only four votes.[90]

The problems associated with the maintenance of Japan's pro-Pretoria policy were outlined in a speech by the Director-General of the Middle Eastern and African Affairs Bureau at a meeting of the Keidanren Executive Council on 8 September 1987. It merits quoting at length:

> It has recently become necessary to exercise more caution in trading with South Africa for several reasons. Last October, the United States Congress passed an anti-apartheid bill. This bill is intended to strengthen restrictions on trade with South Africa and it

---

[89] *Asahi Shimbun,* 19 August 1991.
[90] Japan has run for a non-permanent seat on the UN Security Council eight times and has been elected seven times: 1958-9; 1966-7; 1971-2; 1975-6; 1981-2; 1987-8 and 1992-3. The *Daily Yomiuri* (9 September 1991) also notes that as a tactic to assure Black African support in the autumn 1991 election, Japan postponed lifting sanctions against South Africa until after the UN election.

(1) prohibits the importation of coal and uranium;

(2) bans new investment in that country;

(3) allows the US President to exercise import restrictions on third nations which benefit from these restrictive measures; and

(4) allows the US President to demand compensation from foreign enterprises that profit at the expense of US companies which observe the restrictions.

Secondly, due to the rise in the value of the yen in relation to the dollar, our trade figures with South Africa have increased greatly in dollar terms. In 1986, we surpassed the United States by a small margin to become South Africa's number one trading partner. In the first half of this year, the gap will grow even wider.

The tone of the press concerning the problem of Japan's trade expansion problem with South Africa can be seen in a 4 September *New York Times* report which states that if this trend continues, it is inevitable that the President will introduce trade restrictions against Japan outlined in the Anti-Apartheid Bill. Such criticism of Japan is becoming more evident. In response to this, the Foreign Ministry has argued that the trade is actually declining slightly when calculated in yen terms; in any case, it is not appropriate to give the United States and other countries the impression that Japan is deeply involved. Also, when Foreign Minister Kuranari visited the United Nations, various African foreign ministers and other leaders indicated to him in informal exchanges that they found Japan's South Africa policy problematic. One criticism was that while American companies have to take their own country's tough domestic human rights demands into consideration in their operations, Japanese companies, while they may be influenced by outside pressures, do not seem to face domestic pressure to consider human rights. It has been pointed out that this is linked with problems within Japan itself.

The United States has recently issued its first report since the Anti-Apartheid Bill came into effect. This report states that there are strong grounds to suspect that Japanese businesses have been taking the places of American business in South Africa, although it did not go so far as to cite

names. Next year there is a US presidential election so we
are concerned Japan's trade with South Africa may provide
another spark to fuel the fires of what is regarded as the
Japan problem in the United States.

At present, Japan has announced a ban on the export of
computers for military or police use but otherwise, basically
free trade is being carried out. While expanding trade is the
logic of business, it is also necessary to consider international circumstances. The growth of trade with Africa has
been based on the efforts of individual companies and it is
not for us to make judgements. However, considering the
above factors, we are asking the industries concerned to
proceed cautiously in their trade with South Africa.[91]

The intensification of criticism forced the Japanese government to begin some gradual revision of its policy in the latter
half of the 1980s. Faced with this dysfunctional dual diplomacy system, Japan made the shift from a policy of confrontation with the ANC to an opening of dialogue with that
group and this was one of the first and biggest changes. This
occurred in January 1986 when the Director of the Second
Africa Division was secretly dispatched to Zambia to make
Japan's first official contact with the ANC leadership.[92]
Through the Africa Society of Japan the government issued
an invitation in April 1987 to Oliver Tambo, President of the
ANC, to visit Tokyo. While there, Tambo was able to get
the government's approval for the establishment of an ANC
office in Japan, which later opened in 1988. The dialogue
culminated in the visit to Japan in November 1990 of ANC
Vice-President Nelson Mandela, who was treated as a government guest.

However, it is important to note that Japan's dialogue with
the ANC and the improvement of its relations with Black
Africa was not accompanied by a cooling of relations with
Pretoria. Japan's traditional support for the White regime re-
mained basically unchanged from 1910 onwards. While Nelson
Mandela was in Japan, he strongly requested financial support

---

[91] *Keidanren Shuho,* 26 October, 1987, pp. 2-3.
[92] Morikawa, *Minami Afurika to Nihon,* p. 120.

for the ANC, but the Japanese government's answer was a clear 'no.' This left Mandela feeling that the situation was hopeless, despite the VIP treatment he had received. In contrast, when President de Klerk visited Japan in June 1992, he was treated as a state guest and given an audience with the Emperor, an opportunity Mandela was not offered. The ANC approach had considered Japan's economic presence in post-apartheid South Africa as a sort of long-term economic life insurance policy but de Klerk's treatment as a state guest shows that even in post-apartheid South Africa, White society will hold an economically dominant position for Japan.

Thus by the dawn of the 1990s, dual diplomacy was, in general, no longer a viable policy but certain elements of dual diplomacy still remain in Tokyo's attitude towards Pretoria and the Japanese government has yet to find a new policy to replace it.

4

ACTORS IN THE EXTERNAL DECISION-MAKING STRUCTURE

The formulation of post-war Japanese foreign policy has been achieved mainly through the interaction of three major actors: the LDP, the bureaucracy and the *'zaikai'*.[1] The relationship between these three actors is aptly described by Yanaga Chitoshi:

> Organised business initiates and proposes policies. It sponsors and supports the party in power. The party in turn forms the government and selects candidates for the Diet, who function as legitimatisers of government policy.
>
> The administrative bureaucracy proposes, drafts, modifies, interprets, and implements policies under the surveillance of the party and the goverment. The most important functions of the bureaucracy involve the protection and promotion of business and industry, in whose behalf it formulates long-term economic plans, makes forecasts, sets goals and establishes priorities.
>
> Organised business provides members for the cabinet, the Diet and government advisory councils and administrative commissions. It hires retired government officials as corporation executives and trade association officials.[2]

However, the power exerted by these actors is not always uniform. With its policy planning ability, supported by organisational strength and a wide-ranging network of information sources, the Foreign Ministry in particular has played a leading role in policy formulation and implementation. On politically important issues, the LDP may prevail,[3] while on

---

[1] For more on this subject, see Hosoya and Watanuki (eds), and Watanabe Akio *et al.*, *Koza Kokusai Seiji — Nihon no Gaiko*, vol. 4, University of Tokyo Press, 1989. See also Fukui, 1981.

[2] Yanaga Chitoshi, *Big Business in Japanese Politics*, New Haven, CT: Yale University, 1968, p. 28.

[3] Hosoya in Hosoya and Watanuki (eds), p. 10.

economic issues, the *zaikai* tends to wield great influence on the foreign policy decision-making process. This chapter examines the degree and the extent of the participation of these three major actors in the construction of Japan's African diplomacy.

The Liberal Democratic Party

For almost four decades from its formation in 1955, the Liberal Democratic Party monopolised politics in Japan. The LDP was the majority party (and thus the governing party) in Japan from 1955 till August 1993, when a coalition of opposition parties took power. In this situation of uninterrupted rule, it became normal for the decisions of the LDP to become in effect the decisions of the cabinet and the Diet itself.[4] The LDP proudly stressed this point in its English-language promotional brochures.[5]

In African affairs, however, the LDP generally remained an important but limited   player. The party's interest in and

---

[4] In *Liberal Democratic Party and Its Central Office* (undated) the LDP defines itself as follows: 'The Liberal Democratic Party, or the LDP, represents the single most influential political force in contemporary Japan. The LDP has continuously maintained a stable majority in both houses of the Diet — the supreme state organ of Japan — from the time of its formation in 1955. In the House of Representatives, 295 of the 512 members belong to the LDP (as of August 1989). In the House of Councillors, the LDP holds 108 of the 252 seats. The LDP is also enormously powerful at the local level: 44 of the 47 governors, 570 of the 656 mayors and 1,833 of the 2,910 prefectural assemblymen were elected on the LDP ticket. Except for a very brief period in 1947 and 1948, the LDP and its predecessors have run the government of Japan for over 40 years. During this period, not only have all prime ministers been appointed from among LDP Diet members, but almost all Cabinet ministers as well.'

[5] The Policy Process section of the LDP-produced brochure states: 'Article 41 of the Constitution of Japan stipulates that the Diet is "the sole law-making body of the State". However, legislation submitted for deliberation by the Diet is not formulated by that body — bills are introduced by individual Diet members or the government, and are taken up for deliberation. Legislative proposals originating in . the government express the desires of the Cabinet or central government agencies.

'Under a parliamentary system, the will of the party controlling the Cabinet, and thus the government, is reflected in draft legislation. In the final analysis, it can therefore be said that government policy is no more than the will of the party in power, at present the LDP.' *Ibid.*, p. 8.

Fig. 4.1. JAPANESE OFFICIAL VISITS TO BLACK AFRICA

The Royal Family

Nov. 1960	Crown Prince Akihito, Princess Michiko	Ethiopia
March 1983	Crown Prince Akihito, Princess Michiko	Zambia, Tanzania, Kenya
Feb.-March 1984	Crown Prince Akihito Princess Michiko	Zaire, Senegal

Foreign Ministers

Oct.-Nov. 1974	Kimura	Ghana, Nigeria, Zaire, Tanzania
July 1979	Sonoda	Nigeria, Ivory Coast, Senegal, Tanzania, Kenya
Nov. 1984	Abe	Zambia, Ethiopia

Parliamentary Vice Ministers for Foreign Affairs

July 1981	Aichi	Zambia, Zimbabwe, Zaire, Ghana, Ivory Coast, Liberia
June-July 1982	Tsuji	Rwanda, Tanzania, Zambia, Kenya, Gabon
July 1983	Ishikawa	Guinea, Senegal, Ethiopia
June-July 1984	Kitagawa	Madagascar, Zimbabwe, Malawi, Central African Republic, Somalia
July 1985	Moriyama	Cameroon, Kenya, Uganda
Sep.-Oct. 1987	Hamano	Ghana, Ivory Coast
June 1988	Hamada	Uganda, Madagascar

Source: Ministry of Foreign Affairs, *Afurika Binran*, 1990, pp. 132—3.

knowledge of African issues in general has been minimal. Its basic stance was to leave most day-to-day policy formulation and implementation to the Foreign Ministry. Yet on occasion it has played an important role in the process, as was demonstrated by the formation of the Japan South Africa Parliamentarians Friendship League (JSAPFL) by LDP Diet members in June 1984. The formation of the League came at a crucial time in South African history and in the context of Japan's anti-Communist strategy, the League's support for the White minority regime reflected the clear policy orientations that have guided the country's African diplomacy.

The post-war ruling party's lack of enthusiasm for African issues is clearly seen in the absence of official visits and exchanges with African countries. No post-war Japanese prime minister has visited Africa while in office and since the prime ministership has traditionally been held by the president of the LDP, this also means that no top LDP official has visited the continent (see Fig. 4.1 for a full list of Japanese official visits to Black Africa). This lack of enthusiasm is further demonstrated by the fact that the LDP's supreme policy-making body, the Policy Affairs Research Council (PARC) has no section dealing specifically with Africa. 'Although PARC includes approximately 100 research commissions and special Committees, the only direct connection with the African continent is found in the Special Committee on External Economic Co-operation's *ad hoc* subcomittee on Zaire, which existed between April 1983 and January 1988.[7]

The LDP has never clearly revealed its reasons for establishing this Subcommittee but the following factors can be considered significant. First, cobalt, an essential ingredient in steel, ceramic and glass manufacture, was of vital importance for Japan's economic security and the country depended on Zaire for 80 per cent of its cobalt imports.[8] After the Shaba incident in 1978, when Angolan forces invaded Zaire, these cobalt purchases were temporarily interrupted, causing difficulties for Japan as the price of cobalt increased sixfold in 1978-9. A factor was that after the new Cold War era had emerged at the end of 1979, Japan felt it had become necessary to strengthen support for the Mobutu regime in Zaire in order to counterbalance the evident advance of Eastern (i.e. Communist) forces in Southern Africa as well as to secure stable

[6] *Ibid.*, p. 5: 'The Policy Affairs Research Council conducts research in all fields of national policy, and initiates new policy measures. All matters which are to be adopted as policy by the party must be approved by this council. The chairman of the Policy Affairs Research Council is appointed by the president with the approval of the General Council. The post is one of the three top party executive posts, together with those of the secretary-general and chairman of the General Council.'

[7] Nihon Keizai Shimbunsha, *Jiminto Seichokai*, Tokyo: Nihon Keizai Shimbunsha, December, 1983 p. 223. In a telephone conversation with a LDP PARC official on 25 June 1993, this author was informed that the predecessor to the Subcommittee on Zaire was formed by LDP members on 3 April 1972.

[8] Ministry of Foreign Affairs, Public Information Bureau, *Warera no Sekai*, 219, May 1984, p. 9.

[9] See Charts 2-3, MITI Sangyo Kozo Shingikai (ed.), *Keizai Anzen Hosho no Kakuritsu o Mezashite* Tokyo, 16 August 1982, p. 38.

supplies of cobalt from Zaire.[10] The disbanding of the sub-committee after the United States-Soviet Union confrontation ebbed in the late 1980s adds credence to this view. The LDP's lack of interest in Africa has also been demonstrated in other ways. One is the inactivity of parliamentary friendship leagues. Although many have been formed for the promotion and enhancement of friendly and co-operative relations (see Fig. 4.2), exchanges between parliamentarians have been unremarkable, except, of course, for JSAPFL. That group was both active and aggressive until public opinion forced it to terminate its activities. Even so, it is not clear whether the JSAPFL ever officially disbanded or whether it only pretends to be dead. It appears almost certain that an unofficial network continues to exist.

Fig. 4.2. BILATERAL PARLIAMENTARIAN FRIENDSHIP LEAGUES WITH BLACK AFRICA, MARCH 1990

	Established	*Chairman in 1990*
Japan-Guinea	29 May 1974	Abe Shintaro (LDP)
Japan-Nigeria	16 May 1977	Harada Shozo (LDP)[a]
Japan-Ethiopia	21 June 1985	Okuda Keiwa (LDP)
Japan-Ivory Coast	21 June 1985	Okuda Keiwa (LDP)
Japan-Zambia	27 February 1986	Hosoda Kichizo (LDP)
Japan-Kenya	12 February 1988	Tsuchiya Yoshihiko (LDP)
Japan-Zimbabwe	16 October 1989	Yamanaka Sadanori (LDP)
Japan-Tanzania	12 December 1989	Hata Tsutomu (LDP)[a]

(a) These men were also members of JSAPFL.

Source: Afurika Binran 1990, p. 131.

[10] *Ibid.*, pp. 187-8. In the short English summary to this report, it is noted: 'Mineral resources are indispensable for people's lives and for industrial activities of the modern world. Nickel, chromium and other rare metals, in particular, are of critical importance since they are known as the vitamins of contemporary society. Thus, as has been previously mentioned, a curtailment in their supply would have a tremendous impact on the national economy. Supply structure of these metals is unstable with geographically concentrated deposits and production sites (certain rare metals were concentrated in Communist countries or — still today — politically unstable developing countries), and with low supply and demand price elasticities. For this purpose, it is necessary to consolidate the relations of interdependence with nations possessing resources and to promote resource exploration, development and technological advancement. In addition to these long-range structural measures, measures for unexpected threats, namely to establish national stockpiles as well as further efforts to consolidate private stockpiles, must be implemented.'

As noted earlier, a number of LDP Diet members formed the Diet Association for African Economic Development in April 1970 immediately after the Kono mission's return from Black Africa with the idea of increasing official development assistance (ODA) to the region. It served as a pressure group to exert influence on the government but after the policy of extending and expanding ODA to key countries in Africa materialised in the latter half of the 1970s, the Diet Association lost momentum. Since then, it has mainly carried out ceremonial functions. While technically the Association still functions, it in fact does very little.[11]

This was made clear in May 1992 by the Associations office itself when the OAU was preparing to celebrate its twenty-ninth anniversary. To commemorate the event, the Diet Association sponsored a half-page congratulatory advertisement in the 25 May 1992 edition of the *Asahi Evening News*. This included an article on the OAU by the Dean of the African diplomatic corps in Tokyo and congratulatroy messages from Nakayama Taro, president of the Association, and Sato Takao, its administrative director. A call to Sato's office the next day to find out more about the Association's activities was answered by one of his secretaries who said that while the organisation existed, it carried out no substantial activities.

However, when discussing the role of parliamentary friendship leagues, there is another important aspect that should not be overlooked. Diet members who are members of such leagues sometimes act as mediators or go-betweens when contracts are signed between Japanese companies and aid-recipient countries for ODA projects. For this service they then charge the Japanese companies large introduction fees. Yajima Mitsuhiro, a political secretary to LDP Dietman Ishihara Shintaro, frankly admitted the existence of such a system in his book *Hai Kochira Ishihara Shintaro Jimusho Desu* (Yes, this is Ishihara's Shintaro office).[12]

[11] See Afurika Keizai Kaihatsu Kyoryoku Giin Renmei, April 1970. Also verified by a call to the office of the administrative director of the Association, Sato Takao, 26 May 1993.

[12] Yajima Mitsuhiro, *Hai Kochira Ishihara Shintaro Jimusho Desu*, Tokyo: Nihon Bungeisha, 1991, pp. 188-92. See also the *Mainichi Shimbun* newspaper's *Kokusai Enjo Bijinesu - ODA wa do Tsukawarete Iru Ka?* Tokyo: Aki Shobo, 1990, pp. 150-78 which discusses the questionable involvement of LDP Diet members in ODA.

Fig. 4.3. ORGANISATION OF THE MINISTRY OF
FOREIGN AFFAIRS, 1992

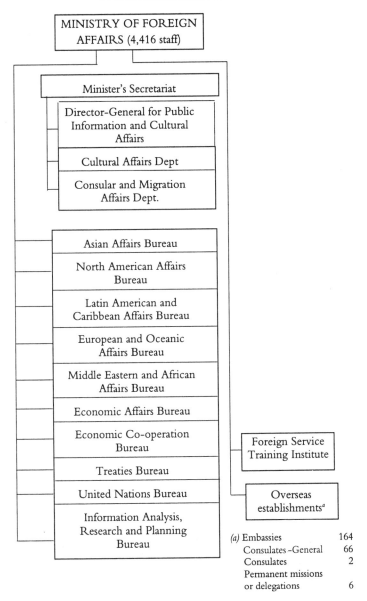

MINISTRY OF FOREIGN
AFFAIRS (4,416 staff)

Minister's Secretariat

Director-General for Public
Information and Cultural
Affairs

Cultural Affairs Dept

Consular and Migration
Affairs Dept.

Asian Affairs Bureau

North American Affairs
Bureau

Latin American and
Caribbean Affairs Bureau

European and Oceanic
Affairs Bureau

Middle Eastern and African
Affairs Bureau

Economic Affairs Bureau

Economic Co-operation
Bureau

Treaties Bureau

United Nations Bureau

Information Analysis,
Research and Planning
Bureau

Foreign Service
Training Institute

Overseas
establishments[a]

(a)		
Embassies		164
Consulates –General		66
Consulates		2
Permanent missions or delegations		6

Source: *Organisation of the Government of Japan*, Tokyo, 1992, p. 14.

Apart from this lucrative interest, LDP Diet members have in general taken little interest in international affairs, especially in areas such as Africa which are regarded as 'the end of the world'. With re-election constantly in mind, most Diet members concentrate their time and energy on the problems of their own local constituencies. If Diet members are regarded by their supporters as not having contributed sufficiently to the solution of such local problems, they will face difficulty in being re-elected. This reality has led to the popularity of the slogan '*Gaiko wa hyo ni naranai*' (Diplomacy wins no votes).[13]

The bureaucracy

Various ministries and agencies outside the Foreign Ministry are also involved in Japan's African diplomacy. The MITI's International Trade Policy Bureau's Europe, Africa and Middle East Division deals with issues of trade and commerce concerning Africa. The Ministry of Finance is involved with investment finance and ODA policy. The Ministry of Agricultural Forestry and Fisheries overseas imports of agricultural and marine products from Africa as well as food-related economic assistance programmes.

The Imperial Household Agency plays a role through its agreement to the pursuit of active court diplomacy with Africa. In 1993, even the Defence Agency entered the picture with the decision to send Japanese troops to take part in the UN peace-keeping operation in Mozambique. This resulted in the dispatch of a fifty-three-member Self-Defence Forces (SDF) unit.

All of these bodies maintain direct or indirect involvement in Japan's African diplomacy, yet the focus of our analysis must be centred on the Foreign Ministry, which plays the essential role

---

[13] Although the LDP itself has shown little extended interest in Africa, several LDP leaders have had a strong personal interest in the continent. Among them were the late foreign ministers Kimura Toshio and Abe Shintaro as well as Ishikawa Yozo, former Parliamentary Vice-Minister for Foreign Affairs, who published *Watashi no Afurika Monogatari* (Tokyo: Banseisha, 1984), in which he emphasised the vital importance of rare metals for Japan's economic survival (pp. 128-35). Perhaps best known of the LDP leaders to take an interest in Africa is Ishihara Shintaro.

of co-ordinating inter-ministry policy, integrating the activities of all these bureaucratic entities and presenting Japan's overall foreign policy to the outside world. (see Fig. 4.3)

, The Foreign Ministry's Middle Eastern and African Affairs Bureau is directly responsible for the formulation and implementation of Japan's regional policy towards Sub-Saharan Africa and the Middle East, as well as research and information gathering activities.[14] The Bureau contains four divisions: First Africa, Second Africa, First Middle East and Second Middle East.

According to the *Diplomatic Blue Book*, the First Africa Division deals with thirty states: Mauritania, Mali, Niger, Senegal, Gambia, Guinea-Bissau, Cape Verde, Guinea, Sierra Leone, Liberia, Ivory Coast, Burkina Faso, Ghana, Togo, Benin, Nigeria, Chad, Cameroon, Central African Republic, Equatorial Guinea, São Tomé and Principe, Gabon, Congo, Zaire, Rwanda, Burundi, Madagascar, Mauritius and the Comoros. The Second Africa Division covers seventeen countries: South Africa, Namibia, Botswana, Swaziland, Lesotho, Zimbabwe, Angola, Mozambique, Zambia, Malawi, Tanzania, the Seychelles, Kenya, Uganda, Ethiopia, Somalia and Djibouti.

The First Middle East Division includes Algeria, Israel, Egypt, Jordan, Syria, Sudan, Tunisia, Turkey, Morocco, Libya and Lebanon.[15]   It should be noted that on issues such as the South Africa problem and colonial questions, this division has played an important role in the co-ordination of Japan's Africa policy.

In order to conduct a systematic and unified African diplomacy, the First and Second Africa Divisions had to adjust and integrate their two sub-policies, i.e. the Black Africa and White Africa policies; this was achieved through daily consultations between division chiefs and reliance on past precedents. The importance of past precedents in the formation of Japan's Africa policy is enhanced by the

---

[14] Ministry of Foreign Affairs, *Gaiko Seisho — Waga Gaiko no Kinkyo*, 1991. See also Fig. 4.3.

[15] *Ibid.* The Second Middle East Divison includes Afghanistan, the United Arab Emirates, Yemen, Iraq, Iran, Oman, Qatar, Kuwait, Saudi Arabia and Bahrain.

Ministry's personnel rotation practices, by which staff involved in the decision-making process are likely to work in the Africa Divison for only two years before being transferred elsewhere. According to testimony from Foreign Ministry staff, the First Africa Division chief plays a central role and serves as co-ordinator of these meetings. When issues of political importance arise, the degree of involvement of the Director-General, the deputy minister for Foreign Affairs and even the Foreign Minister may increase. However, the exercise of influence by the higher echelon of the Foreign Ministry in Japan's African policy (or other policies, for that matter) is not terribly significant. Factors such as Cold War considerations, harmonious co-operation with the United States and Europe and adherence to the dual diplomacy framework greatly limited the range of policy options even on politically important issues.

Other regional departments within the Foreign Ministry that contribute significantly to African diplomacy are the North American and the European and Oceanic Affairs Bureau. An example of the former's involvement in Africa diplomacy can be seen in United States State Department's Assistant Secretary for African Affairs Herman Cohen's 14 November 1989 visit to Japan for consultations with Foreign Ministry officials. The Ministry has declined to make public details of Cohen's meeting with the bureau but the main points of his informal discussions with members of the Keidanren's CCA were outlined in that organisation's weekly newsletter.

It was reported that Cohen emphasised the impression of the United States that South Africa was becoming more forward-looking; thus the United States was maintaining economic sanctions to encourage change in South Africa's apartheid policy. Cohen asked for Japan's co-operation over this.[16] He also noted that with the ending of competition between the United States and the Soviet Union, America intended to encourage constitutional rule and support economic growth in Africa by stressing the importance of investment. He concluded that the United States was making greater efforts to support countries such as Zimbabwe and Cameroon, which it saw as having the economic

---

[16] *Keidanren Shuho,* 27 November 1989, p. 9.

potential to 'kickstart' development in neighbouring states too.[17]
Other Foreign Ministry bodies that play a role in the formulation of policy include the Economic Affairs Bureau (trade, energy and natural resources issues), the Economic Co-operation Bureau (aid policy) and the self-explanatory UN Bureau involving UN diplomacy. Making contributions also are the Minister's Secretariat, the Public Relations Division and the Foreign Nationals' Affairs Division in the Ministry of Foreign Affairs.[18]

The participation of these other sectors is important since the staff allocated to the Middle Eastern and African Affairs Bureau is relatively small and appears to be far from sufficient. As of 19 October 1992, there were twenty-two staff in the First Middle East, sixteen in the Second Middle East, fifteen in the First Africa and nine in the Second Africa. Thus the total staff for Sub-Saharan Africa (including the bureau chief and the deputy minister for Foreign Affairs) was only twenty-six.[19] For a listing of the 138 ministry employees posted to Sub-Saharan Africa, see figure below.

Such staff limitations inhibit policy implementation and have

Fig. 4.4. JAPANESE DIPLOMATIC STAFF DESPATCHED TO
EMBASSIES IN AFRICA, MARCH 1993
(*figures include ambassadors*)

Ethiopia	9	Kenya[b]	17
Cameroon	5	Zaire[c]	—
Guinea	5	Zambia	10
Tanzania	10	Zimbabwe	9
Central Africa Rep.	5	Senegal	13
Nigeria	10	Ivory Coast	10
Ghana	7	Madagascar	8
Gabon	9[a]	South Africa	11

(*a*). Includes two employees temporarily removed from Zaire.
(*b*). Includes Japanese UN employees in Kenya.
(*c*). Temporarily closed due to political instability.
Source: Interview with a Foreign Ministry official, Tokyo, 10 March 1993.

[17] *Ibid.* p. 9.
[18] The Foreign Ministry's African diplomacy was also supported by public corporations such as the Japan International Co-operation Agency and the Japan Foundation (both affiliated with the Ministry of Foreign Affairs) the Export-Import Bank of Japan (Ministry of Finance) and JETRO (MITI).
[19] Information obtained in interview with a Foreign Ministry official.

helped pave the way for the *zaikai's* participation in Japan's African policy. The important role of this third major actor will now be considered.

The zaikai

Just what is the *zaikai*?[20] Along with the LDP and the bureaucracy, it is one of the three governing elites of post-war Japan and is generally considered to be composed of four major economic organisations and their leaders: Keidanren, Nikkeiren, Keizai Doyukai (the Japan Committee for Economic Development) and Nissho (the Japan Chamber of Commerce and Industry).[21]

In short, the *zaikai's* justification is to create a favourable political and economic climate, both inside and outside Japan, for the stability and long-range development of Japanese capitalism.[22] In order to realise these goals, the *zaikai* — centred around its most powerful economic organisation, Keidanren — carries out activities to co-ordinate, consolidate

---

[20] The word *zaikai* has been translated in many ways: business circles, financial circles, the business community, etc. As this book emphasises the *zaikai's* role as a political actor, the term 'organised business' is most appropriate. The term was used first in English in Yanaga. For more on the *zaikai's* history, structure and functions, see Heiwa Keizai Keikaku Kaigi Dokusen Hakusho Iinkai (eds), *Kokumin no Dokusen Hakusho* (People's White Paper on the Japanese Economy — Zaikai, 6, Tokyo: Ochanomizu Shobo, 1982; Hara Akira 'Zaikai' in Nakamura Takafusa and Ito Takashi (eds), *Kindai Nihon Kenkyu Nyumon*, University of Tokyo Press, 1977, pp. 170-92; and Misawa Shigeo 'Taigai Seisaku to Nihon Zaikai' in Hosaya and Watanuki (eds), pp. 179-211.

[21] Keidanren's 1991 English-language brochure (Keidanren, Public Affairs Dept., Tokyo: Keidanren, 1991) describes the organisations this way: Nissho is a nationwide confederation of local Chambers of Commerce and Industry throughout Japan and deals with various national as well as international economic problems. One characteristic feature of Nissho, founded through special legislation, is its interest in regional economic problems, including those pertaining to small and medium-scale businesses. In this regard, Nissho undertakes various vocational or technical training programmes, business consultation services and overseas trading referral service for small and medim-scale businesses. Nikkeiren is composed chiefly of regional employers' associations and various trade associations and is a specialised group concerned with the problems of wages, working conditions and labour-management relations. Keizai Doyukai is made up of individual members who are business executives. It provides a forum for officers of business corporations to meet individuals and speak out freely on various economic and social problems.

and unify the various interests, opinions and conflicts within the Japanese businesss community. The *zaikai* then works to have the united will and interests of the business community reflected in government policy. The methods for such pressure group activities include presentation of policy proposals, participation of *zaikai* leaders in consulatitve councils, and periodic informal discussion meetings with government officials. Other 'informal' activities include providing political parties, especially the LDP, with huge donations of political funds,[23] private meetings with LDP leaders at exclusive tea-houses, and the offering of key posts in private companies to high-ranking retired government officials, a practice known in Japan as '*amakudari*' (descent from heaven).[24] These second career holders help strengthen the intimate

[22] See, for example, the English-language edition of the Keidanren Constitution, Tokyo, n.d., p. 1., Article 1: 'The purpose of Keidanren shall be to maintain close contact with various economic sectors, to sound out opinions of the business circles on economic problems both domestic and international, and to endeavour to obtain practical solutions to these problems, thereby to promote the self-sustenance and sound development of the national economy.'

[23] The *zaikai's* donation of political funds to the LDP is carried out through Keidanren, as revealed in the *Daily Yomiuri* (12 Feburary 1990) just six days before the Lower House election: 'Fearing that the LDP may lose its majority in the Lower House, as it did in the House of Councillors last July, Keidanren is doing all it can to support the ruling party. . . . Last Friday, Keidanren organised a meeting for its member at a Tokyo hotel, inviting Nakamura Kichiro, head of the LDP's Affairs Bureau, who is in charge of election campaigns. . . . Keidanren held a similar gathering in late January, inviting about 200 businessmen, but this time it invited about fifty executives from major firms to consolidate its support for the LDP in "crucial constituencies", top Keidanren officials said. . . . Keidanren is expected to donate ¥13 billion, or ¥1 billion more than the average year, to the LDP this year.'

[24] For a comprehensive study of the *amakudari* phenomenom, see *Amakudari Hakusho*, Seifu Kankei Tokushu Hojin Rodokumiai Kyogikai, Tokyo, 1986; Chalmers Johnson, 'The Re-employment of Retired Government Bureaucrats in Japanese Big Business', *Asian Survey*, 14, 11 (November 1974), pp. 953-65; and Karel van Wolferen, *The Enigma of Japanese Power*, London: Macmillan 1989, p. 45: 'Some three hundred bureaucrats annually join the business world as directors or senior advisors of corporations they monitored during their government career. Since the retirement age is fifty-five, such bureaucrats will have another twenty years or so in which to help ensure smooth communications between industry and the ministries or the central bank.'

network of personal connections between the bureaucracy and the *zaikai*, connections that can be used to exert pressure officially — and unofficially — to influence government policy.

The third function of the *zaikai* is participation and co-operation in the process of implementation of foreign policy, generally known as *'minkan keizai gaiko'* or private business diplomacy, i.e. complementary efforts aimed at creating a favourable climate for big business and providing supplementary support for government diplomacy. This third function — the central focus of our study — is examined in detail in Chapter 4.

As part of Japan's African diplomacy, this activity was carried out first by the Afurika Kyokai (Africa Society of Japan) and later by the Keidanren's CCA. The Africa Society was established by the *zaikai* with the strong backing of the Japanese government as a part of the preparations necessary to expand Japan's economic presence in Africa and help to strengthen its fledgling diplomacy with the continent. The society's own documents best explain its aims and origins:

> In May 1958, the establishment of an organisation to strengthen   political, economic and cultural ties with the countries of the African continent was advocated by a number of influential people in the political and business worlds and the media and this led to the establishment of the organising committee.
>
> In December 1959, permission was given for the formation of the society as an organisation affiliated with the Ministry of Foreign Affairs and in January 1960, it was registered as a corporate body. Foreign Minister Fujiyama Achiro asked the Keidanren Vice Chairman Uemura Kogoro to select a chairman and at his request, Tashiro Shigeki, the chairman of Toyo Rayon Co. Ltd, agreed to take the post. His appointment was approved at a Keidanren meeting on 29 August 1960 and in November of that year, the secretariat opened in Tokyo and the recruitment of members, public relations and information gathering began.[25]

---

[25] Shadan Hojin Afurika Kyokai (ed.), *Gyomu Hokoku 90-91*, Tokyo, 1991, p. 4.

This short passage reflects how closely Keidanren and the Foreign Ministry can work together.[26] It is also revealing that the head of Toyo Rayon was chosen as the first chairman of the association, for at that time (1960) textile-related products were still dominant among Japanese exports. Other initial officers of the Africa Society were vice presidents Nishi Haruhiko, former ambassador to Britain, and Furukaki Tetsuro, former ambassador to France.[27]

Committee on Co-operation with Africa (CCA)

Along with this joint effort between government and big business of course went the establishment of Keidanren's CCA (Afurika Iinkai) in August 1970. The origins and aims of the CCA were described this way in the Kono African Economic Mission report published in October 1970:

> The importance of Africa for Japan and requests for the enlargement and intensification of co-operative relations with the countries of Africa have become generally recognised. On its return, our economic mission expressed the view to Keidanren officials that there is a need for a place — a centralised channel — where Japanese industry as a whole can consider African policy. With the understanding of Keidanren officials, the decision to form the Committee was approved at the 25 May general meeting and on 30 June, Mission Head Kono Fumihiko was selected to serve as chairman. After this, the Committee proceeded with the selection of a total of seventy-one members — representatives of corporations, economic organisations and others. To mark the commencement of its activities, the Committee invited Mr Kimoto, the Japanese ambassador to Ghana (then home on temporary leave) to speak at the first meeting of the Committee held 31 August 1970.[28]

---

[26] Although the Africa Society became affiliated with the Ministry of Foreign Affairs in 1959, this does not necessarily mean that the society became a subordinate organisation of the Ministry. In order to get corporate juridical person status, organisations interested in the promotion of international exchange, like the Africa Society, must, as a matter of form, be affiliated with the Foreign Ministry.

[27] *Africa-Japan*, 1(1963).

[28] Africa Economic Mission *Hirake yuku Burakku Afurika*, p. 58.

Keidanren explained its own aims as follows:

> Keidanren thinks it is important to develop more diversified
> and multi-level exchanges between Japan and African coun-
> tries while also promoting mutual understanding and closer
> relations. In this conection, it established the Committee on
> Co-operation with Africa in August 1970 under the chair-
> manship of Kono Fumihiko. The Committee has since been
> actively at work to promote the trade and economic relations
> with Africa on a private basis.[29]

Clearly, then, the aims of the Committee were to act as a
central conduit for the consideration of African policy and to
co-operate in the economic development of Black African countries as well as to promote economic exchange and deepen
Japan's relations with African nations.

The existence of such diverse goals is not strange, considering
they reflect the various aspects of the *zaikai*'s overall role — most
specifically, co-ordination of the various interests and opinions of
the membership, with the aim of having these interests reflected in
government policy and at the same time attempting to promote
friendly relations with foreign countries. In short the CCA serves
not only as the headquarters for Japan's systematic economic
advancement into Africa but also as a channel to help formulate and
execute the government's policy towards the continent.[30]

With this background in mind, it is useful now to examine
the Committee's organisational structure and activities. The
Keidanren Committee on Co-operation with Africa consists of
seventy four members (see Fig. 4.5). Most of them are the
presidents or chairmen of major corporations in the industrial
sector. Representatives of several government-related
organisations, such as the Export—Import Bank, JICA and Japan
Natrional Oil Corporation, are also allowed to participate as full
members, demonstrating that the *kanzai ittai* system is built into
the very structure of the committee. Nevertheless, in the management of the committee, a dozen private companies predomi-
nate and play leading roles in the two steering committees set
up within the CCA.

---

[29] *Keidanren Review on Japanese Economy*, 67 (1981), p. 11.
[30] In effect, the CCA is taking over the main functions of the Africa Society of
Japan, except for public relations activities.

Fig. 4.5. MEMBERS OF THE KEIDANREN COMMITTEE ON
CO-OPERATION WITH AFRICA, 17 JUNE 1986

> *Chairman* Kobe Steel Corp.; *Vice Chairmen* Toyota Motor Corp., Fuji
> Bank Ltd., Nippon Steel Corp., Sumitomo Chemical Co., and
> Hanamura Nihachiro of Keidanren

Nippon Kokan K.K.
Sumitomo Metal Industries Ltd
Kawasaki Steel Corp.
Kobe Steel Ltd
Yodogawa Steel Works Ltd
Nippon Kokan K.K.
Mitsubishi Heavy Industries
Ishikawajima — Harima Heavy Industries
Hitachi Zosen Corp.
Daiichi Sekiyu Kaihatsu Japan National Oil Corp.
Nissan Motor Co. Ltd
Bridgestone Corp.
Sankyu Inc.
Kubota Corp.
Hitachi Ltd
Toshiba Corp.
NEC Corp.
Sanyo Electric Co. Ltd
Yuasa Battery Co. Ltd
Matsushita Electric Industries Co. Ltd
Mitsubishi Chemical Industries Ltd
Showa Denko K.K.
Sekisui Chemical Co. Ltd
Sumitomo Bakelite Co. Ltd
Kuraray Co. Ltd
Unitika Ltd
Toyobo Co. Ltd
Fuji Spinning Co. Ltd
Sakai Textile Manufacturing Co. Ltd
Japan Mining Industry Association
Nippon Mining Co. Ltd
Mitsui Mining & Smelting Co. Ltd
Sumitomo Metal Mining Co. Ltd
Mitsubishi Kinzoku
Dowa Mining Co. Ltd
Furukawa Kogyo
Mitsui Mining Com.
Mitubishi Kogyo Cement
Nippon Suisan Kaisha Ltd
Kyokuyo Co. Ltd
Nippon Yusen K.K.

Mitsui OSK Lines Ltd
Mitsui & Co. Ltd
Mitsubishi Corp.
Marubeni Corp.
C. Itoh & Co.
Kanematsu Corp.
Toyo Menka Kaisha Ltd
Kawasho Corp.
Nissho Iwai Corp.
Nichimen Corp.
Sumitomo Corp.
Nomura Boeki
Tokyo Boeki
Bank of Tokyo Ltd
Suruga Bank
Kajima Corp.
Konoike Gumi
Tokyo Marine and Fire Insurance Co. Ltd
Taisho Marine and Fire Insurance Co. Ltd
Nippon Koei Co. Ltd
Ebara Corp
Japan Export—Import Bank
Japan International Co-operation Agency (JICA)
Kokusai Kensetsu Gijutsu Kyorokukai
Association of African Economy and Development
Africa Society of Japan

Note: The companies are listed in the order that they appeared on the CCA membership list.

The first of these is the Special Committee (Senmon Iinkai) established in 1978 as a follow-up to the February 1978 African Economic Mission,[31] and made up of the department heads or section chiefs directly in charge of their companies' African affairs.[32] The group is concerned with concrete examination of specific issues involved in the *zaikai's* economic co-operation with Africa.[33] The fifteen corporate members of the committee, as well as three advisers from government- related organisations, are listed in Fig. 4.6.

The Policy Committee (Seisaku Iinkai) was formed in August

[31] See *Keidanren Shuho* 18 May 1978, p. 13.
[32] Noted in an internal document dated 17 June 1986, titled 'Keidanren Afurika Iinkai ni Tsuite Shiryo Ichiran', Keidanren Economic Co-operation Department. It is this department that is in charge of matters relating to the CCA.
[33] *Keidanren Shuho*, p. 13. Includes such issues as economic co-operation, technical co-operation, trade and investment and Southern African problems.

1984 of the presidents or vice presidents of eleven major corporations (see Fig. 4.6). [34] It is like a task force in charge of overall management and is regarded as the highest decision-making body within the CCA.[35] Nine of the eleven Policy Committee member corporations are also represented on the Special Committee. This overlapping reflects the influence these companies exert on the overall activities of the committee. Almost all are industry-wide leaders in the fields of iron and steel, non-ferrous metals, machinery, electronics, electrical appliances or banking, as well as the major trading companies. Mitsubishi Heavy Industries, one of the core companies of the Mitsubishi group, virtually monopolised the overall chairmanship for sixteen years, from the CCA's inception in 1970 until June 1986 (see Fig. 4.7). The absence of textile companies in the upper echelons of the steering committees reflects the shift Japan's economic advancement into Africa has taken since the 1960s.

A CCA document described the group's major activities as being the despatch of economic missions and the presentation of

[34] Keidanren Economic Co-operation Dept internal document, 17 June 1986, p. 2. This author also learned much about the committee's structure and activities from Prof. Masudo Kinya, a former Keidanren official.

[35] The *Journal of Japanese Trade and Industry* describes the general decision-making style of Keidanren committees this way: 'Keidanren also has bilateral committees to promote exchange with countries around the world. Just a few examples are the Committee on Japan-EC Relations, the Japan-Canada Economic Committee, the Committee on Co-operation with Indonesia and the Committee on Co-operation with Africa. The member of these committees are corporate executives, and the chairmen are the chief executives of big companies. The committees also frequently hold closed-door meetings of corporate middle management and corporate staff in charge of specific matters in order to discuss problems in greater detail. Miyoshi Masaya, Keidanren senior managing director, explains that the organisation makes it a rule to discuss problems exhaustively at four levels in order to form a consensus. Any issue will be addressed by corporate chairmen and presidents, board directors in charge of the matter under study, division and department managers and the working staff directly involved. The Secretariat provides behind-the-scenes support for the Executive Council, the Board of Directors, the Board of Executive Directors, and the various committees. Keidanren's policy is to employ only the graduates of four universities — the two top state-run universities, Tokyo and Hitotsubashi, and the two top private universities, Waseda and Keio. The 170 Secretariat staffers, 100 of them male, are the young elite of the business community.' 3 (1985), p. 15.

Fig. 4.6. POLICY AND SPECIAL COMMITTEE MEMBERS,
DECEMBER 1985

Policy Committee (Seisaku Iinkai) Members
Top officials of the following companies:

Mitsubishi Heavy Industries	C. Itoh & Co. Ltd
Nippon Mining Co. Ltd	Nippon Koei Co. Ltd
Bank of Tokyo	Marubeni Corp.
Mitsui & Co. Ltd	NEC Corp.
Mitsubishi Corp.	Kobe Steel Ltd
Mitusi OSK Lines Ltd	

Special Committee (Senmon Iinkai) Members
Department heads or section chiefs in charge of Africa from:

Mitsubishi Heavy Industries	Mitsubishi Corp.
Nippon Mining Co. Ltd.	Sumitomo Corp.
C. Itoh & Co. Ltd.	NEC Corp
Bank of Tokyo	Marubeni Corp.
Nissho Iwai Corp.	Mitsui & Co. Ltd
Nippon Koei Co. Ltd.	Nichimen Corp.
Kawasaki Heavy Industries	Kajima Corp.
Nippon Yusen K.K.	

Advisers, officials or department heads in charge of Africa from:

Japan Export-Import Bank
Overseas Economic Co-operation Fund
Japan International Co-operation Agency (JICA)

Source: 'Afurika Iinkai Seisaku Iinkai Meibo', internal CCA document, 11 Dec. 1985, p. 2.

Fig. 4.7 CHAIRMEN OF THE KEIDANREN COMMITTEE ON
CO-OPERATION WITH AFRICA

Aug. 1970-June 1982	Chairmen, Mitsubishi Heavy Industries (Kono Fumihiko)
June 1982-June 1986	Chairman, Mistubishi Heavy Industries (Kanamori Masao)
June 1982-Oct. 1991	President, Kobe Steel Ltd (Maki Fuyuhiko)
Oct. 1991-June 1994	Sumitomo Metal Mining Co Ltd (Fujimori Masamichi)
July 1994-	Japan Energy Corp. (Yukio Kasahara)

Source: Compiled from information published in *Keidanren Shuho*, a weekly newsletter.

policy proposals to the government upon their return. The same
document also summarised the CCA's main activities for the year
1985, revealing the committee's actual broader functions. They
were: informal meetings with visiting African officials, African
ambassadors in Tokyo and Foreign Ministry officials such as the

Director-General of the Middle Eastern and African Affairs Bureau; dealing with a request from the Foreign Ministry (with which the CCA complied) to introduce someone in the *zaikai* willing to work in the Zambian embassy as an economic co-operation specialist,[36] and despatch of project-seeking missions for agricultural irrigation projects to Kenya, Tanzania and Zambia as part of follow-up activities related to the 1984 African Economic Mission.

Listed under other miscellaneous activities were co-sponsorship with the African Society of Japan of an African investment seminar; a reception for and participation in an OAU seminar organised by African ambassadors in Tokyo; and joint sponsorship (with JETRO, the Tokyo Chamber of Commerce and the Japan Foreign Trade Council Inc.) of the annual meeting of the Japanese ambassadors to African states held in Tokyo. Informal meetings were also held with the ambassadors to garner information on what was going on in Africa and to express to the ambassadors the *zaikai*'s views on economic co-operation. The CCA also met members of the UN Council for Namibia during its visit to Tokyo in 1985.

The above activities involve aspects of both the policy formulation and implementation processes. The former includes policy proposals and informal meetings with various government officials. Although informal, these meetings cannot be underestimated, since the *zaikai* is able to use these opportunities to convey requests on certain issues to the government and thus influence policy. In order to conduct effective business diplomacy, it is essential for the government and the *zaikai* to share common perceptions on various issues and common views on what responses should be taken. Through these periodic meetings, such mutual understanding can evolve.[37]

Committee activities concerning implementation of policy fall into two categories — personnel exchange and economic co-operation — discussed in detail in Chapter 5.

The CCA's activities are supported by several parallel organisations, the most important being SATA, as well as the

---

[36] Keidanren Economic Co-operation Department, internal document 17 June, 1986, p. 5.

[37] Similar efforts were also being undertaken externally with advanced capitalist countries. See Ministry of Foreign Affairs, Public Information Bureau, *Sekai no Ugoki,* Tokyo, November 1982, p. 22.

Fig. 4.8 KEY CORPORATIONS INVOLVED IN JAPAN'S AFRICAN DIPLOMACY

	CCA 1986	CCA Policy Committee 1985	CCA Special Committee 1985	ASJ 1986	SATA	NCSA
C. Itoh & Co. Ltd	★	★	★	★		★
Hitachi Ltd	★			★	★	★
Marubeni Corp.	★	★	★	★		★
Matsushita Electric	★			★	★	
Mitsubishi Corp.	★	★	★	★	★	★
Mitsubishi Heavy Industries	★	★	★	★	★	
Mitsui & Co. Ltd	★	★	★	★	★	★
Mitsui OSK Lines Ltd	★			★	★	
NEC Corp.	★	★	★	★		
Nippon Koei Co. Ltd	★			★		
Nissan Motor Co. Ltd	★			★	★	
Nissho Iwai Corp.	★		★	★	★	★
Sumitomo Corp.	★		★	★	★	★
Toyota Motor Corp.	★			★	★	★

Note: Due to the difficulty of obtaining this internal data there is some variation in the years examined, but as this chart shows, all of these companies played major leadership roles in these organisations in the mid-1980s.

Source: CCA membership list for 1986, Policy and Special Committee membership for 1985, Africa Society of Japan (ASJ) Board of Directors for 1986, SATA membership for 1989 and Nippon Club of South Africa (NCSA) officers for 1988.

Africa Society of Japan and overseas organisation of Japanese companies involved in economic advancement into Africa, such as the Nippon Club of South Africa.

In fact, the key posts in all these organisations are held by a small group of key corporations, as can be seen in Figure 4.8. Chief among them are the Big Six trading houses (Mitsui, Sumitomo, Mitsubishi, Nissho Iwai, C. Itoh & Co and Marubeni), all of which are represented on SATA's executive board and the CCA's Policy and Special Committees. Their pervasive presence is not surprising, as these six companies alone handle over 50 per cent of Japan's trade with South Africa.[38] In 1987, this broke down to: Mitsui, $6 billion; Nissho Iwai, $5 billion, Sumitomo, $3 billion, Mitsubishi and C. Itoh & Co., $2.5 billion each and Marubeni, $2 billion.[39]

Of the CCA's sister organisations, perhaps the most significant is the Southern Africa Traders Association (SATA). As noted earlier, SATA was formed very quietly, almost secretly, in April 1985 for the purpose of promoting mutual understanding and smooth trade and commercial relations with the countries of Southern Africa. The first secretary, general was Makiura Toshio who also happened to be the secretary general of the Springbok Club, the Tokyo 'old boy network' of businessmen and diplomats who had once served in South Africa, as well as the Tokyo representative of the South Africa Foundation and an employee of South African Airways.

Very little infomation about SATA's activities have been made public but an article in the Springbok Club newsletter described it as a 'consultative and liaison institution [40] for trade and commerce issues concerning Japan and Southern African nations, supported by relevant industries. The article went on to say that SATA co-ordinated its activities with other private organisations and focused on the countries of Malawi, Zambia, Zimbabwe, Mozambique, Botswana, Lesotho, Swaziland and South Africa.[41] However, the Springbok article also neglected to clarify several points.

[38] 'Trading Companies Fear Criticism of Their Trade with South Africa', *Daily Yomiuri*, 22 February 1988.
[39] *Ibid.*
[40] *Springbok Club Kaiho,* 10 (1 November 1987), p. 42.
[41] *Ibid.*

For example, it did not mention that the CCA had been directly engaged in the promotion of trade relations with Black Southern African countries since 1970; in commercial terms, only two of them, Zambia and Zimbabwe, were important trading partners, and compared with South Africa they were of minor significance. Nor did the article mention that until SATA was established, there was no *zaikai* organisation aimed specifically at smooth trade relations with South Africa. Makiura's presence in the post of secretary-general clearly emphasised SATA's orientation and the main focus of its interest, South Africa, but this was not explicitly acknowledged in the article.

SATA's organisation and activities also reflect this focus. It has its headquarters in Tokyo and has a branch office in Johannesburg. Of the twenty original member companies, nineteen have an office or liaison office in South Africa; eleven companies (including the Big Six trading companies) are on the executive board that manages SATA's affairs. The Mitsui OSK Lines' representative has held the post of chairman of SATA since its inception. Vice chairmen have been elected for three-year terms. From 1985 to 1988, Nissho Iwai and Toshiba officials held these posts and in the next three-year term they were occupied by Mitsui and Toyota officials.[42]

The SATA branch in Johannesburg, the only branch in Southern Africa, is organisationally interwoven with the Nippon Club of South Africa, which is composed of Japanese firms operating in the country. The president of the Nippon Club has also served as the chief secretary of the Johannesburg branch of SATA. Constant communication and information exchange exist between the branch office and the Tokyo headquarters.

In an interview, Shibayama Gosuke, the chairman of SATA, revealed that SATA strives to achieve its goals by maintaining close and active consultations and exchange via four major channels of communication, between headquarters and the branch office and among SATA members in Tokyo; between SATA and the Japanese government, especially the Foreign Ministry

[42] Information obtained during an interview with SATA chairman Shibayama Gosuke at the Mitsui OSK Lines headquarters, Tokyo, 18 January 1989.

and MITI; between SATA and the Pretoria government, including day-to-day contact with South African representatives in
Tokyo; and between SATA and counterpart South African companies and business organisations which operate within Japan,
such as South African Airways, SATOUR and de Beers.

Although it appears that initially SATA had avoided contact
with South African Blacks, SATA's focus widened in 1986 to
include direct contact with non-White South Africans, especially the Black community. SATA became involved in the
campaign to raise funds for the Japan—South Africa Fund (described in detail in Chapter 5) and also began to meet with
leaders of the anti-apartheid movement who visited Japan, such
as Donald Woods, as well as the ANC Tokyo representative
Jerry Matsila. While still giving low priority to these new activities, they have accelerated such encounters in recent years in
hopes of smoothing the way for Japan's economic presence in
post-apartheid South Africa.

As demonstrated in this chapter, Japan's post-war foreign policy
has for the most part been determined by the interaction of three
major actors — the Liberal Democratic Party, the bureaucracy
and the *zaikai*. Japan's African diplomacy also has been achieved
mainly within this triangular framework and as this examination
of the *zaikai* has shown, an inner triangle also exists within this
larger triangular framework. The Foreign Ministry's Africa Divisions, a few members of the LDP and PARC and a handful
of key corporations form the inner group that guides Japan's
African policy. These key companies include the Big Six trading
houses, Mitsubishi Heavy Industries, Nissan, Toyota, Nippon
Koei, NEC, Mitsui OSK Lines, Matsushita and Hitachi. The
next chapter examines this inner triangle in action.

STATE VISITS

Emperor Haile Selassie I of Ethiopia, with Emperor Hirohito of Japan and Empress Nagako, May 1970.

President Mobutu Sese Seko of Zaire, accompanied by his wife, with the Japanese Emperor and Empress, April 1971.

President Nelson Mandela of South Africa with Emperor Akihito, July 1995.

All these photos are reproduced courtesy of Kyodo Photo Service.

5

DUAL DIPLOMACY: CASE STUDIES OF BIG BUSINESS INVOLVEMENT

Economic co-operation

What has been the contribution of the *zaikai,* and what has been the involvement of the business community in the actual implementation of Japan's policy of economic co-operation with Africa?

To understand the *zaikai* role during the years of LDP rule, it is necessary to reiterate the LDP government's basic understanding of the concept of aid. Its aid policy has placed a high value on the role of private corporations. This is made explicit in the English-language Foreign Ministry pamphlet, *The Developing Countries and Japan*:

> Active Co-operation on the Private-Level: Private Flows (PF) — Long-term export credits and direct investment constitute major parts of private flows (PF). However, these are primarily aimed at seeking profits through export promotion and overseas investment, and they are different in character from Official Development Assistance (ODA), which aims at extending assistance to the developing countries. At the same time, they are significant in that they are intended to supplement the shortage of capital in a developing country and to gain profits through the transfer of management know-how and technical information. It is in this sense that they are considered to be a part of economic co-operation.[1]

The *zaikai* echoes the government's view. In a July 1990 edition of the *Keidanren Weekly Newsletter,* it was pointed out that 'economic co-operation is broadly understood to include grants from NGOs, private flows such as direct investment and import expansion of products from developing countries; these

118

all play an effective role in the economic development of the developing countries'.[2]

The attempt by Japan to suggest that investment, trade and other profit-seeking activities carried out by private companies can be seen as a part of official aid activities has, of course, been criticised by the recipient countries and other aid-donor nations. The government's response when confronted with such criticism is especially noteworthy. It chose to minimise use of the term 'economic aid', with its altruistic implication, and began to refer to its actions instead as 'economic co-operation', a vaguer term which allows the government to maintain its position.[3]

Secondly, Japan views economic co-operation not as a goal in itself, but as a diplomatic means to achieve a larger goal — national and Western interests. This idea, noted earlier, is expressed clearly in a statement made in 1981 by Matsuura Koichiro, then director of the Aid Policy Division of the Ministry of Foreign Affairs' Economic Co-operation Bureau: 'Crisis prevention, crisis preparedness and crisis management have been singled out as security measures and economic co-

[1] Ministry of Foreign Affairs, *The Developing Countries and Japan*, Tokyo, 1979, p. 26. Since the latter half of the 1980s, Japanese decision-makers have actively advocated that private flows, especially direct foreign investment (DFI), can play an important role in the economic development of Third World nations. See, for example, the statement by Matsuura Koichiro, Director-General of the Economic Co-operation Bureau of the Japanese Ministry of Foreign Affairs, made in English at a high-level meeting of the Development Assistance Committee, 5-6 December 1988: 'Compared with other private flows, private direct investment has the merit of enabling a transfer of funds without putting any additional debt burden on the developing countries. However, investment decisions by private enterprises are usually taken after careful consideration of investment circumstances. From our own experience, ODA plays a very important role in preparing a positive investment environment through the improvement of the infrastructure, development of human resources, and so on. In witnessing the influx in investment in developing countries such as Thailand and Malaysia and the consequent economic growth which this investment brings to these developing countries, obviously we need to re-acknowledge the important role of ODA as catalyst for the promotion of private investment.' Matsuura, pp. 353-4. For a detailed study of Japan's direct investment in Africa, see Chiyoura, pp. 83-138.

[2] *Keidanren Shuho*, 9 July 1990, p. 4.

[3] See Yamamota, pp. 10-11.

operation is one of the major means of crisis prevention.[4]

These two points need to be remembered when examining the *zaikai's* role in the government's economic co-operation policy in Africa, especially in White Africa.

Economic co-operation in White Africa

The economic co-operation of Japanese corporations and industries with the Pretoria regime was not limited to the importation of South African products. It also included direct involvement in economic development projects, which were considered an integral part of South Africa's survival strategy. This latter aspect can be critically examined by focusing here on a case-study of the large-scale mineral resources development export project of the 1970s. This was the Sishen-Saldanha Bay Development Project (SSBD) and the Iron and Steel Industrial Corporation (ISCOR) Expansion Plan, which was considered one of South Africa's central industrial development projects.

The Sishen-Saldanha Bay Development Project was designed to develop the Sishen mine, estimated to hold 4 billion tonnes of iron ore, and to construct an 860-km. railway linking the mine to Saldanha Bay, where port facilities were to be constructed as well as a steel mill that would be able partly to process the mined ore.[5] At the time when it was launched, it was considered a core project among the five major development projects being promoted by the government. These included the St Croix Island Port Facilities Expansion plan for iron ore; Richards Bay Expansion Plan for Coal and railway link with Witbank for coal; ISCOR's Expansion Plan; and the Orange River Project for electricity. The SSBD was described by the *South African Digest* as 'one of the biggest development schemes to be undertaken in South Africa for decades'.[6]

However, many major problems had to be dealt with before the project could take off. These included procurement of the

[4] *Keidanren Shuho*, 19 March 1981, Tokyo, p. 24. The newsletter notes this quote was taken from a speech made to the Keidanren Committee on Foreign Economic Co-operation, 10 March 1981.

[5] Pacific-Asia Resource Center, *Aparutoheito e no Nihon no Katan*, Tokyo, October 1975, p. 21.

[6] Kitazawa, *From Tokyo to Johannesburg*, p. 4.

indispensable capital, machinery and equipment and related technology. Equally necessary was a reliable customer for the huge amounts of iron ore that the development would provide, because if an export market could be secured before the project was implemented, Pretoria could use its natural resources as collateral for acquiring the capital and machinery needed for development. Also the capital earned from the massive exportation of iron ore and related processed products could be used over the long term for other development projects, such as the ISCOR Expansion Plan.[7] The partner Pretoria selected to solve these problems was Japan.[8]

In July 1970, South Africa sent a mission to Tokyo headed by Dr T. F. Muller, the chairman of ISCOR. The mission offered attractive incentives to the Japanese iron and steel industry as well as the *zaikai,* and the mission urged their participation and co-operation in the SSBD project. The incentives offered included the following:

> ISCOR was ready to assign a total of 140 million tonnes of Sishen iron ore for export to Japan and would lift further restrictions on the export of coking coal to Japan. Above all, South Africa made it clear that it was ready to launch a joint venture to construct numerous steel mills in addition to the Saldanha mills, including a large number of blast furnaces within the vast projected expansion plan of ISCOR.[9]

The Japanese response to the mission was very positive, especially since at that time Japan was enjoying a period of high economic growth and faced the problem of acquiring a

[7] See Kitazawa Yoko, *Watashi no Naka no Afurika, Han Aparutoheito no Tabi,* (Tokyo: Shakai Shisosha, 1979, p. 206) in which the author notes the Sishen-Saldanha Bay Development Project was carried out in order to make the exportation of industrial plants necessary for the ISCOR Expansion Plan possible.
[8] Nippon Yusen K.K., *Chosa Shitsu, Chosa Shiryo 75-A-8, Minami Afurika,* 27 June 1975. This report observed South Africa's keen interest in exporting minerals to Japan and the construction of the port at Richards Bay to export coal, the Sishen-Saldanha Railway and the St Croix Island construction for iron ore exportation were being carried out with the idea in mind that Japan will be the largest market. See also Ruth First, Jonathan Steele and Christabel Gurney, *The South African Connection: Western Investment in Apartheid,* London: Temple Smith, 1972, pp. 142-6.
[9] Kitazawa, *From Tokyo to Johannesburg,* pp. 4-5.

stable supply of energy and mineral resources from a friendly and reliable supplier. Dr Muller visited Japan again in 1973 and requested it to begin importing Sishen iron ore in 1976, noting that two-thirds of the iron ore from the project would be supplied to Japan. He also asked for a 'long-term contract for purchase of the products and to provide plant and related material for the projects'.[10] Japan did eventually sign a long-term contract for the import of Sishen iron ore and semi-processed steel products, which provided the boost necessary to realise the SSBD project.[11]

By applying Japan's overall natural resources development project policy to South Africa, the importance of the Japanese contribution was described in the 1979 UN Khalifa Report:

South Africa also relies heavily on foreign involvement for

---

[10] *Ibid.*, p. 5.

[11] Japan's assistance to Pretoria was not limited to that of a market and a supplier of capital, plant and equipment and related technology but also extended to the improvement of infrastructure indispensable for the development of mineral resources, their processing and transportation. Assistance with infrastructure, especially in the field of transportation, was revealed in a UN report (Unit on Apartheid, Department of Political and Security Council Affairs, Notes and Documents, January 1972, pp. 47-8): 'In negotiating agreements with Japan, especially in ores and minerals, South Africa has a disadvantage of distance to contend with. It is 7,300 sea miles from Durban to Yokohama and hence freight costs are high. These costs can be partly reduced by using special purpose freighters — but South Africa does not have the harbours to handle these. At present, Port Elizabeth harbour cannot handle anything over 45,000 tonnes, while Durban cannot handle anything over 25,000 tonnes (*Financial Mail*, 18 September 1964). To overcome this problem, the South African government recently announced a major new development programme to develop a harbour at Saldanha Bay in the Western Cape. The new harbour will be able to handle large freight carriers (*Sunday Times*, Johannesburg, 30 July 1970). In conjunction with missions to advise on shipping problems in the Republic, the Japanese have also acted as consultants to South African Railways. A special Japanese mission of railway experts visited the Republic in 1966 and the Japanese have been concerned with the railway problems of the proposed Saldanha Project (*South Africa Digest*, 1966; *Rand Daily Mail*, 30 November 1970). See also Keidanren's English-language publication, *Keidanren 1981*, p. 12, for its general stance on natural resource development projects: 'Japan's co-operation in infrastructure building, natural resources development, and industrialisation is an essential condition for a longer-term supply of their resources to Japan. Keidanren is the central focus of co-operative ties in most of such endeavors.'

the realisation of the Sishen-Saldanha project. The project would be technically, economically and financially feasible only if the co-operation of foreign economic interests was secured. The economic viability of the Sishen-Saldanha scheme is apparently predicated on large-scale, long-term exports of iron ore to Japan. While several Western European countries were reported to have expressed interest in Sishen's production, Japan's involvement was held to be essential for the scheme to approach an economic level. A Japanese withdrawal could therefore severely affect the success of the entire scheme. In July 1975, the Johannesburg *Financial Mail* indicated that ISCOR had concluded an initial contract for the export of 7.5 million tonnes of iron ore a year to Japan.[12]

ISCOR's expansion plan. The Japanese Foreign Ministry has characterised ISCOR as an iron and steel manufacturer which is also a state corporation, established by law in 1928 with 99 per cent of its stock owned by the South African government.[13] State corporations are described as those corporate entities which are centred on basic industries, frontier industries and strategic industries, all of which act as important levers for the government's industrialisation policy.

Kitazawa Yoko has described the origins of the ISCOR expansion plan in this way:

> ISCOR, the state-controlled iron and steel corporation, revealed a R900 million expansion project involving its steel mills at Newcastle and Vanderbijlpark in July 1970. In November 1973, ISCOR announced a new R2500 million, ten-year expansion plan. According to this plan, ISCOR was to invest R200 million in its Pretoria works, R730 million in the Vanderbijlpark works, R1400 million in the Newcastle works and R130 million in mine and quarry extensions.[15]

The role of Japanese enterprises in the plan primarily involved the supply of large-scale industrial plants on a long-term stable basis (see Fig. 5.1). To judge the degree of the

[12] Khalifa, p. 13.
[13] Zai Puretoria Nihonkoku Soryojikan (ed.), p. 89.
[14] *Ibid.*,
[15] Kitazawa, *From Tokyo to Johannesburg*, p. 9.

overall contribution which Japanese enterprises made to the
plan, one must also take into consideration relevant information as found in the views expressed by the Japanese government and the LDP, such as the Foreign Ministry's report on
the 1968-73 South African Economic Development Plan. This
noted the background of the plan, predicted gold production
was likely to decrease and stated that a goal of an annual
growth rate of 5.5 per cent had been targeted in South
Africa.[16] It then pointed out that the following tasks had to
be tackled before the goals of this economic development plan
could be realised: promotion of import replacement
industrialisation; establishment and strengthening of export
industries other than gold; diversification of export markets;
acqustion of more White manpower from Europe and the
United States; procurement of a stable supply of foreign capital, technology, machinery and equipment; creation of a
massive Black skilled labour force by expanding educational and
training opportunities; development of border areas as well as
Bantu homelands; and promotion of economic and technical
co-operation with neighbouring nations. Thus the Foreign
Ministry was well aware that the economic development
programme gave priority to the promotion of industrialisation
and the acquisition of a stable supply of the machinery,
equipment and related technology connected with this.

In a November 1982 report, the LDP expressed the following opinion concerning the role private enterprise can play
in industrial plant export:

> Plant generally refers to large items, such as factories or
> machinery valued at over $500,000; can be considered to be
> a part of overseas economic assistance.[18] . . . While plant
> export has a powerful effect on the economic development of
> the receiving countries, it also increases the credibility of
> Japan's economic power and technical expertise and fosters

[16] Zai Puretoria Nihonkoku Soryojikan (ed.), p. 66.
[17] Ibid., pp. 66-71. For a critical analysis of the active participation and co—
operation of Japanese corporate groups in Border Industrialisation, see Kitazawa,
From Tokyo to Johannesburg, pp. 18-34.
[18] Liberal Democratic Party, Policy Affairs Research Council, Special Committee
on External Economic Co-operation, *Waga To no Keizai Kyoryoku Seisaku ni
Tsuite*, Tokyo, 1982, p. 87.

feelings of expectation towards Japan. Also, it can be expected to widen trade with Japan and diplomatic trust in the future.[19]

In 1979, the Foreign Ministry stated:

The concept of direct investment applies either to a joint project or to a local project in which Japanese companies take part. Direct investment usually involves such elements as the acquisition of securities, obligatory rights, direct overseas projects and the establishment of an overseas branch office, etc.[20]

By this definition, the participation of Japanese corporations in the ISCOR expansion plan, the Sishen-Saldahna Bay Development and other projects for the development of mineral resources or the improvement of infrastructure should have been prohibited. Yet the government conveniently interpreted the definition, supported by the LDP's views, to allow Japanese corporations in South Africa and even the Japanese government itself to behave with a *de facto* free hand. Indeed, an obvious example of the government's own participation can be seen in the long-term export loan made by the Export-Import Bank of Japan for plant exportation for the ISCOR expansion plan.[21]

[19] *Ibid.*

[20] Ministry of Foreign Affairs, *The Developing Countries and Japan*, p. 26.

[21] Kitazawa, *From Tokyo to Johannesburg*, p. 11. See also 'Bank of Tokyo has Deposits in South Africa Despite Curbs', *Japan Times*, 19 December 1986: 'The Bank of Tokyo said Thursday it has engaged in interbank Eurodeposit lending to South Africa despite the Japanese government's restrictions on loans to that country because the transaction was "not a loan, but a deposit". ... The official said the deposits, which are different from loans because they are made on a "verbal basis" and do not involve a signed agreement, are not "purely direct loans in the sense prohibited by the Japanese government". . . Meanwhile, according to the *Plant Export Yearbook* since 1983, Japanese companies have exported at least •¥16.2 billion worth of plant equipment to ISCOR using deferred payments, a type of loan, and in 1983 the Export—Import Bank of Japan provided suppliers credits to the governmental Iron and Steel Corp. (ISCOR) for equipment on a contract valued at ¥1.5 billion. A banker, who wished to remain unidentified, described the voluntary restrictions as a "grey area". We can make our own interpretation as there is no precise definition," he said. A report on international bank lending to South Africa by the US California Nevada Interfaith Committee on Corporate Responsibility issued in April estimates that Japan had $2 to $3 billion worth of loans to South Africa when the moratorium was imposed.'

Fig. 5.1. INDUSTRIAL PLANT EXPORTS TO SOUTH AFRICA

	User	Type of plant	Delivery date	Value (¥100m.)	Condition of sale	Contractor (manufacturer, trading co.)
1969	ESCOM	200,000 KVA power generating equipment		5	Cash	Toshiba, Mitusi
1969	ISCOR	Oxygen equipment		7	ªDP	Hitachi, Marubeni
1971	ISCOR	Hot strip mill	1974	126	DP	Mitsubishi Heavy Ind., Mitsubishi Corp.
1971	ISCOR	Billet mill	1974	36	DP	Hitachi, Marubeni
1971	ISCOR	Coke furnace	1974	61	DP	Nihon Otto, Tomen
1971	ISCOR	Bar mill related equipment		15	DP	Hitachi, Nissho Iwai
1971	ISCOR	Roll grinder		5	DP	Toshiba, Nissho Iwai
1972	Mobil Oil	Durban oil refinery expansion	1974	110	Cash	Chiyoda Chem. Eng.
1972	ISCOR	Converter	1974	90	DP	Kawasaki Heavy Ind., Nissho Iwai
1972	ISCOR	Converter	1974	90	DP	Nippon Steel, Mitusi
1972	ISCOR	Tandem cold mill	1974	43	DP	IHI, Nissho Iwai
1972	ISCOR	Converter	1974	36	DP	Kawasaki Heavy Ind., Nissho Iwai
1972	ISCOR	Electrical parts for large-size steel mills		61	DP	Toshiba, Nissho Iwai
1972	ISCOR	Grinder		7	DP	Toshiba, Nissho Iwai
1972	ISCOR	Electrical parts		18	DP	Hitachi, Marubeni,
1972	ISCOR	Oxygen equipemnt				Kobe Steel, Nissho Iwai
1973	ISCOR	Temper mill	1974	32	DP	Hitachi, Marubeni
1973	ISCOR	Billet mill		85	DP	Hitachi, Marubeni

Date	Buyer	Product	Date	Amount	Payment	Supplier
1973	ISCOR	Electrical parts for medium-size steel mills		40	DP	Mitsubishi Electric, Mitusbishi Corp.
1973	ESCOM	Hydroelectric power generating equipment		18	DP	Toshiba, Mitsui
1974	Postal Min.	Satellite ground station	1975	6	Cash	NEC, Marubeni
1974	SAPO	Cable for city use	1975	3.3	Cash	NEC, Marubeni
1975	ISCOR	Electric furnace for Fe,Cr		17	DP	Toshiba, Mitsui
1975	ISCOR	Power generating equipment		1.5		Toshiba, Mitsui
1975	ISCOR	Electric furnace equipment		46.5		Kawasaki Heavy Ind, Mitsui
1975	JCI	Ferrochrome pelletising plant	1976	40	DP	Kobe Steel, Mitsui
1975	JCI	Electric furnace for ferrochrome	1976		DP	Tanabe Kakoki, Mitsui
1976	Richard Bay Iron and Titanium	Electric parts for industrial plant use		8	Cash	Kita Shiba Electric, Mitsui

ª DP = deferred payment

Source: *Puranto Yushitsu Nenkan*, Tokyo: Jukagaku Kogoyo Tsushin Sha, 1980, pp. 156–7.

As noted earlier in this study, the Japanese Foreign Ministry espoused a pro-Pretoria policy as a means to achieving an anti-Communist and economic expansionist end. The importance of the Foreign Ministry influence in financial affairs is reflected in a revealing statement that appeared in the *Japan Times* (14 May 1984): 'But a Finance Ministry spokesman said, financial policy toward South Africa remains under the control of the Foreign Ministry.'

The policy of investment in South Africa clearly demonstrates the large gap that exists between the Japanese government's assertions and its actions, a dichotomy that has led to severe international criticism. The 1979 UN Khalifa Report summed up the situation succinctly:

> The Japanese Government officially prohibits permanent investment in South Africa. However, according to the *Financial Mail* of 30 October 1970, the Japanese definition of 'investment' seems to be very loose, so that Japanese firms have increased their overall stake in South Africa. In addition, some Japanese concerns invest in South Africa through European outlets. The ban on direct Japanese investment has also been circumvented by South Africans setting up their own plants to make goods under licence, partially with components imported from Japan.[22]

Finally, the contributions that the Japanese government and businesses have made to South Africa's militarisation should not be overlooked. In addition to the aforementioned large-scale

[22] Khalifa, p. 10.

[23] On the problematic aspects of exporting dual-use products to Pretoria, American Friends Service Committee researcher Thomas Conrad has noted: 'The 1977 arms embargo imposed by the UN Security Council had "stopped the flow of most official government-to-government arms transfers to South Africa", said Conrad, a member of the staff of NARMIC, the research arm of the independent Quaker organisation. But, he said, South Africa "is presiding over brisk invisible military trade with a number of TNCs (transnational corporations)". According to Conrad, South Africa had been able to build up the largest arms industry in the southern hemisphere by gaining access to "the high-tech building blocks of modern weaponry which include computers, microprocessors, instrumentation equipment, electronic components and sub-assemblies for use in larger systems." This, he said, was being done with the tacit approval of the government in which the trading companies are based.' (*Daily Yomiuri*, 20 September 1985)

Fig. 5.2. EXPORTS: COMMODITY BY COUNTRY, 1987
(*Unit: US $1,000*)

Commodity	Africa	Nigeria	South Africa	Soviet Union
Office machines	80,550	1,235	51,390	7,095
Automatic data-processing machines	47,584	717	30,990	6,179
Electrical machinery	824,224	73,373	232,549	214,930
Heavy electrical machinery	89,173	10,945	19,657	18,851
Telecommunications equipment	304,912	3,272	66,160	59,208
Semi-conductor crystals	3,636	157	1,507	318
Precision instruments	146,763	3,662	74,187	25,183
Scientific and optical instruments	110,124	3,499	65,700	24,896
Cameras (assembled)	8,583	130	4,358	974

Source: MITI, *Tsusho Hakusho* [MITI White Paper] *Kakuron*, Tokyo, 1988. This chart is a portion of a larger chart included in the Appendix of this publication.

supply of industrial plant and related technology, Japan has also been a major supplier of dual-use products: high-tech goods, parts and materials that have the capacity to be diverted for military use.[23] Many high-tech Japanese products developed and produced for general sale are widely acknowledged to be often of a higher quality than equivalent American products developed for military use. During the Vietnam war the US military's smart bombs used Sony small-size television cameras and as Ishihara Shintaro boasts, Japanese-made integrated circuits play an important role in current American military strategy.[24] The commodity export chart (Fig. 5.2) reveals the wide range of products that Japan exported to South Africa in 1987. The problem of the export of products with the potential for dual use gains added credence from the fact that many of the major corporations involved in business transactions with South Africa are also engaged in defence industries (see Fig. 5.3).[25]

First, it is important to point out the possibility of using the knockdown export of trucks, passenger cars, motor-cycles and other transport equipment for military logistical support. On African military affairs, an expert, Dr Robin Luckham heard directly from high government officials in South Africa that although Japanese companies did not provide weapons, they did produce and sell products such as trucks to South Africa, knowing that they would be used for military purposes.[26] During a research trip to South Africa in 1982, this author observe at first hand that Japanese vehicles such as Nissan cars and Honda motor-cycles were being used by the police and that buildings in Johannesburg were monitored with Hitachi surveillance cameras.

[24] Morita Akio and Ishihara Shintaro, *No to Ieru Nihon*, Tokyo: Kobunsha 1989, pp. 13-18.

[25] Japan's pro-South Africa policy can be considered to have supported the development of the military industry in Japan, for a stable supply of rare metals is indispensable for the research and development and production of weaponry, especially high-tech weapons. Japan's post-war militarisation has progressed in parallel with knowledge-intensive industrialisation. For more on this subject, see Maeda Tetsuo, 'Nihon no Gunsan Fukugotai' *Gunshuku Mondai Shiryo*, 131 (October 1991), Tokyo, pp. 35-42; and Yoshihara Koichiro, Nihon no Heiki Sangyo, Tokyo: Shakai Shisosha, 1988. See also Sekai (ed.), *Gunjika Sareru Nihon Gunji Taikoku Nihon*, Tokyo: Iwanami Shoten, 1987.

[26] Sekai, *June* 1982, p. 131.

Fig 5.3. JAPAN'S TOP 20 DEFENCE CONTRACTORS (1990)

(unit: ¥1 million)

Rank	Company	No. of contracts	Value	Share of defence contracts total (%)
1.	Mitsubishi Heavy Industries	238	440,829	28.1
2.	Kawasaki Heavy Industries	132	146,469	9.3
3.	Mitsubishi Electric	268	100,348	6.4
4.	Ishikawajima—Harima Heavy Ind.	70	78,604	5.0
5.	Toshiba	204	59,904	3.8
6.	NEC	376	54,456	3.5
7.	Japan Steel Works Ltd	43	34,819	2.2
8.	Komatsu	61	22,438	1.4
9.	Fuji Heavy Industries	54	21,677	1.4
10.	Hitachi Ltd.	74	20,096	1.3
11.	Oki Electric Industries Co.	73	16,834	1.1
12.	Daikin Industries	64	16,622	1.1
13.	Fujitsu	189	15,081	1.0
14.	Sumitomo Heavy Industries	32	15,052	1.0
15.	Shimadzu Corp.	95	14,708	0.9
16.	Kosumo Oil Co.	313	13,160	0.8
17.	Nissan Motors	42	13,145	0.8
18.	Mitsubishi Precision Co.	34	12,383	0.8
19.	Nippon Oil Co.	222	11,631	0.7
20.	Nihon Koki	102	11,231	0.7
	Total	2,686	1,119,387	71.3

Source: Maeda, p. 40.

Japan's contribution to South Africa's militarisation can also be seen in the large supplies of high-tech products, such as automatic data processing machines, electronic calculators, semi-conductor crystals, telecommunication equipment and scientific and optical instruments.[27] These products can be assumed to have contributed not only to the research and

[27] When considering Japan's involvement in South Africa's militarisation, the possibility of co-operation in the nuclear weapon development programme should not be overlooked. Unfortunately, this subject is cloaked in secrecy and little concrete information is available. However, during the 8 March 1985 session of the Budget Committee of the Japanese Diet's Second Sub-Committee, it was reported that an opposition party member stated there were suspicions that Hitachi, Toshiba and Mitsubishi were involved in equipment and material exports to South Africa's Valindaba Uranium Enrichment Plant and asked for an explanation. The record of the session notes that the government side was unable to give a convincing explanation. Shugiin Jimukyoku, *Shugiin Iinkaigi Roku 13, Yosan 2, Bunkakai, 1984-85*, Tokyo, 25 March 1985, pp. 31-2.

development, production, maintenance and improvement of weapons, but also substantially to the formulation and strengthening of the comprehensive command, control, communication and intelligence system of Pretoria's 'Total Strategy' programme.[28]

The introduction of sanctions in Japan on 1 November 1985 prohibiting the export of computers which might assist the activities of apartheid-enforcing agencies, notably the armed forces and the police, indirectly admitted the problematic aspects of the export of dual use products. But these sanctions, as well as other measures introduced at the same time, were mere diplomatic lip-service. They came too late and there were no penalty clauses within the sanctions to enforce compliance by the corporations.

The lack of enthusiasm shown by the Japanese government for these sanctions is made clear in a report from the *Daily Yomiuri* (3 December 1985):

> It was unclear what impact the sanctions would have on computer sales to South Africa. The ban aims to deny South African security forces sophisticated means to control the majority Black population. The Foreign Ministry official said he was uncertain exactly how much of the $45 million worth of computers sold to South Africa went to the government but estimated 'It is a very small percentage.'

With the government taking such an attitude, Japanese companies continued to export computers to the White minority forces unhindered even after November 1985. However, the sanctioned yet sanction-breaking activities of Japanese corporations did not go unnoticed. An article in the *New York Times* 11 (August 1986) led to further criticism of Japan's actions:

> Any foreign company that takes commercial advantage of American sanctions — in other words, that sells goods to South Africa that American companies cannot sell because of an embargo — could be denied access to the United States market through the 301 provision.

---

[28] For more on the subject of Total Strategy, see Hayashi Koji (ed.), *Minami Afurika —Aparutoheito Taisei no Yukue*, Tokyo: Institute of Developing Economies, 1987, pp. 170-88, and Kenneth W. Grundy, *The Militarization of South African Politics*, Bloomington; IN: Indiana University Press, 1986.

The Senate committee's measure would ban the import of uranium, coal and steel, revoke landing rights for South African Airways, bar new loans to the Pretoria Government and allow visas to South African Government officials only on a case-by-case basis.

The measure would also continue sanctions imposed by President Reagan last year, including a ban on exports of computers or related software to some South African Government agencies.

According to widespread reports here, Hitachi of Japan is among the foreign companies selling computer products to the South African police. Should the Senate Foreign Relations bill become law, Hitachi could become subject to Section 301 sanctions."[29]

Hitachi became a target of criticism as it moved rapidly to expand its market share by filling the vacuum left by the withdrawal of American computer companies from South Africa. Strong suspicions also arose that Hitachi's computers were being sent via the West German company BASF to the South African company Persetel for use by the police and the military in South Africa. These charges were outlined in a report written by Richard Leonard for the Oil, Chemical and Atomic Workers' International Union in October 1986, titled 'BASF's Strategic Role in South Africa':

> BASF, as the distributor of Hitachi mainframe computers and peripheral equipment to Persetel of South Africa, is playing a key role in providing strategic products to a company with ties to South Africa's military industrial complex. . . . Once computers are supplied to distributors and users in South Africa (particularly government agencies), there can be no guarantee that they will not be passed on to restricted agencies or that these agencies will not gain access to them through time-sharing arrangements. Again, the ties of Persetel's parent corporation Reunert to the military make this all the more possible. Even without these links, South African laws empower the government to secretly procure goods and services from corporations.[30]

[29] Nathaniel C. Nash, 'Washington Watch', *New York Times*, 11 August 1986, p. D2.

[30] Richard Leonard, 'BASF's Strategic Role in South Africa', report prepared for

The report concludes:

> Because of its role in South Africa, BASF (and also Hitachi) should face increasing scrutiny and pressure. BASF should be called on to provide full information on its business in South Africa, including employment practices under the EC code and also an accounting of users of computers provided to Persetel, and then to end all business there.[31]

When Japan's trade with Pretoria was criticised, the Japanese government often responded that business transactions considered to be ordinary trade were no problem, and assertions that the export of large-scale industrial plant and dual-use products with strong military implications could be regarded as ordinary trade was highly unreasonable. Indeed on 7 August 1963 the Japanese government prohibited the export of weapons to South Africa and in 1967 it introduced prohibitions on exporting weapons to states in the Communist bloc, states to which the export of weapons was forbidden by a UN resolution, and parties involved or likely to become involved in international disputes.

Another excuse that the government has offered is the contention that as a trading nation without natural resources, it conducts trade and commerce with countries with different ideologies and political systems on the principle of the separation of politics and economics. Japan's trade with the former Soviet Union was often cited an example of this; however, this trade was carried out under strict COCOM (Coordinating Committee for Export to Communist Areas) controls and at the end of 1979, after the Red Army invaded Afghanistan, Tokyo introduced very tough economic sanctions against Moscow. Obviously, the assertion that politics and economics can be separated was merely a diplomatic tool.

Economic co-operation in Black Africa

The Japanese economic co-operation policy directed towards Black Africa required the *zaikai's* support not only via import expansion, direct investment and technical co-operation but also

---

the Oil, Chemical and Atomic Workers' International Union, October 1986, pp. 19-20.
[31] *Ibid.*, p. 20

through its positive participation in ODA projects. We consider this latter aspect first.

The *zaikai's* involvement in the bilateral ODA implementation process was large and came about through trading companies, construction companies, manufacturers, consulting firms specialising in development and private economic co-operation organisations sponsored by it.[32]

The importance of the contribution made by the trading companies in particular can be seen in Fig. 5.4. Furthermore:

> The twelve largest trading companies have approximately 15,000 employees (including local employees) and when dispatched to developing countries, they can use their excellent information-gathering network to play a major role in project identification, formulation and proposal preparation.[33]

Another reason for the significant role of the trading companies here[34] is that, in theory at least, Japan's ODA policy employed the method of offering assistance on the basis of requests from the aid-recipient nations. Yet it was generally far from easy for many Black African countries to identify projects and formulate policy proposals with a high probability of being approved by Tokyo. Under these conditions, it became inevitable that the recipient nations came to depend upon the trading companies which are experienced in the field of ODA and maintain strong connections with the Japanese government. Although aid is in theory offered on request, the reality is quite different.

In the case of facility construction included in grant and yen loan projects, construction companies, as contractors,

[32] Engineering Consulting Firms Association, Japan, *Keizai Kyoryoku Enjo ni Okeru Kigyo to Kokka no Arikata*, Tokyo, April 1990, p. 5. See also Alan Rix, *Japan's Economic Aid Policy-Making and Politics*, London: Croom Helm 1980, especially Chapter 6.

[33] *Ibid.* P. 5

[34] For more on the role of Japanese trading companies (*sogo shosha*) in general, see JETRO, *The Role of Trading Companies in International Commerce*, Revised edn. Tokyo: JETRO 1982; Alexander K. Young, *The Sogo Shosha Japan's Multinational Trading Companies*, Tokyo: Charles E. Tuttle, 1979. For a critical, analytical examination of *sogo shosha*, see also Heiwa Keizai Keikaku Kaigi Dokusen Hakusho Iinkai (ed.), *Kokumin no Dokusen Hakusho*, Tokyo: Ochanomizu Shobo, 1984.

Fig.5.4. ASSIGNMENT OF ROLES IN O.D.A
DEVELOPMENT PROJECTS

	Japan Essential: A, B, D Subordinate: C					USA and Europe Essential: A, C		
Project identification Project formulation	A	B	C	D	E	A	C	B
Project design	A	B	C		DE	A	C	B
Project implementation	A	B/D			C	A	C	B
Project evaluation	A					A	C	

A = Government
B = Contractors (construction companies, manufacturers, suppliers)
C = Development consulting firms
D = Trading companies
E = Industry organisations

Source: Kaigai Consarutingu Kigyo Kyokai, Japan, *Keizai Kyoryoku Enjo ni Okeru Kigyo to Kokka no arikata*, p. 40.

along with the trading companies, are deeply involved in project identification, formulation and implementation processes. Also, a segment of the manufacturing sector become involved through their role as procurers of materials and equipment.[35]

The degree of involvement by Japanese corporations in

[35] Kaigai Consarutingu Kigyo Kyokai, p. 98.

bilateral ODA can be seen in Zaire's Matadi Bridge construction project, completed in May 1983.[36] The bridge was initially conceived as part of a total infrastructure project that would include construction of a new port at Banana on the Atlantic coast and a 150 km. rail line that would extend to Matadi near the mouth of the Zaire river. If the plan had materialised, it would have provided a direct rail link from Kinshasa to the Atlantic, and it was expected to provide a big boost to Zaire's social and economic development. The initial request for co-operation was made by President Mobutu when he visited Japan as a state guest in April 1971, and with Japanese government support the project moved towards the implementation stage.[37] In November 1973, an exchange of notes was signed between the two governments and a year later, in November 1974, a ¥34.5 billion loan was extended to Zaire.[38]

Behind the positive response to the Zairean request was Japan's own resource strategy, which considered co-operation in the improvement of Zaire's infrastructure important for securing its abundant mineral resources. However, the project came to a standstill in the mid 1970s when the 1973 oil crisis caused a steep increase in construction costs, and the price of copper — Zaire's main foreign exchange earner — decreased on the international market. In 1977 Tokyo and Kinshasa reviewed the project, as the result of which the railway line plan was scrapped but it was agreed that the monumental Matadi bridge would be built as originally planned.[39] It is 722 metres long, 12 metres wide and 53 metres high, and is the largest suspension bridge in Africa.[40]

In Japanese bilateral ODA projects, Japanese corporations are accorded a leading role, and in the case of grant

[36] This project is described in *Enjo Tojokoku Nippon*, edited by *Asahi Shimbun* reporters assigned to covering aid, Tokyo: Asahi Shimbunsha, 1985, pp. 27-8.
[37] Tomiyama Kintaro 'Zaire', in Fukunaga Eiji (ed.), *Nihon Kigyo no Taiken-teki Afurika*, Tokyo: Yuhikaku 1986, p. 247.
[38] *Ibid.*
[39] *Ibid.*
[40] Ministry of Foreign Affairs, Public Information Bureau (ed.), *Warera no Sekai*, p. 9.

138   *Japan and Africa*

Fig. 5.5. THE GRANT MECHANISM

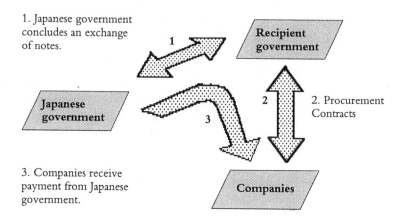

1. Japanese government concludes an exchange of notes.

Japanese government

Recipient government

2. Procurement Contracts

3. Companies receive payment from Japanese government.

Companies

Source: Ministry of Foreign Affairs, Gaimu Hodokan (ed.), *Keizai Kyoroku Q & A*, Tokyo: Sekai no Ugokisha, 1989, p. 29.

projects only Japanese corporations can tender bids (see Fig. 5.5 above).[41] Because the Matadi bridge project was a yen loan project, it was not necessarily tied to Japanese companies alone, but even so Japanese companies were given the contracts for the project.

Ishikawajima-Harima Heavy Industries (IHI) was at the centre of a consortium of Japanese companies that worked on the project, and in the company history published in 1992 it was noted that 'IHI won a contract from the Zairean government in 1979 for the planning, design and total construction of the Matadi Bridge and the project was completed in 1983 by a consortium of Japanese companies with IHI at its head.'[42]

However, besides revealing the important role played by Japanese companies in bilateral ODA, this project also raises some serious questions. First, would the construction of such

[41] Kaigai Consarutingu Kigyo Kyokai, p. 47. It is important to note that a large percentage of Japan's bilateral ODA to Africa (50.6 per cent in 1986) was comprised of grants. See Yoshida Masao, 'Nihon no Afurika Enjo' in Hayashi Koji (ed.), *Afurika Enjo to Chiiki Jiritsu*, Tokyo, Institute of Developing Economies, 1988, p. 129.

[42] Ishikawajima-Harima Heavy Industries (IHI), *IHI Jukogyo Shashi-Gijutsu Seihin Hen*, Tokyo: Ishikawajima-Harima Heavy Industries, 1992, p. 345.

a bridge without a connecting railway link really bring about a positive change in the social and economic development of Zaire as a whole? It should be remembered here that this project was not completed on the basis of a grant but under a yen loan that would eventually have to be repaid. As it turned out, repayment was even more costly than expected due to the increased value of the yen.

Secondly, who was the main beneficiary of the project? Just who was aiding whom? One report noted that 'the bridge construction required 14,000 tonnes of steel products, all shipped from Japan, and of the total cost of ¥34.5 billion, approximately ¥25 billion was returned to Japan.[43] Private Japanese companies have certainly made an important contribution to the implementation of ODA projects, but as the Matadi bridge case demonstrates, this does not necessarily mean Japanese corporations have acted solely with the promotion of the interests of Black African countries in mind.

The *zaikai's* contribution to the economic co-operation policy in Black Africa has also been carried out through import expansion, foreign direct investment and technical assistance. But since import expansion to the region has proved difficult to realise due to the low demand for products from Black Africa, and the level of technical co-operation to the region has been relatively insignificant,[44] the focus here has to be on direct foreign investment (DFI).

The Japanese government's belief that DFI was an effective means of promoting African economic development was clear

[43] *Enjo Tojokoku Nippon*, Asahi Shimbunsha, p. 30.
[44] When considering the degree and extent of technical assistance by the *zaikai* towards Africa, it is useful to examine the activities of the Association for Overseas Technical Scholarship. In its publication *Guide to AOTS* (Tokyo: AOTS, June 1991), it notes: 'AOTS, a non-profit organisation, was established in 1959 with the support of the Japanese Ministry of International Trade and Industry. Its main purpose is to promote technical co-operation for the industrialisation and development of developing countries and enhance mutual understanding and friendly relationships between those countries and Japan. To date, AOTS has trained nearly 48,000 persons in Japan from about 150 countries and regions. In addition, it has organised various training programmes in developing countries involving more than 6,000 participants. The activities of AOTS are financed by Japanese government subsidy, company contributions, and other sources' (p. 2). The AOTS chart below (Appendix H) shows only 2,399 trainees from Africa have participated between 1959 and 1990.

in a speech made by former Foreign Minsiter Kimura Toshio
at a reception held in the Keidanren Hall in Tokyo on 23
May 1975 to commemorate OAU Day:

> I believe that obtaining investments from private Japanese
> enterprises is an important element for African nations in
> the development of their respective economies . . . . Direct
> investments by the private sector not only supplement lim-
> ited government-based economic aid but also include the
> transferring of technologies both for management and manu-
> facturing. From this point of view, I believe that direct
> investments by private enterprises should be greatly accel-
> erated in the future. However, private enterprises which
> make such investments, unlike the government, are all
> motivated by the making of reasonable profits. Therefore,
> I believe that African countries which hope to see an
> increase in investments by Japanese private enterprises should
> prepare a good investment environment in their respective
> countries to make such investments attractive to the Japa-
> nese side.[45]

The ambassadors from OAU member nations undoubtedly
had mixed feelings when listening to this speech. Despite the
fact that the gathering was held to mark OAU Day, Kimura
avoided any concrete mention of Japan's stance on either
Southern Africa issues or the new international economic
order. Even if Kimura's claim that direct investment could bring
about a positive influence on economic development could be
justified, many problematic aspects still existed in Japan's plan
for investment in Black Africa.

First, Japan was offering only a relatively small amount of
DFI and this was concentrated in just a few resource-rich
countries (see Figs 5.6 and 5.7). Investment in Liberia was
almost all due to its flag of convenience companies; when this
amount is excluded, Japan's Black Africa DFI figures decrease
substantially. The second problem was that a considerable
portion of Japan's DFI was allocated to areas relating to natural resources development (see Fig. 5.8). Fig. 5.9 reflects the
overall picture of Japanese corporations' natural-resources-related

[45] Kimura Toshio, 'On the 16th Anniversary of the Inauguration of the OAU',
Africa-Japan, 1979, pp. 9-10

Fig. 5.6. JAPAN'S OVERSEAS DIRECT INVESTMENT
BY REGION, 1951-80 (*unit: US$1m.*)

		%
Asia	9,830	26.9
North America	9,798	26.8
South and Central America	6,168	16.9
Europe	4,471	12.3
Oceania	2,525	6.9
Middle East	2,259	6.2
Africa	1,445	4.0
Total	36,497	100.0

Fig. 5.7. JAPAN'S DIRECT INVESTMENT IN SUB-SAHARAN
AFRICA BY COUNTRY, 1951-80 (*unit: US$1m.*)

		%
Liberia	791	55.8
Zaire	244	17.2
Nigeria	153	10.8
Niger	73	5.1
Zambia	45	3.2
Other countries	112	7.9
Total	1,418	100.0

Source (5.6 and 5.7): Ministry of Foreign Affairs, Public Information Bureau, *Nihon to Afurika — Sahara Inan no Kuniguni,* Tokyo, 1982, p. 21.

Fig. 5.8. JAPAN'S DIRECT OVERSEAS INVESTMENT
BY INDUSTRY, 1951-80 (*unit: US$1m.*)

Manufacturing	*World*	*(share %)*	*Africa*	*(share %)*
Chemicals	2,626	7.2	14	1.0
Iron and non-ferrous metals	2,619	7.2	20	1.4
Textiles	1,637	4.5	38	2.6
Electrical machinery	1,579	4.3	4	0.3
Transport machines	979	2.7	6	0.4
Machinery	894	2.4	—	—
Lumber-pulp	758	2.1	0	0.0
Foods	587	1.6	8	0.6
Other	894	2.4	6	0.4
Subtotal	12,573	34.4	96	6.6
Resource-related				
Mining	7,071	19.4	471	32.6
Other	910	2.5	58	4.0
Subtotal	7,981	21.9	529	36.6
Other				
Commerce	5,409	14.8	3	0.2
Finance/Insurance	2,426	6.6	2	0.1
Other	8,108	22.2	815	56.4
Subtotal	15,943	43.7	820	56.7
Total	36,497	100.0	1,445	100.0

Souce: Ministry of Foreign Affairs, Public Information Bureau, *Nihon to Afurika—Sahara Inan no Kuniguni,* Tokyo, 1982, p. 2. Compiled with data from the Bank of Japan.

investments in the latter half of the 1970s.

As a result the investment in the manufacturing sector for which the black African side had held high expectations was in fact very small. Much of what there was of this investment was aimed at the manufacturing sector in Nigeria to enable that nation, which had a large domestic market and oil dollars, to pursue its ambitious industrialisation and new capital construction projects.[46] Finally, Japan's DFI in Black Africa in the early half of the 1980s moved into a phase of stagnation and then reduction.[47] This trend arose in part from the deterioration of the investment climate in Africa, as symbolised by the serious accumulated debt problem, and a shift in the interests of Japanese investors toward the Asia Pacific region and EC nations after the upward valuation of the yen after the 1985 Plaza Accord (see Figure 5.10).

More specific factors in the decline of investment were the failure of the large-scale mineral development project in Zaire,[48] which considerably cooled the enthusiasm of Japanese mining

[46] JETRO, *Kaigai Shijo Hakusho Toshi* Tokyo: JETRO, 1984, p. 204. This book describes Japan's investments in Nigeria: 'The cumulative figures on Japanese investment in Nigeria had reached $156 billion as of the end of March 1983. Forty Japanese companies were involved in joint ventures. The presence of Japanese companies is still small compared to Europe and America but in some areas such as galvanised sheet metal and motor-cycles, Japanese companies now occupy almost 100 per cent of the market. Despite this, Japanese companies faced difficulties in 1983 because of the overall worsening of economic conditions.' It should also be noted that while Japanese companies have invested in the manufacturing sector in the Ivory Coast, Kenya, Tanzania and other African nations, it has been mainly on a small scale.

[47] For example, Japan's exports to Nigeria, which were $2.2 billion in 1981, had by 1984 decreased by 80 per cent to $450 million. See Nakatsuka Seizo, 'Businessman no Mita Afurika' in Fukunaga (ed.), p. 10.

[48] On 31 May 1983, Nihon Kogyo and five other Japanese corporations (Sumitomo Metal Mining Co., Mitsui Mining and Smelting Co., Furukawa, Mitsubishi and Dowa Mining Co. announced their decision to withdraw from the copper ore development project in Zaire in which they had invested a total of ¥60 billion. The reasons for the withdrawal included the stagnation in the international price of copper, the influence of the civil war in Angola and the large deficit caused by transporting copper ore by railway via East London in South Africa. Losses to the Japanese side totalled ¥53 billion. For more on this subject, see *Asahi Shinbun*, 8 January and 1 June 1983 and the Shadan Hojin Afurika Kaihatsu Kyokai, *Nyu Afurika* (14, July 1983), pp. 2-3.

companies for capital investment in Africa, and the oil glut that hit Nigeria in the latter half of 1981, causing serious economic difficulties there. As interest waned, the *zaikai* did carry out various activities designed to encourage investment in Black Africa. Starting in November 1981, the Keidanren CCA held a series of seminars on the investment environment in Africa which were conducted by various African ambassadors. It also sent major and minor economic missions to Black Africa to study the possibility of import expansion and technical assistance along with joint ventures. However, these efforts did not succeed in revitalising investment in Black Africa, and the *zaikai's* reluctance to invest became a problem for the Japanese government: in its view, ODA, DFI and trade were closely linked to both the economic development of pro-Western and non-aligned Black African states as well as the realisation of Japan's desire to maintain and expand its economic presence in the whole region.

Former Ministry of Foreign Affairs Middle Eastern and African Affairs Director-General Hatano Yoshio expressed such concern at an informal meeting of the CCA on 4 March 1983:

> Japan's ODA towards Africa is certainly not sufficient but it is growing. However, the advancement of private Japanese corporations into Africa is moving a little slowly. In many regions of the world, a pattern can be seen wherein private corporations advance first and the government follows. But in the case of Africa, it appears that ODA comes first. It sows the seeds and if private corporations tend them properly, they can come to bear fruit. Perhaps it is inevitable that many problems will arise but currently the interest of private corporations in Africa is not increasing at all . . . . Finally, I would like to request that Keidanren send a high-level economic mission to Africa as soon as possible to look at the continent for themselves.[49]

Yet despite the government concern, the *zaikai's* contribution to economic co-operation with Black Africa in the

---

[49] Hatano, pp. 12, 15.

Fig. 5.9. JAPANESE MINING-RELATED COMPANIES IN AFRICA, MARCH 1977

		Company	Capital	Started	Japanese investors (% holding)
Copper	Zaire	SODIMIZA	$6 million	Oct. 1972	Zaire Kozan Kaihatsu (Nikko 52, Furukawa 9, Mitsubishi Kinzoku 6, Dowa 4, Nissho Iwai 5)
Copper	Zaire	Société Minière de Moba	250,000 Z	Jan. 1972	Marubeni 16
Copper	Zaire	SMTF	200,000 Z	Jan. 1972	Mitsui Corp. 14
Iron ore	Liberia	Liberia Iron & Steel	$100,000	April 1966	Kawatetsu, NisshoIwai, Tomen, Marubeni, C. Itoh 24.9,
Iron ore	Senegal	MIFERSO	150 m. CFA	July 1975	Kanematsu Gosho 24
Petroleum	Zaire	Japan Petroleum Co. (Zaire)	¥4.87 bn.	1970	Zaire Sekiyu (Teikoku Sekiyu 32.28, Sekiyu Kaihatsu Kodan)
Petroleum	Nigeria	Japan Petroleum Co.	6 m.		Nigeria Sekiyu
Chrome	Kenya	Unknown	¥100 m.	Planned 1977	Nihon Kokan, Kokan Kogyo, C.Itoh
Chrome	Madagascar	Unknown	¥2.5 m.		C. Itoh and 7 other companies
Uranium	Niger	COMINAK	3.5 bn. CFA	Planned 1980	Kaigai Uranium Shigen Kaihatsu 25
Uranium	Mauritania	Compagnie Francaise des Petroles			Tokyo Uranium Kaihatsu (Marubeni, Nikko and others 20)
Uranium	Niger	Afasto-ouest	2.5 bn. CFA		Kaigai Uranium Kaihatsu 33.3
Uranium	Niger	Akborun-Azelick	1.7 bn. CFA		Nihon Sekiyu Yushitsunyu 50
Manganese	Upper Volta (Burkina Faso)	SOMITAM		July 1975	Tambao Mangan Kozan Kaihatsu 30
Fluorite	Kenya	Iwatani-Lonata Vermiculite Co. Kenya	8.1 m. KSH	Feb. 1974	
Non-ferrous	Zaire	SIMZ	2 m. Z	Jan. 1972	Mitsui Corp. 14.2
Other	Sierra Leone	Jafricon	$50,000	1969	Sewa Kaihatsu 91

Source: Chart compiled by Chiyoura, pp. 96–7.

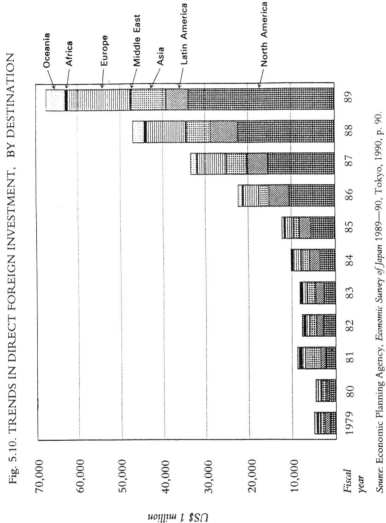

Fig. 5.10. TRENDS IN DIRECT FOREIGN INVESTMENT, BY DESTINATION

US$ 1 million

Source: Economic Planning Agency, *Economic Survey of Japan 1989—90*, Tokyo, 1990, p. 90.

1990s has remained limited, and the situation does not appear likely to change in the near future. The focus of Japan's investment activities is now on the Asia—Pacific region and if there should be a revitalisation of interest in investment in Africa at all, it is highly likely that priority will be given to South Africa.[50]

Personal exchange activities

The *zaikai's* support of Japan's pro-White Africa policy through personal exchange activities has two facets. It calls for the maintenance of intimate connections with the White ruling class while at the same time keeping its contacts with anti-apartheid forces, such as the UN, OAU and ANC, to a bare minimum.

[50] The *zaikai's* strong expectations of South Africa are clear from the fact that Keidanren despatched a study mission to that country 21—27 April 1991 two months before de Klerk's visit to Japan. In an English-language report, Mission Leader Yamaguchi Tamotsu, deputy president of the Bank of Tokyo, summarised the Mission's aims and activites: 'Keidanren has co-operated in the strict enforcement of the Japanese government's sanctions against South Africa through various means, including voluntary restraint on trade. Japan's trade with South Africa, which was the largest in the world in 1987, had dropped to fourth or fifth place by 1990.

In view of the changes that have taken place inside and outside South Africa, however, Keidanren decided to send a study mission to that country 21-27 April of this year to survey the political, economic and social conditions there. An additional purpose of the mission was to examine the progress that has been made in the implementation of assistance schemes for non-White entrepreneurs and university students in South Africa, which Keidanren has been implementing in cooperation with the Southern Africa Trade Association (SATA) since 1989, and to consider priorities for the future. During our visit, the members of the mission held discussions with numerous senior government officials, including State President F.W. De Klerk, Foreign Minister R.F. Botha, Finance Minister B.J. du Plessis, and Trade, Industry and Tourism Minister Dr G. Marais, as well as Foreign Affairs Committee chiarman Geldenhuys.

We also had opportunities to exchange views with representatives of different political parties, business leaders and local European and US business groups, representatives of the Black business and education communities, representatives of Black political movements (including ANC deputy president Nelson Mandela and leaders of the Inkatha Freedom Party, the largest Zulu-based political organisation in South Africa), and senior officials of Japanese-affiliated companies there. Some members of the mission also visited local factories.' Keidanren, International Economic Affairs Department, *Keidanren Nan A Keizai Shakai Shisatsu Mission Hokokusho*, Tokyo, June 1991, pp. 9-10.

In Tokyo personal exchange activities with the former Pretoria regime were carried out through the CCA, SATA and the Springbok Club. In Johannesburg this function is performed by the Nippon Club of South Africa. As mentioned earlier, the activities of the CCA and SATA have been heavily veiled in secrecy, as are the activites of the Springbok Club (discussed in Chapter 6). The best available case-study of how the *zaikai's* personal exchange activities have worked is revealed in the history of the Nippon Club of South Africa, established in Johannesburg in 1961. According to the Club's revised by-laws (effective 19 December 1979), its goals, activities and membership qualifications are:[51]

BY-LAWS

1. The association shall be known as the Nan A Nihonjinkai. The English name shall be the Nippon Club of South Africa and the club office will be in the home of the club president.

2. *Goals and activities*
The goals of the club are as follows:
—to promote friendship and the common interests of the members:
—to promote friendly relations between Japan and South Africa; and
—to contribute to the growth of trade and commerce between the two nations.

The club year will run from 1 April until 31 March of the following year.

To achieve the above goals, the club will undertake the following activities:

(a) hold periodic meetings to cultivate mutual friendship and exchange information;

(b) hold social gatherings to bring together distinguished guests from both countries;

(c) promote health, welfare and cultural activities;

[51] Nan-A Nipponjin-kai, *Nan-A Nipponjin-kai Kaisoku*, revised edn., Tokyo: Nan-A Nihonjin Kai, 19 December 1979.

(d) assist with the education of the children of Japanese residents of South Africa (including management of the private Japanese school in South Africa);

(e) other activities that are deemed necessary to fulfill the goals of the association.

3. *Membership qualifications*

(a) Corporate members. Japanese corporations in South Africa can become corporate members. Non-Japanese corporations that employ Japanese staff members and that are deemed suitable for membership can also become corporate members. However, if the foreign corporation's Japanese staff members should withdraw from the club for reasons outlined in Article 5 of these by-laws and another Japanese staff member does not take the place of the withdrawing Japanese member, the foreign corporation will lose its corporate membership status but could, if it wishes, be qualified to become a corporate supporting member.

(b) Individual regular members. Japanese residents of South Africa can become regular members of the association but this membership status does not apply to their families or to diplomatic personnel and their families.

(c) Associate members. The families of Japanese residents of South Africa and Japanese visitors to South Africa can become associate members and participate in the association's activities.

(d) Honorary members. Diplomatic personnel and their families as well as other suitable candidates can be granted honorary memerbship and participate in the association's activities.

(e) Corporate supporting members. Corporations other than Japanese corporations can be granted this status if they are considered suitable for membership.

(f) Individual supporting members. Non-Japanese can also be granted individual supporting membership and participate in the association's activities if they are approved for membership.

4. *Procedures for enrolling new members*

(*a*) Corporate and regular individual members shall submit applications for membership.

(*b*) Other members must be recommended by two regular members and be approved by the club's executive committee. It is not necessary for the committee to provide a reason for denying membership to a prospective member. Corporate supporting members can register only two individual members.

5. *Withdrawal from membership*

One shall be considered to have withdrawn one's membership in the following cases:

(*a*) death or transfer;

(*b*) if a letter of withdrawal is submitted to the association and it is approved by the executive committee;

(*c*) if dues are not paid for a period of six months or more;

(*d*) if a decision to expel the member is made by the executive committee.

The dues paid by withdrawing members will not be refunded.

[Articles 6-8 deal with annual and extraordinary meetings and quorums.]

The Executive Committee

The Executive Committee will be the governing body of the Nippon Club of South Africa and will be in charge of the management of the club and will decide the club's activities. The nine members of the committee will be chosen at the annual general meeting. Whenever necessary, the chairman may call a meeting of the Executive Committee and resolutions can be passed with the approval of six members (except for the selection of members of the Executive Committee outlined in Article 12).

[Articles 10-21 deal with technical matters concerning the administration of the club — officers, membership, budget — and the management of the Japanese School of Johannesburg.]

The by-laws make clear that the nine-member Executive Committee (comprising seven members and the chairman and vice chairman) plays the decisive role in the management of the Club. Once again, the central leadership positions of chairman and vice chairman usually fall to a small handful of powerful corporations, especially the Big Six trading companies:

Fig. 5.11. THE BIG SIX TRADING COMPANIES' ROLE IN THE
NIPPON CLUB OF SOUTH AFRICA, 1975-80

	Chairman	Vice chairman	Presence on the 7-member Executive Committee
1975	Mitsui	Mitsubishi	C. Itoh, Marubeni, Nichimen[a]
1976	Mitsui	Mitsubishi	C. Itoh, Sumitomo, Nissho Iwai
1977	Mitsubishi	Mitsui	C. Itoh, Sumitomo, Marubeni
1978	Mitsubishi	Mitsui	C. Itoh, Marubeni, Tomen[a]
1979	Mitsui	Marubeni	C. Itoh, Sumitomo, Mitsubishi
1980	Mitsui	Marubeni	Mitsubishi, Sumitomo, Nishho Iwai

(a) These are not members of the Big Six but are major Japanese trading companies.

Source: Compiled from Nan-A Nihonjin-kai, *Springbok — Minami Afurika Nihonjinkai Gekkan Shinbun Hyaku go Kinen Soshuhen*, Tokyo, 1981.

There are two points concerning the personal exchange activities undertaken by the Nippon Club that cannot be overlooked. First, there is the presence of Japanese government officials as honorary members in a club whose stated goals are 'to promote friendly relations between Japan and South Africa and to contibute to the growth of trade and commerce between the two nations.'[52] Secondly, in June 1974 the Japanese government announced restrictions on sports, cultural and educational exchanges with South Africa. Yet shortly after this, the Nippon Club stated its clear intention to ignore such restrictions, and in fact it intensified its exchange with the White ruling class in South Africa.

Nippon Club chairman Kumagai Naohiko of Mitsui made this explicit in his inaugural greetings to the membership published in the club newsletter 28 April 1975:

This year, I would like to enhance the activities of the Nippon Club of South Africa and also strengthen one of

[52] *Ibid.* p. 1.

its goals, that of the exchange and promotion of friendly relations with the local community.

Last year, our country imposed restrictions on sports, cultural and educational exchanges with the Republic of South Africa. However, those of us who are actually in South Africa — living in this society, trying to adapt to it and deepen friendly relations — must go beyond political problems. I believe it is the responsibility of Japanese who live overseas to increase the number of people who like and understand Japan and, through exchange with South Africans, we can do this.[53]

Under the leadership of Chairman Kumagai, active exchange with the White community in Johannesburg progressed, and in November 1975 the club by-laws were revised to allow non-Japanese corporations and individuals to participate in the club's activities. Kumagai proudly mentions this point in his review of the club during 1975:

When I took over the chairmanship of the Nippon Club of South Africa last year, I said that to achieve our biggest goal now (i.e. friendly relations with South Africa and an increase in trade and commerce), the deepening of mutual understanding between South Africa and Japan should be the task we undertake in 1975.

Through golf invitations and the sports festival, we have been able to garner information on the situation here from influential South Africans. The women's auxiliary group tour of Soweto provided a chance for them to observe the country's largest problem — the reality of how Black people live. With the approval of all the members, the by-laws were amended to allow membership to South African corporations with close connections to Japan and I believe this will be useful for creating even deeper mutual understanding.[54]

---

[53] Nan-A Nihonjin-kai, *Springbok-Minami Afurika Nihonjinkai Gekkan Shimbun Hyaku go Kinen Soshuhen*, Tokyo, 1981, p. 125. Note this digest of past issues of the *Springbok* newsletter of the Nippon Club of South Africa was completed with the assistance of the Tokyo-based Springbok Club, composed of businessmen and bureaucrats who had once served in South Africa, further proof of the close relations between the two clubs.

[54] *Ibid.*, p. 159.

The drive to recruit supporting members was extremely successful, as a report in the club newsletter reveals (21 March 1979):

> The existence of the club has attracted attention again this term and a distinctive feature was the large number of club membership applications from local corporations and individuals. At the end of this term, there are now eleven supporting member corporations and supporting individual memberships have grown to 1,000.[55]

Such a large number of supporting members had no direct influence on the management of the club, which was in the hands of the Executive Committee, but their active participation does take on a larger dimension when it is realised that at that time, the club consisted of only fifty-six Japanese corporate members and just 140 Japanese individual regular members.[56]

The Nippon Club's clear emphasis on personal exchange with the White community in South Africa is obvious in the club activities recorded in *Springbok:* a 13 March 1975 golf tournament with Gary Player in attendance;[57] a guest lecture by the chief editor of the *Financial Gazette* on 17 September 1975; and the list goes on and on.[58] Guest speakers for 1977 included a representative of Barclays Bank, an employee of the South Africa Tourist Corporation and staff of the Institute for Medical Research and the University of South Africa.[59] On 5 July 1978, the club hosted a luncheon at the Carleton Hotel for South African ambassador to Japan von Hirschberg.[60] The club newsletter noted that von Hirschberg was very much interested in things Japanese and that the members of the Springbok Club in Tokyo were always receiving his assistance.[61] The 18 October 1978 issue notes a meeting was held with the Minister of Community Development to exchange opinions on the subject of honorary

55 *Ibid.*, p. 273.
56 *Ibid.*, p. 274.
57 *Ibid.* p. 124.
58 *Ibid.* p. 141.
59 *Ibid.*, p. 237.
60 *Ibid.*, pp. 252-3.
61 *Ibid.*, p. 253.

White status and the Immorality Act (which prohibited inter-racial sexual and marital relationships). During that meeting, the Minister stated that he wanted to increase contacts with the Japanese; he also hoped that the Japanese would rapidly increase meetings with other South African ministers for the exchange of opinions.[62]

The Japanese School of Johannesburg, the first Japanese school on the African continent, is another means of contact and exchange with White South Africans.[63] In fact, the first exchange activity with Black schools did not take place until the autumn of 1987.[64]

The school began as an attempt to provide supplementary education in the Japanese language for the children of Japanese businessmen, and it subsequently grew in parallel with the rapid growth of the Japanese business community. Established in 1966 by the club and the Japanese government, with the co-operation of the South African government in an all White area, the school began with only sixteen pupils.[65] By 1981 it had become an accredited overseas school with ten teachers sent out by the Japanese Ministry of Education, three local staff and ninety-five pupils. The school helped to promote trade by allowing businessmen to bring their families along for the standard postings of three to five years.[66]

Technically considered a private school set up by the business community, it had as its first principal the Consul-General; teachers are sent by the Ministry of Education and over 60 per cent of the school's running costs come from the government.[67] It is revealing that only 11.6 per cent comes

---

[62] *Ibid.*, p. 259.

[63] See Morikawa Jun, 'Nihon-Minami Afurika Kankei Kenkyu Noto-Nihon no Tai Nan-A Seisaku to Nihonjin Gakko' (Japan's South African Policy and the Japanese School of Johannesburg) in JAAC, *Nanbu Afurika Nenpo* Tokyo: Afurika Kodo Iinkai, 1984, pp. 58-67. See also Kusuhara, *Afurika no Ue to Aparutoheito*, pp. 96-116.

[64] Based on an interview with Suseki Tomoaki, a former teacher at the Japanese School of Johannesburg.

[65] Morikawa, p. 59.

[66] *Ibid.*, pp. 61-3. The school serves not only as an educational institution but also functions to assist trade promotion and cultural exchange.

[67] *Gakko Yoran 1982*, pp. 1-2, points out that the Consul-General served as principal from the establishment of the school in August 1966 till March 1973.

from the business community in Tokyo and just 21.9 per cent from tuition.[68] The cost of a new school building which was constructed in the all-White suburb of Emmarentia in 1984 was also subsidised by the government. The Nippon Club contributed ¥6.4 million, the Tokyo business community ¥120 million, and the Japanese government ¥229 million.[69]

The *zaikai's* attempts to limit its contacts with the anti-apartheid forces have to be considered in parallel. The methods by which this was accomplished become especially clear when the activities of the CCA are examined.

Contact between the anti-apartheid forces and the *zaikai* were limited to *ad hoc*, informal meetings (*kondankai*) with the CCA, most of them restricted to a mere exchange of opinions. However, these meetings provided the *zaikai* with an opportunity to help soften criticism of the Japanese government's South Africa policy. By co-operating in the diplomatic tactic of allowing the anti-apartheid movement to direct its criticism at big business, the *zaikai* deflects the same criticism away from the government, which in turn willingly allowed the business community to shoulder the responsibility for Japan's dual African policy. There is a strong tendency for the *zaikai* to serve as a sort of shock absorber for the government by accepting the role of the erring party.[70]

One example of such 'diplomatic drama' came on 12 May 1975 when members of the UN Council for Namibia visited the Tokyo headquarters of the CCA. At that meeting the mission chief, Rupiah Banda, remarked that Namibia's early liberation would be possible if members of the international community supported the UN decision. On this point, he said, the Japanese government had announced full support for the UN resolution and made a donation to the Namibia Fund — gestures which the commission recognised and appreciated. The problem he stressed, was Japanese business.[71]

---

[68] These figures are for 1981. See Springbok 100th Anniversary edn, p.84.

[69] *Springbok,* 19 May 1982, p. 2.

[70] This same type of relationship can be seen in the interaction between the Foreign Ministry, which strongly proposed economic sanctions against Pretoria, and MITI, which resisted them. See Morikawa, *Minami Afurika to Nihon.*

[71] *Keidanren Shuho,* 22 May 1975, p. 10.

According to the Keidanren record of the discussion, Banda stated that Japanese companies maintained economic relations with South Africa in a variety of forms and this gave the impression that Japan supported apartheid and colonialism. If Japanese companies did not quickly cut their contacts with South Africa, he warned, anti-Japanese sentiments would intensify in Namibia and other African countries; when the battle was eventually won in South Africa, Japan's position would change greatly. Banda also noted that the actions of Japanese businesses suggested they were not aware of the suffering of the Namibian people, and he encouraged them to increase their understanding of the situation.[72]

The UN Commissioner for Namibia and one-time Nobel Peace Prize winner, Sean McBride, also strongly criticised the actions of Japanese businesses in relation to UN attempts to protect the natural resources of Namibia.[73] The CCA chairman Kono Fumihiko did not respond directly to the criticism of Banda and McBride. Rather he countered:

> We understand the situation in Namibia and understand and approve of the sentiments of the UN Council on Namibia but for Japan — a country without natural resources of its own — suddenly to lose an important source of natural resources is a big problem. We will convey your opinions to corporate leaders and ask them to think favourably about them, but to change their source of importations will take time.[74]

Kono then ventured a complaint of his own:

> As a coloured race, the Japanese well understand the position of the African people but while carrying out the same economic activities as Whites, it seems we have been singled out for criticism even more than Whites. Perhaps it is because we are also a coloured race and it is expected that we should be on the same side.[75]

Needless to say, the Kono response to the UN mission was

---

[72] *Ibid.*
[73] *Ibid.*, pp. 10-11.
[74] *Ibid.*, p. 11.
[75] *Ibid.*

unsatisfactory and the illegal importation of uranium, which symbolised the unacceptable actions of Japanese corporations, continued unabated. Four years later, the UN Council on Namibia sent another mission to Japan (6-9 March 1979) to revisit the CCA and ask for its co-operation. Again the CCA listened but took no action.[76]

The zaikai, especially the CCA, has played a very major role in the government's personal exchange activities with Black Africa. It has done this by hosting meetings with state and official guests from Black Africa; holding regular meetings with the ambassadors of African states, both individually and as a group (in June 1991, there were twenty-seven African ambassadors in Japan, of whom twenty-one were from Black Africa); and sending economic missions to Africa, which also fulfilled the function of paying reciprocal courtesy calls on foreign governments.

On the hosting of meetings, the CCA itself noted:

> Recently, the number of officials from African countries visiting Japan has increased greatly and most of them are official guests whose goal is exchange with government leaders. But, of course, during these visits they also visit Keidanren without fail and it has become customary for them to hope for exchanges with the CCA.[77]

This statement is certainly no exaggeration. For example, of the number of official African visitors to Japan between October 1988 and April 1989, almost all held meetings with members of the CCA, while key figures have also been guests at luncheons hosted by CCA officials.

The Keidanren visits were partly for the promotion of friendly bilateral relations or requests for ODA but requests for direct investment and import expansion were also received during these meetings, according to Keidanren reports.[78]

During such official visits, the close relationship between

---

[76] *Keidanren Shuho*, 15 March 1979, pp. 3-5.

[77] CCA (ed.), *Seifu Haken Afurika Keizai Mission Hokokusho*, Tokyo, December, 1988, p. 2.

[78] For example, at a breakfast meeting on 18 September 1988 with members of the CCA, Ike Nwachukwu, Nigeria's Minister of External Affairs, requested investments from Japanese corporations in large-scale agricultural projects, food processing, mineral resources development, LNG and electric power. See *Keidanren Shuho*, 31 October 1988, pp. 12-13.

business, government and the LDP is impressed upon such guests as they busily shuttle between the three main focuses of power — the Foreign Ministry in the Kasumigaseki section of Tokyo, LDP headquarters in nearby Nagata-cho, and Keidanren headquarters in the Otemachi business district.

The *zaikai* also contributes to personal exchange activities with Black Africa by serving as an alternative channel for dialogue and the improvement of relations, with guests from countries or political forces with which Japan does not yet have formal relations. The visit of the ANC president Oliver Tambo in April 1987 was such an example.

As the relaxation of tensions between the United States and the Soviet Union became obvious in the late 1980s and clear signals of the approaching end to the apartheid system in South Africa began to appear, it was necessary for the Japanese government to begin a positive dialogue with the ANC, which was rapidly expanding its political power and influence. At the same time, it was difficult for the government to invite a group that had been considered antagonistic. Taking this fact and the positions of Washington and Pretoria into consideration, the government avoided a political dilemma by having the Africa Society of Japan invite Tambo.[79]

The effect of the Tambo visit on both the Japanese government and the ANC was summarised by Shiba Minoru of the *Asahi* newspaper. Tambo was able to meet with Prime Minister Nakasone and Foreign Minister Kuranari and, more important, he managed to get their promise to bring up the subject of the ANC's desire for strengthening of economic sanctions against South Africa at the Venice summit of the Group of Seven in June of that year. He also obtained a promise that an ANC office could be opened in Tokyo and a pledge of $400,000 in aid for Black non-governmental organisations in South Africa. Tambo was also able to meet with *zaikai* leaders and attend anti-apartheid meetings and events in Tokyo and Osaka.[80] For the Japanese government the

---

[79] Ministry of Foreign Affairs, *Gaiko Seisho-Waga Gaiko no Kinkyo* 1988, p. 67. See also Amaki Naoto (Director of the Ministry's Second Africa Division), 'Oliver Tambo ANC Gicho Honichi no Igi', *Gekkan Afurika*, 27, 7 (1987), pp. 9-11.

[80] Shiba Minoru, 'Semarareru Afurika Gaiko no Kyoka', 27, 7 (1987), p. 14.

visit served to soften OAU criticism of Japan's Africa policy and to establish a channel of communication with the ANC in preparation for the post-apartheid era.[81]

The CCA's regular contact with African ambassadors in Japan, especially those from OAU member states, was also quite important. They began in 1974 and their informality provided a valuable opportunity for the participants to discuss directly many of the problems that existed in Japan-Africa relations. They also provided the *zaikai* with an opportunity to stress their pro-Black Africa stance. The first such meeting was held at Keidanren headquarters on 16 April 1974 and was attended by ambassadors from Algeria, Egypt, Central African Republic, Ethiopia, Gabon, Ghana, Guinea, Ivory Coast, Liberia, Libya, Madagascar, Morocco, Nigeria, Sudan, Tanzania, Uganda and Zaire.[82] Excerpts from that initial discussion were reported in the Keidanren newsletter and it is remarkable that to a large extent they remain valid in the 1990s.

Judging from Japan's Africa policy to date, the Egyptian ambassador noted that he could observe no genuine efforts to co-operate for African economic development. He urged Japan not only to have trade relations with Africa but also to participate actively in economic development as well.[83] The Libyan ambassador stated that Japan was advanced industrially and economically and had the ability to assist in African economic development. Unfortunately, Japan looked to Africa only for natural resources and sources of energy, and such exclusively materialsitic relations were not healthy.[84] Commenting that such meetings could not be found in the United States or Western Europe, the Algerian ambassador noted that the gatherings were meaningful for deepening mutual understanding. He felt that Japan gave more attention to Africa since the war in the Middle East, and that future relations appeared

---

[81] *Ibid.*

[82] *Keidanren Shuho*, 25 April 1974, p. 10.

[83] *Ibid.*, p. 11.

[84] *Ibid.*, p. 12. It is interesting to note that this meeting between the CCA and the African ambassadors in Tokyo took place after the autumn 1973 oil shock and against the background of a heightening of natural resources nationalism in various Third World nations. For more on Japanese corporations' concern over natural resources nationalism, see Ministry of Foreign Affairs, *Waga Gaikono Kinkyo*, 1975, pp. 4-5 198-209.

promising. Even so, he urged Keidanren to plan concrete projects for Africa and to make them known to the Japanese government.[85]

The Ghanaian ambassador expressed the view that past Japan-Africa trade had been carried on via third parties, a legacy of the colonial period; in future, he wanted Japan to trade directly. He also remarked that co-operative relations between Japan and Africa should be based on mutual trust, understanding and friendship. He said that efforts were being made in Africa to present a correct image of Japan, but in Japan itself there seemed to be mistaken images of Africa. He then asked the committee's help in correcting such attitudes.[86] The acting Nigerian ambassador warned that in the context of the economic co-operative relations between Africa and Japan, the existence of the South African and Rhodesian problems could not be overlooked: it was incompatible to promote co-operative relations with Black African states while at the same time widening trade with South Africa and Rhodesia. He wanted the Japanese business community to understand that Black African countries were battling against the racial discrimination policies of South Africa.[87] On a more general note, the ambassador from the Central African Republic noted that there were many Japanese television programmes that depicted Africa as an underdeveloped area inhabited only by barbarians, and he hoped such programmes would be stopped.[88]

Kono Fumihiko, the CCA chairman, responded to these opinions as follows:

> In 1970, I visited nine African countries and heard about the various problems African nations faced from the governments of each of these countries. These can be summed up as: (1) the trade imbalance between Japan and the African nations; (2) the effect that the severity of Japanese loan conditions has on economic co-operation; (3) the interest of the African countries in direct investment and technological transfer rather than trade; and (4) the desire

[85] *Keidanren Shuho*, 25 April 1974, p. 12.
[86] *Ibid.*, pp. 12-13.
[87] *Ibid.*, p. 14.
[88] *Ibid.*, pp. 14-15.

Fig. 5.12. MAJOR JAPANESE ECONOMIC MISSIONS TO AFRICA

	Sponsorship	*Head of mission*	*Countries visited*
February 1970	Government-sponsored Africa economic mission	Kono Fumihiko, chairman, Mitsubishi Heavy Industries, Ltd	Ethiopia, Kenya, Ghana, Tanzania, Zambia, Zaire, Nigeria, Ivory Coast, Senegal
May 1976	Keidanren Nigeria mission	Ichikawa Tsuneo, senior adviser, Kobe Steel	Nigeria
February 1978	Government-sponsored Africa economic mission	Kono Fumihiko, chairman, Committee of Economic Co-operation with Africa	Tanzania, Ivory Coast, Nigeria, Senegal
November 1980	Keidanren Africa mission	Kono Fumihiko, chairman Committee on Economic Co-operation with Africa	Senegal, Gabon
April 1984	Government-sponsored Africa economic mission	Kanamori Masao, chairman Mitsubishi Heavy Industries Ltd and of Committee on Economic Co-operation with Africa	Zambia, Zimbabwe, Kenya, Nigeria, Zaire
November 1988	Government-sponsored Africa economic mission	Maki Fuyuhiko, managing director, Kobe Steel	Zimbabwe, Cameroon, Nigeria
9-23 May 1992	Government-sponsored Africa economic mission	Fujimori Masamichi, chairman, Sumitomo Metal Mining Co. and of CCA	Zambia, Zimbabwe, South Africa, Botswana
27 November – 1 Dec. 1994	Keidanren South Africa mission	Kasahara Yukio, chairman, Japan Energy Corp. and of Committee on Sub-Saharan Africa	South Africa.

Source: Compiled from data in the Keidanren Economic Co-operation Department internal document 'Keidanren Afurika Iinkai ni Tsuite Shiryo Ichiran', pp. 2-4, and CCA (ed.), 'Seifu Haken Afurika Keizei Mission Hokokusho'.

for emancipation from racial discrimination.

When the opportunity arises, I have been conveying the requests of the African nations to the Japanese government and the business world but they are not yet sufficiently understood. Meetings like this for the exchange of opinions with ambassadors are a first step, but rather than adhere to this format, I would like to hold meetings as often as possible in future from many perspectives and hope we may thus deepen mutual understanding.[89]

The third element in the *zaikai's* contribution to the personal exchange approach is what the Japanese government likes to call 'visiting diplomacy' (*homon gaiko*). The close relations between the Foreign Ministry and the *zaikai* and the Ministry's role in encouraging the sending of missions began in earnest from 1970, with seven high-powered missions to Africa over twenty-two years, beginning with the first Kono mission in February 1970 (see Fig. 5.12). It is important to remember here that whether carrying the 'official government-despatched mission' designation or not, the missions, composed of business leaders, performed the function of paying return courtesy calls on African governments — an important diplomatic role in which they took the place of political leaders. A description of this function is found in the 1980 Keidanren Africa Mission Report:

In December 1978, President Bongo of the Republic of Gabon visited Japan unofficially on his way to China. In April 1979, President Senghor of the Republic of Senegal visited Japan for the first time as a state guest. During their visits, both presidents had a chance to meet with CCA chairman Kono Fumihiko and other Keidanren leaders and both strongly urged Keidanren leaders to visit their countries. Later, both conveyed official requests for visits through their ambassadors in Japan.

Similarly, the Foreign Ministry repeatedly encouraged Keidanren to send a mission and to strengthen relations with and promote an understanding of Japan in the important former French colonies of Senegal and Gabon. Thus,

---

[89] *Ibid.*, pp. 15-16.

Keidanren felt such a mission was a chance to see actual conditions in these countries, to exchange opinions with government leaders on Japanese economic co-operation and with these questions in mind, to study what role Japanese business should play. From this perspective, a visit was considered quite meaningful, the invitations of both nations were accepted and the decision to despatch an economic mission was made.[90]

Senden gaiko (PR diplomacy): White Africa

This section examines the *zaikai*'s involvement in Japan's *senden gaiko* (PR diplomacy) towards South Africa through an analysis of the business community's contributions to the Japan—South Africa Fund, begun in 1989 for the purpose of assisting the non-White population in the Republic. The project, and the *zaikai* involvement in it, was elaborated in a report by Shibayama Gosuke, the chairman of SATA:

> The current situation inside and outside of South Africa is in a state of great flux. In order to bring about a peaceful and realistic change of apartheid, raising the living and educational standards and social position of the 75 per cent of the population that is non-White is a major issue.
>
> Therefore, SATA started fundraising activities as of March 1989 in order to improve the position and skills of the Black population in South Africa. Receiving co-operation from Keidanren and advice from MITI and the Foreign Ministry. The main aim of this aid activity is the promotion of Black enterprises, improvement of welfare and scholarships for Black students to assist and encourage their self-help efforts.
>
> SATA and Keidanren have called for donations, setting ¥400 million as a goal. The programme will be implemented by Japan Overseas Development Corporation (JODC) and the Association for the Promotion of International Co-operation (APIC). Close consultations between these organisations, SATA, Keidanren, MITI and the Foreign Ministry will be maintained to ensure the effective opera-

[90] Keidanren, *Keidanren Ho Afurika Shisetsudan Hokoku*, Tokyo, December 1980, p. 5.

tion of the fund, which is known in South Africa as the Japan-South Africa Fund, as well as a gradual increase in the understanding of the fund.[91]

The development of the Japan-South Africa Fund provides an excellent example of how government and business work together to implement commonly perceived goals and also demonstrates how economic assistance can be manipulated for public relations purposes. Significantly, the initiative for the project came first from the Foreign Ministry.[92] The co-operation of Keidanren and SATA was needed to fill a gap in the Ministry's own economic assistance plans and to help counter criticism of the Japanese government and corporations by the anti-apartheid movement which became increasingly severe after 1985. Japan's narrow victory in the 1986 election for a non-permanent post on the UN Security Council impressed on the government the dissatisfaction of the Black African countries. Criticism heightened further as Japan became the largest trading partner of South Africa, and thus the worst violator of economic sanctions, for two consecutive years in 1986 and 1987. The government's concern was not confined to the South African question. In the United States demands for punitive measures against Japan had also begun to surface. Complaints arose that Japan's behaviour in South Africa symbolised an unfairness that could also be linked to the problematic aspects of the US-Japan trade relationship.[93]

The Japanese government was eager to minimise or even neutralise such international criticism. One of the means chosen was the extension of economic assistance to South African Blacks; public relations activities were used to publicise this assistance. Japan began to make contributions to medical, educational and other projects designed to aid South African Blacks victimised by apartheid in fiscal 1987.[94] In that year Japan gave $400,000 but this had a negative rather than positive public relations effect since it served only to emphasise the 'too

---

[91] *Keidanren Geppo,* November 1989, p. 46.

[92] See Keidanren Economic Co-operation Department, pp. 6-7.

[93] 'Japan: Playing Both Sides'. See Newsweek, 6 April, 1987, p. 12 Also see *Keidanren Shuho,* 26 October 1987, pp. 2-3.

[94] Ministry of Foreign Affairs, *Diplomatic Blue Book 1989,* p. 237.

little, too late' nature of the Japanese contribution. This was especially apparent when contrasted with the United States' contribution of $25 million, the EC's $23 million, and the $6 million each from Britain and Canada. Even the Gillette Company, the large American conglomerate, had pledged $500,000-$100,000 more than the world's second greatest economic power.[95]

Japan also faced technical difficulties in increasing its official assistance. It regarded South Africa as a developed country and except for emergency relief funds, it was therefore difficult to justify the extension of economic assistance. Japan also felt that it had to consider the interests of the Pretoria government. There was a strong possibility that the Black community would suggest that Japan minimise or cut altogether its trade with the Republic rather than extend economic assistance.[96] For Japanese businesses, and by extension the government which had been maintaining huge trade relations with South Africa such a scenario was a nightmare. As an alternative, the Ministry decided to seek the participation and co-operation of the *zaikai*, which up till that time had not been involved in assistance to South African Blacks, despite the precedents set by Western companies such as Mobil, NCR and Gillette.

Until the Japan-South Africa Fund intiative, big business had indeed been reluctant to get involved. As Makiura Toshio of SATA noted in a report on aid projects for non-Whites in South Africa, while government and private organisations in the United States and Europe had been extending active assistance to Black people, the contributions of private organisations in Japan, which had a shallow historical relationship with non-White South Africa, have been nil.[97] A similar view was expressed by Akagawa Yasuji, the Marubeni Corporation branch manager in South Africa, who reported that Japanese companies had been approached for aid three or four years before, but there had been debate within SATA over

[95] *Keidanren Shuho*, 3 April 1989, pp. 2-3.
[96] See *Asahi Shimbun*, 24 January 1988 in which Cyril Ramaphosa, the General Secretary of the National Union of Mineworkers (NUM), was quoted as saying 'The Japan-South Africa Fund is utter nonsense'.
[97] *Springbok* Club Kaiho 13 (1 December 1991), p. 31.

whether or not to support Blacks in South Africa.[98]

Perhaps it was to this period of internal debate that Makiura referred when he noted that the idea of the project had first arisen in 1986 when SATA officials, together with Japanese Consul-General Sezaki, visited South Africa and toured facilities in Soweto run by the Urban Foundation.[99] In any case, the *zaikai's* response to the government's request for assistance was favourable, partly because the *zaikai* itself was aware of a sense of crisis. An official of SATA revealed this concern in an interview with the *Daily Yomiuri* newspaper:

> According to the secretariat of the organisation, the association has shied away from the apartheid problem in the past. Now, however, it has realised it has to act. Member corporations have began feeling a 'sense of crisis' as Japan-bashing by other countries on the South African trade issue has increased.[100]

The time had come for the *zaikai* also to consider its long-term strategy for securing an economic position in post-apartheid South Africa.

As for the degree and extent of SATA's actual involvement in the Japan—South Africa Fund, according to Shibayama's description of the project, JODC and APIC were officially in charge of implementation of the project. Both are semi-governmental aid organisations.[101] JODC is a non-profit organisation, set up under the auspices of the government in 1970 and funded by private organisations. APIC is a non-profit foundation, established in 1975 with the full support and under the direction of the Ministry of Foreign Affairs.[102]

Even so, it appears that SATA played an important role at

[98] *Ibid.*, 15 November 1989, p. 1.

[99] *Ibid.,* 13 (1 December 1991), p. 3.

[100] See 'Keidanren Moves at Last to Help South African Black's, *Daily Yomiuri*, 20 March 1989.

[101] Japan Overseas Development Corporation, *JODC*, Tokyo: p. 1.

[102] See Association for Promotion of International Co-operation brochure, *APIC* (undated): 'In order to have Japan's international co-operation make a true contribution to the development of the recipient country, one of APIC's primary objectives has been to perform a pipeline function between the government and private sectors in Japan in furnishing a wide range of information and data on international co-operation to all concerned.'

each stage of the implementation process, including fundraising, project identification, project selection and approval, management of the project funds, and follow-up and the establishment of future projects. The *Daily Yomiuri* noted that 'the main organ in charge of the fund-raising campaign is SATA' and that 'SATA will ask for the co-operation of all its member corporations and about eighty other Keidanren member companies directly or indirectly connected to trade with South Africa'.[103]

Makiura Toshio has also stated that the SATA branch in South Africa investigates projects implemented and planned by social welfare organisations; it then selects candidates for assistance based on their report to SATA headquarters.[104] Akagawa's statements also corroborate SATA's central position. He noted that the selection of recipient programmes is discussed with the Johannesburg branch of SATA after receiving advice from the consul general's office. Proposals are then sent to SATA's Tokyo office and implemented upon its approval.[105] Except for the actual distribution of the funds, SATA has clearly been in control of the project. But the important question here is why has the government attempted to present the fund in this complicated way, using JODC and APIC as a Trojan horse to conceal the united efforts of the Foreign Ministry and the *zaikai*?

In terms of promoting a positive public relations campaign, JODC and APIC, as aid organisations, had the public image the government wanted to project. Widespread awareness that the pro-Pretoria business organisation SATA was in charge could have caused a reverse effect, and created the kind of negative publicity the government wanted to avoid. For although it was geared to the non-White population in the Republic, the Japan-South Africa Fund was also focused on larger public relations goals.

Senden gaiko (PR diplomacy): Black Africa

This same *'senden gaiko'* approach, with the government and private big business working in harmony (*kanzai ittai*), can be

[103] *Daily Yomirui*, 20 March 1989.
[104] *Springbok Club Kaiho* 13 (1 December 1991). p. 32.
[105] *Springbok*, November 1989, p. 1.

seen in Japan's relations with Black African countries. PR diplomacy has been carried out here by propelling the Africa Society of Japan centre-stage, although the real direction comes from the Foreign Ministry and support from the *zaikai*.[106] The extent of the *senden gaiko* function the society performs was revealed in a speech given in English at a UN symposium on Africa held in Tokyo in 1985. Nakahira Noboru, then Director-General of the Foreign Ministry's UN Bureau, said:

> Particular mention should be made of the Africa Society of Japan, which has contributed substantially to expanding knowledge about Africa in Japan. In brief, its role consists of selling Africa to Japan and Japan to Africa. With the support of business (more than 140 major Japanese companies working in Africa and some 40-50 small companies) and of the Minister of Foreign Affairs, this dynamic society organised an exchange of economic information, arranged meetings with African personalities and organised exhibitions of African art. It organised market studies of demand, and published a monthly bulletin of general information (*Africa*), as well as an African annual dealing with political and economic subjects. This activity marked a turning point in a country where the press had paid little attention to Africa. In this connection, only *Asahi* and *Yomiuri*[107] had correspondents in Africa, in Dar es Salaam and Nairobi respectively. Japanese interest in Africa was accelerated by membership in the major institutions for international co-operation and development.[108]

---

[106] The society established four regional branches in the Hokkaido, Tohoku, Chubu and Kansai regions of Japan in 1986 which sponsor lectures and local exhibitions relating to Black Africa. The society is governed by a chairman and an executive board. In 1991, the chairman of Suruga Bank served as the society's head and board members included the former Japanese ambassador to Ghana, the chairman of Hattori Seiko Co., the vice chairman of the Kajima Corp. and the chairman of Nippon Koei Co., who until recently had been the acting chairman of the Keidanren Africa Committee. The society board includes 31 members, composed of the heads of major enterprises from across the business spectrum.

[107] *Asahi* and *Yomiuri* are Japan's two largest newspapers.

[108] 'New Orientations for the Reinforcement of Co-operation between Africa and Japan', UN Symposium on Africa, Tokyo, 4-5 Dec. 1985.

The society's 1991 annual report substantiates the organisation's *senden gaiko* functions. The list includes interchange with Africans who visit Japan; lectures and exhibitions; farewell and welcome-back parties for Japanese ambassadors posted to Africa; charitable activities; '*kondankai*' (informal meetings) between the business coummunity and ambassadors currently posted in Africa; seminars for African ambassadors in Japan; publications; despatch of various missions to Africa; general meetings and board meetings; and contact with regional branches of the Africa Society.[109] While all these activities are attributed to the Africa Society, it is clear that the most important of these functions — those related to economic matters — are more thoroughly carried out by the CCA. It is the public relations, publications and charitable activities that are chiefly left to the Africa Society of Japan.

Two clear examples of how the Africa Society of Japan has been involved in Japan's *senden gaiko* are the 'Africa Month' held from 28 September to 28 October 1984, and the 'Send Blankets to Africa' campaign, from 15 December 1984 till February 1985.

Africa Month was the largest project ever conceived to introduce Black Africa to the Japanese public, with events held in Tokyo as well as Osaka, Nagoya and Sapporo, which have Africa Society of Japan regional branches. Many activities were included in the month-long programme: an inaugural reception, exhibitions of nature conservation posters, artefacts, stamps, photography and art, a book fair, a fashion show (in which the wives of African diplomats took part), movies, performances by dance troupes from Zaire and Tunisia, and a concert by the Nigerian musician King Sunny Ade. Also scheduled was a visit by the Central African Republic basketball team, a symposium entitled 'Poor Africa, Rich Africa', and several easy-to-understand seminars on trade and investment, economic co-operation and the political situation in Africa.[110]

Although the event was called Africa Month, the

---

[109] Africa Society of Japan, *Gyomu Hokoku*, Tokyo, May 1991, p. 2.

[110] Ministry of Foreign Affairs, *Nihon to Afurika: Afurika gekkan o Kinen Shite*, Tokyo: Sekai no Ugokisha, September 1984. This booklet contains the schedule of Africa Month activities and general information on the continent and Japan's relations with Africa.

programme clearly emphasised Black Africa's nature, culture and society rather than anything that could be considered controversial, such as Japan's own Africa policy or even environmental issues such as the ivory trade.[111] This did not occur by chance. The aim of the Africa Month programme was to project Japan's pro-Black Africa posture and to influence domestic public opinion by encouraging interest in Africa while at the same time distracting attention away from Japan's problematic White Africa policy.

The official Africa Month publicity brochure stated that the event was being held under the auspices of the Africa Society of Japan and the APIC, with the assistance of the Foreign Ministry, the Japan Foundation, Japan Broadcasting Corporation (NHK), the Japan Newspaper Editors and Publishers Association, and the National Association of Commerical Broadcasters in Japan. Other forms of co-operation came from businesses involved in Africa, such as the Big Six trading companies, Nippon Koei, NEC, Seiko and Matsushita.

While the Africa Society of Japan did serve as the secretariat for the month's activities, it is clear that the real producer of the event was the Foreign Ministry, which was involved in the planning, decision-making, overall command of the proceedings and follow-up activities.

The Foreign Ministry was undoubtedly interested in the *senden gaiko* aspects of Africa Month. During an informal meeting on 11 July 1986 with Keidanren and other business leaders at the annual conference of Japanese ambassadors to African states, Miyake Wasuke, Director-General of the Ministry's Middle Eastern and African Affairs Bureau, stated: 'In order to continue to expand public relations activities about Africa in

---

[111] 'Japan imports 40 per cent of the total ivory produced and is the world's largest importer. Although Japan has voiced its wish to give top priority to the protection of elephants, in reality it is also interested in protecting its 300-year-old ivory handicraft industry. . . . Considering that Japan is a big consumer of all kinds of resources, it should take a clear-cut position on the ivory problem, since 80 per cent of the ivory on the market is poached or smuggled. . . . The world will be carefully watching Japan's moves. It should refrain from making last minute ivory purchases before the ban takes effect.' *Daily Yomiuri*, 18 October 1989. Japan imported about 100 tons of ivory every year until 1989, when it banned all ivory imports. 'Battle over Elephants Appears Likely in Kyoto', *Asahi Evening News*, 3 March 1992.

170   *Japan and Africa*

Japan, an Africa Month was held in 1984, an Africa Week in 1985. This year we are also planning to hold an African Festival as well.'[112]

Sunaga Kazuo of the First Africa Division pointed out in his report on Africa Month that Africa was important for Japan both as a source of natural resources, especially rare metals, and in UN diplomacy, since the African states command one-third of the votes. Thus it was necessary to activate and strengthen African policy but due to history and geographical distance, Japanese people in general are not much interested in Africa. He went on to note that the aims of the Africa Month project had been to strengthen African diplomacy by increasing interest in Africa among the Japanese as well as increasing support for the famine aid fundraising campaign.[113] Summarising the results of Africa Month, he remarked that these two goals had been achieved and that the starvation lunches hosted by the Foreign Minister had been widely reported not only in Africa but also in the Middle East, South-East Asia and Western Europe. Furthermore, so greatly had the African countries appreciated Japan's active stance towards Africa that Japan was unanimously recommended by them to serve as the co-ordinator of the UN General Assembly session on 2 November 1984 on the critical economic situation in Africa.[114]

Africa Month was part of a Foreign Ministry autumn agenda clearly designed to focus on Africa. On 27 September, the day before the Africa Month inaugural reception, Foreign Minister Abe Shintaro hosted a starvation lunch at the UN attended by 380 people which raised $6,000. The next day he hosted a luncheon in New York to which the UN General Assembly chairman and representatives of thirty-six countries (including twenty-one African foreign ministers) were invited.

From 14 November to 23 November, Abe visited Zambia, Egypt and Ethiopia, and while in Ethiopia he declared Japan's intention to increase food aid. After his return to Japan he held a breakfast meeting with African ambassadors in Tokyo on 28 November. The following day, he hosted yet another

[112] *Keidanren Shuho*, 17 July 1986, pp. 11-12.
[113] Sunaga Kazuo, 'Afurika Gekkan Hokoku' *Gekkan Afurika*, vol. 25, no. 1 (January 1985), p. 35.
[114] *Ibid.*, p. 36.

starvation lunch at the Foreign Ministry, attended this time by 550 political and business leaders and representatives of the African embassies in Tokyo. Abe also issued an emergency appeal at this luncheon for support of the famine relief campaign. On 3 December, the UN General Assembly adopted a declaration on the critical economic situation in Africa and Abe's emergency appeal was introducted into the UN official record by the Japanese representative.[115]

All these activities were designed to project Japan's concerned, pro-Black Africa image, but there also seems to have been another hidden motive. In November 1984, the Japanese representative on the International Court of Justice, Oda Shigeru, was up for re-election and the Foreign Ministry was doing everything possible to support his candidacy and increase his vote-count. Their autumn pro-Black Africa agenda seems likely to have been a part of this initiative.[116]

The Diplomatic Blue Book for 1985 reported that as early as August 1983 the Foreign Ministry, under the direction of Foreign Minister Abe, had established an election task force headed by the Vice Minister for Foreign Affairs and designed to ensure Oda's re-election.[117] It also noted that the Foreign Ministry united its efforts on many levels to conduct a highly organised election campaign for Oda, requesting support through Japanese embassies abroad and calling for appeals by Japanese government leaders on foreign visits and key foreign visitors to Japan.[118]

The election was held on 7 November 1984. Eight Security Council votes and eighty General Assembly votes were needed to win. Oda, with twelve Security Council and 114 General Assembly ballots cast in his favour, came top of the poll, and a large majority of his votes came from Asian, Latin American and African states. The Foreign Ministry campaign had been a notable success.[119]

But why was the Foreign Ministry content to call itself

---

[115] For more on Foreign Minister Abe's activities during Africa Month, see *Gekkan Afurika*, vol. 25, no. 5 (May 1985), p. 23.

[116] See *Asahi Shimbun*, 24 December 1984.

[117] Ministry of Foreign Affairs, *Waga Gaiko no Kinkyo*, 1985, p. 321.

[118] *Ibid.*

[119] *Ibid.*

just one of the supporters of the Africa Month project rather than reveal its central role to the public? Quite simply, a private economic organisation such as the Africa Society of Japan, projecting an image that emphasised the strengthening of friendly relations and co-operation with Africa, created a much more effective image for Japan than the Foreign Ministry, but it also achieved the Ministry's cherished objectives.

A similar style of presentation can also be seen in the 'Send Blankets to Africa' campaign, carried out as a follow-up to Africa Month. The Foreign Ministry recognised the public relations value of the campaign and included a summary of the project in an official government bulletin, presented as a half-page English-language advertisement in the *Asahi Evening News* (27 March 1985) titled 'Japanese Youth Extend Hands across the Seas'. It read:

> When the plight of Africans, especially the Ethiopians, was publicised last year, various organisations immediately started campaigns to collect contributions and goods to send to the afflicted people of Africa. During Africa Month in September-October 1984, the Africa Society of Japan collected contributions, and many concerned young people, including primary school children, sent in contributions. The contributions were used to buy and send ¥70 million worth of medicine and food to Africa.
>
> The Society established the Society to Send Blankets to Africa and with the backing of the Ministry of Foreign Affairs, began collecting blankets on 15 December 1984. The chairman of the blanket society is veteran actor Morishige Hisaya, who has always been active in charity.
>
> The drive collected 1.7 million blankets for Africa, and they were shipped out prior to 10 March.

This public pronouncement suggested that the Africa Society of Japan spontaneously set up the campaign on its own initiative. However, the Foreign Ministry's role becomes clear in a statement by Africa Society of Japan chairman, Okano Kiichiro. He noted that on Foreign Minister Abe's return from Ethiopia, the African aid campaign was intensified, and that under the Foreign Minister's direct instruction the Society

to Send Blankets to Africa was created inside the Africa Society.[120]

In short, the Africa Society of Japan has played an important 'sub-contracting' role in the implementation of Japan's *senden gaiko* towards Africa.[121] More important, the *zaikai* has been called upon to play a significant supplemental role in the diplomacy process and has in fact made an important contribution to the smooth implementation of Japan's Africa policy.

[120] *Gekkan Afurika*, vol. 25, no. 4 (April 1985), p. 3.
[121] From the point of view of presenting a unified, well-balanced image and understanding of Africa, the Africa Society's activities, which have been strongly influenced by *senden gaiko*, have displayed certain clear limitations. Yet the Society has made a contribution in its own way. Through its educational activities it has increased interest, knowledge and understanding of Africa in Japanese society, an achievement that should be acknowledged.

6

RACISM IN JAPAN'S AFRICAN DIPLOMACY

Japanese attitudes towards race were typified in a speech made by the former Japanese Prime Minister Takeshita Noboru on 18 July 1990: 'If chloroflurocarbons destroy the ozone layer, people will be susceptible to skin cancer. So far, only White people [*hakujin no kata*] have suffered from skin cancer . . . Neither Blacks [*kuro*] nor we, the *madra* [those in between, i.e. Asians], have had the disease.'[1] '*Kuro*' is a derogatory term very close to the English term 'nigger', while adding '*no kata* to the word '*hakujin*' (White) denotes respect.

The Japanese public's reaction to the comment was one of indifference, perhaps precisely because the public shared the same perceptions on racial questions. A mentality of 'difference' exists that leads to feelings of inferiority towards Whites and superiority towards Blacks; this attitude is illustrated in Japanese perceptions of the United States.[2]

> Scholar John G. Russell describes Japan as a hierarchical society in which prestige of all kinds is paramount. 'When the Japanese look at America', he explains, 'they see White people at the top of the social ladder and Blacks and other minorities at the bottom, and judge people accordingly.' That is one reason why twisted and confused images continue to predominate here.[3]

[1] 'Kokujin no koto o kuro to hyogen', *Asahi Shimbun*, 19 July 1992; 'Former Premier Uses Derogatory Term for Blacks', *Daily Yomiuri*, 20 July 1992.
[2] For a detailed study of Japanese perceptions on race in general, see Wagatsuma Hiroshi and Yoneyama Toshinao, *Henken no Kozo—Nihonjin no Jinshukan*, Tokyo: Nihon Hoso Shuppan Kyokai, 1967. For Japanese attitudes towards Blacks, see John G. Russell's two studies *Nihonjin no Kokujinkan — Mondai wa Chibikuro Sanbo Dake Dewanai*, Tokyo: Shin Hyoron, 1991 and 'Narratives of Denial: Racial Chauvinism and the Black Other in Japan', *Japan Quarterly*, October-December 1991, pp. 416-28.
[3] Michael Berger, 'Blacks in Japan', *PHP Intersect*, August 1991, pp. 34-8.

This image of race relations and confused self-identification pointed out by Russell and others can be described as a negative legacy of the '*Datsu A, nyu O*' (Out of Asia, into the West) course the Japanese government, and to a certain degree, Japan as a whole, followed after 1868, when Japan began to 'modernise'. This stressed that Japan should pursue its own development and not stay with 'backward, stagnant' Asia. Instead, it should use the advanced Western powers as a model for nation-building and empire management.

The goal of catching up with the West was achieved gradually, beginning in the late nineteenth century and continuing through the twentieth. First came the abolition of extra-territoriality for foreigners and the restoration of tariff autonomy. Next, Japan became a regional power with its victories in the Sino-Japanese (1894-5) and the Russo-Japanese (1904-5) wars. Finally, Japan's membership in the Allied forces in the First World War led to it becoming one of the five major world powers at the time of the Paris Peace Conference in 1919.

Parity with the West was achieved in many ways, but the problem of eliminating discrimination against Japanese nationals among the Western powers and their dependencies remained to be solved. One of the Japanese government's efforts to rectify this situation was the proposal to introduce an anti-racial discrimination clause into the Covenant of the League of Nations (discussed below). Another was the demand for the improvement of the conditions of Japanese nationals in the United States and British dominions. This long-cherished dream of the Japanese governing elite finally came partly true in October 1930, when Japan won a political concession from the Pretoria regime allowing Japanese people to be treated as *de facto* Whites.

Another consequence of the '*Datsu A*' policy was the formation of a superiority complex towards other coloured peoples, especially Blacks. That process was accelerated when Japan itself became a colonial empire and subjugated other Asian peoples. This superiority complex towards coloured people carried over into the post-war Japanese society despite the defeat of Japanese imperialism and colonialism in the Second World War and subsequent democratisation. However, the racist tendencies of Japanese society have begun to be challenged on many fronts: by the growing importance of human rights issues in international relations, through criticism of the problematic behaviour of Japanese companies overseas and by the anti-discrimination movements within Japan, such as the anti-apartheid movement, which was active from the 1960s. To understand the relationship between Japan's African diplomacy and racism more clearly, we should now examine some of these key issues.

Historically, the Japanese government's stance on racism can be traced back to the Paris Peace Conference of 1919, where Japan proposed amending the Covenant to include an abolition of the racial discrimination clause, an anti-racist act that was in reality actually racist.

It is first important to note the exact wording of the proposal which the Japanese representative, Baron Makino, introduced on 28 April 1919:

> I had first on the 13th of February an opportunity of submitting to the Commission of the League of Nations our amendment to the Covenant embodying the principle of equal and just treatment to be accorded to all aliens who happen to be the nationals of the States which are deemed advanced enough and fully qualified to become Members of the League, making no distinction on account of race or nationality.
>
> On that occasion I called the attention of the Commission to the fact that the race question being a standing grievance which might become acute and dangerous at any moment, it was desirous that a provision dealing with the subject should be made in this Covenant.[4]

A few paragraphs later he concludes:

> If just and equal treatment is denied to certain nationals, it would have the significance of a certain reflection on their quality and status. Their faith in the justice and righteousness which are to be the guiding spirit of the future international intercourse between the Members of

[4] US Department of State, *Papers Relating to the Foreign Relations of the United States, The Paris Peace Conference 1919*, vol. III, House Document no. 874, Washington, DC: US Govenment Printing Office, 1943, pp. 289-90.

the League may be shaken, and such a frame of mind, I am afraid, would be most detrimental to that harmony and co-operation, upon which foundation alone can the League now contemplated be securely built. It was solely and purely from our desire to see the League established on a sound and firm basis of good-will, justice, and reason, that we have been compelled to make our proposal. We will not, however, press for the adoption of our proposal at this moment.

In closing, I feel it my duty to declare clearly on this occasion that the Japanese Govenment and people feel poignant regret at the failure of the Commission to approve of their just demand for laying down a principle aiming at the adjustment of this long-standing grievance, a demand that is based upon a deep-rooted national conviction. They will continue in their insistence for the adoption of this principle by the League in future.[5]

Most important of the motivations for proposing such an anti-racial discrimination clause was the strong anti-Japanese sentiments that existed in the United States, Canada, Australia and other countries at that time. Ironically, they existed alongside the movement to promote the actual practice of the internationalist and idealist currents embodied in President Woodrow Wilson's Fourteen Points by incorporating them into the charter being established for the League of Nations.

The work of the scholar Ikei Masaru sheds light on the situation in the United States at that time:

Due to the opposition of Presidents Theodore Roosevelt and William Taft, bills proposed by the California legislature to forbid Japanese ownership of land were defeated three successive times: in February 1907, in November 1909 and in March 1911. California's anti-Japanese movement still remained active thereafter and in May 1913, the so-called 'Wafe Bill' was passed by the California legislature with certain amendments. This made land ownership by foreigners who were not eligible to become naturalised citizens of the United States illegal. It came into effect on 10 August

[5] *Ibid.*, p. 291.

of the same year. The California legislature thus resolved
an issue that had concerned the anti-Japanese faction in the
legislature for a long time. For the Japanese living in
America at that time, more than half of whom were engaged in agriculture, the implementation of this state law
was a heavy blow both physically and psychologically . .
. It was only a year after the implementation of this law
that the First World War broke out. Japan participated in
the war on the side of the Allies and some of the Japanese
residents in the United States volunteered to join the army.
For this and other reasons, anti-Japanese feeling became less
pronounced and the anti-Japanese movement temporarily
died down.

Nevertheless, the problem of Japanese immigration
became an ever greater bone of contention between the two
countries in the period leading up to the Paris Peace
Conference. For Japan to take advantage of this situation
and, in conjuction with Wilson's idealism, to propose the
abolition of racial discrimination was only natural.[6]

In addition to these elements was the deep concern of the
Japanese government (and the Japanese people in general) for
their country's national prestige at this point. As a result of the
First World War, Japan became one of the five Great Powers,
and along with the other four one of the prime diplomatic
goals was to maintain and enhance its national prestige. These
factors must all be considered when attempting to understand
why Japan took such an active stance against anti-Japanese
movements and promoted the clause on abolition of racial
discrimination. In other words, '. . .in order to assert her
complete equality with the other Powers, Japan had little
choice but to refuse to recognise and formally oppose the
difference in treatment given to her own immigrants and
European immigrants into the United States.[7]

There is also the question of Japan's motives for sponsoring

---

[6] Ikei Masaru, 'Pari Heiwa Kaigi to Jinshu Sabetsu Mondai', in *Nihon Kokusai Seiji Gakkai* (ed.), *Kokusai Seiji Nihon Gaiko Shi Kenkyu-Dai Ichiji Sekai Taisen*, Tokyo: Yuhikaku, 1963, p. 45.

[7] Iriye Akira, *Nihon no Gaiko — Meiji Ishin kara Genzai made*, Tokyo: Chuo Koronsha, 1966, p 57.

the abolition of this clause. The Japanese govenment was not motivated by a desire to encourage the realisation of universalist and idealist principles in order to help liberate those peoples suffering from discrimination, opression and exploitation by imperial and colonial powers. Instead, Japan's motives were: to affirm the equality of both the Japanese nation and its people with the Western nations and their peoples; to try and counter the manifestation of extremely humiliating anti-Japanese sentiments as soon as possible; and to help realise the aim of promoting the narrow interests of the nation by extensive overseas expansion.

A statement by Shidehara Kijuro, the Vice Minister of Foreign Affairs, makes these motives clear:

> When consideration is given to the harmful effects which the rise of anti-Japanese sentiments in the United States, Canada and Australia have had over the previous twenty or thirty years, we must be sure to take advantage of the situation to resolve this problem.[8]

The first part of Minister Plenipotentiary Makino's speech made at the conference also destroys the validity of the Japanese govenment's claim that its actions were meant to support universalist and internationalist principles. It refers to the principle of equal and just treatment to be accorded to all aliens who happen to be the nationals of the States which are deemed advanced enough and fully qualified to become Members of the League, making no distinction on account of race or nationality.'[9]

Thus the abolition of discrimination between all countries and people was not Japan's intention. Discrimination was to be abolished only between nations having the traits outlined above. Secondly, people in colonies or dependencies that were not 'civilised' (i.e. 'advanced enough') and not members of the League of Nations were not meant to receive 'fair and equal treatment'. This in itself was a kind of discrimination.

From the point of view of colonised peoples, this was indeed a strange distinction to make. It considered that because they were supposedly not far enough along the road to

[8] Ikei, p. 45.
[9] US Department of State, p. 291.

civilisation and were not considered to have the necessary qualifications to become members of the League, they must remain in their existing situation under the rule of colonialists whose idealogy was built around a central core of racial discrimination. It thus perpetuated rather than countered such discrimination.

Finally, the widespread existence at that time of serious forms of discrimination within Japan itself against *burakumin* (the Japanese equivalent of Untouchables) Okinawans, the Ainu, Koreans, Chinese and others as well as in its colonies and dependencies further reduces the plausibility of the Japanese govenment's claim. The forceful suppression of 1 March 1919 Korean independence movement is a prime example of such attitudes. The acquisition of the Shantung Peninsula concession from Germany and the annexation of the former German island territories in the South Pacific through the Versailles Peace Treaty further revealed its imperialistic side. Japan also collaborated with other powers engaged in imperialist and colonial activities in the Middle East and Africa at this time. Thus, the idea that the Japanese government was an oppressed coloured country seeking to help fellow sufferers of racial discrimination was no more than a pretence hiding its own form of imperialism and racial discrimination.

The Japanese government and racism

With this historical background in mind, we will now critically examine the Japanese govenment's more recent racial attitude, as shown in its posture towards the Japan-South African Parliamentarians Friendship League and the related problematic statements made by members of the LDP from the 1980s onwards.

The JSAPFL was formed on 6 June 1984 by forty-five LDP members of the Diet.[10] The chairman was LDP Vice President Susumu Nikaido and Dietman Ishihara Shintaro served as Secretary General. Other influential members included Takeshita Noboru, later to become prime minister, and Moriyama Mayumi, who in 1984 was Parliamentary Vice Foreign Minister and had been the first woman to hold the LDP's second-

---

[10] The list of members was obtained and translated by the JAAC (see Appendix J).

most senior position as Chief Cabinet Secretary.

The group was created to increase friendly relations with South African parliamentarians at a time when anti-apartheid sentiment was growing in much of the rest of the world. Once word of the group's formation became public, the JAAC obtained a copy of the league's prospectus. It then sent an open letter to the league including a list of questions. The reply and the prospectus were then translated into English by the JAAC and circulated nationally and internationally.

The prospectus called on parliamentarians to take more interest in South Africa and while noting that the country had been ostracised by the world for its policy of racial segregation it added: At the same time, social and economic improvements have been taking place, allowing the Black population to reach the highest standards of living on the African continent.[11]

The prospectus also noted the importance of South Africa's rare metals to the Japanese economy and the very important trade partnership between the two countries. The JSAPFL's proposed future activities included exchanges with the South Africa-Japan Parliamentarians' Friendship League of the Republic of South Africa, working to extend direct flights by their respective flag carriers between the two countries and establishing embassies on both sides.[12]

The secretary-general, Mr Ishihara, answered the JAAC letter by noting that Japan should deepen its ties with South Africa and let South African people know about the technological and economic power of Japan. Thus, the door to the international society would be opened through South Africans' recognition of the ability of non-White races. The reply reaffirmed the importance of rare metals and noted that steps towards reform were being taken in South Africa. It concluded: 'We are trying to encourage the process of reform through the exchanges of parliamentarians between the two countries.

[11] Form the Prospectus of the Japan-South Africa Parliamentarians' Friendship League, obtained and translated by JAAC, July 1984.

[12] To understand this last goal, it should be noted that Tokyo and Pretoria already had diplomatic relations and an ambassador had been sent from Pretoria to Tokyo but officially these were still called consular relations. The league considered this state of affairs unnatural and wanted to try to normalise the hidden diplomatic relations.

And we are going to try to deepen the relationship between Japan and South Africa.[13]

In a forty-five minute meeting with four members of the JAAC on 26 October 1984, Ishihara spoke more frankly. According to JAAC records of the conversation, he made the following reply when asked about his view on honorary White status for the Japanese in South Africa:

> I have read a thesis by a Norwegian scholar that says there is a theory that in regards to certain abilities, Blacks have inferior genes to Whites. In America, efficiency drops when Blacks are employed. Even if Blacks are given the vote, South Africa's future will still be chaotic. Even if they are independent, they can't survive.[14]

When the JAAC members argued that it is silly to consider skin colour and neglect to consider historical background, Ishihara replied:

> People said that Nkrumah and Kenya should be examined ten years after independence but African countries and socialism didn't work. I don't think South Africa is good but there is also the threat of Communist domination in Africa. There is no alternative. Confusion in South Africa has a great influence on our national interest and you have to think in terms of security.[15]

During the course of the discussion, Ishihara also admitted he had visited South Africa in 1982. Since the South Africa ambassador's Tokyo office was nearby, Ishihara admitted that he often came to visit. He also admitted meeting members of the South African business community when they visited Japan the previous year and even went as far as to suggest that the JAAC members should visit South Africa themselves.[16]

The Japanese govenment itself gave tacit approval to the league but JAAC and media criticism eventually forced the

[13] From a letter from the secretary-general of the league to JAAC, translated by JAAC, Tokyo, 1984.

[14] JAAC, 'Minami Afurika Mondai Kenkyujo', *Nanbu Afruika Nenpo*, Tokyo, 1985, p. 30.

[15] *Ibid.*

[16] *Ibid.*, p. 31. Ishihara visited South Africa in 1982 at the invitation of the South Africa Foundation.

group to suspend its public activities in 1985. However, some of the league's members did not give up easily. Parliamentary Vice Foreign Minister Moriyama refused to resign from the league and was backed up by the Foreign Ministry's Middle Eastern and African Affairs Bureau Director-General Miyake Wasuke, who told the *Mainichi* newspaper that the league was not an illegal organisation and it was not strange for her to be a member, even though she was the Parliamentary Vice Minister'.[17] Foreign Minister Abe, however, noted that her position restricted her right to membership and so put pressure on her to resign. This she did on 8 December 1984.[18]

The questionable views of Ishihara and Moriyama are certainly not without precedent within the LDP. During the last decade, many of the party's top leaders have made public pronouncements that have caused international criticism and protest.

In March 1984, Prime Minister Nakasone referred to the 'jazz of African natives' by using a Japanese term for native (*dojin*) that is highly pejorative and suggests primitive, uncivilised people.[19] In 1986 he was reported as having said: 'The level of intelligence in the United States is lower than in Japan due to the considerable number of Blacks, Puerto Ricans and Mexicans.'[20]

Two years later, LDP leader Watanabe Michio angered Americans by proclaiming that they 'use credit cards a lot. They have no savings, so they go bankrupt. . . . there are so many blacks and so on, who would think nonchalantly, "We're bankrupt but from tomorrow on, we don't have to pay anything back."'[21]

Next came the very controversial comments of the then Japanese Justice Minister Kajiyama Seiroku. While touring a Tokyo district mainly populated by prostitutes on 21 September 1990, he exclaimed: 'It is like a bad currency driving out a good currency . . . It is like in America, when

[17] *Mainichi Shimbun*, 8 December 1984 (morning edition).
[18] *Ibid.* (evening edition).
[19] *Asahi Shimbun*, 29 March 1984.
[20] Bruce Iwasaki, '*Ongoing Racial Ignorance*', Daily Yomiuri, 17 October 1990.
[21] Wiley A. Hall III, 'Some Racists Wear Kimonos', *Daily Yomiuri*, 29 September 1990.

neighbourhoods become mixed because Blacks move in and Whites are forced out.'[22]

The comment stirred outrage in the United States and brought a demand for an apology from the African Diplomatic Group in Tokyo.[23] In an effort to calm the outcry in the United States, where the Congressional Black Caucus was calling on Kajiyama to resign, the government despatched MITI Minister Muto Kabun to Washington on a damage control mission.[24] After his return, a Diet members' study group on the problems of Black Americans was set up in December 1988. Even so, the group's only activity seems to have been to request the Ministry of Education to consider including more on the history of Black Americans in Japanese textbooks.[25] Ironically, what was not made public at the time was the fact that Muto himself had been a member of JSAPFL. And only a few years later, on 18 July 1990, former Prime Minister Takeshita also got himself into trouble by referring to Blacks with the derogatory Japanese term 'kuro'.

What is the most telling about all these incidents is that such problematic public pronouncements have not impeded the political careers of these leaders in the least. None of them has had to resign. Rather they have moved up the political ladder unhindered. Nakasone was prime minister for eight years and later became a *de facto* political king-maker. Moriyama eventually became the first woman Minister of Education. Watanabe was appointed Foreign Minister and Vice Prime

[22] Eddie N. Williams, 'Japanese Racism Affects American Black', *Daily Yomiuri*, 21 October 1990.

[23] See Appendixes K-L.

[24] Yoshida Shinzo, 'US Black Congress Call for Kajiyama to Quit, *Daily Yomiuri*, 13 October 1990.

[25] Yabe Takeshi, *Nihon Kigyo Wa Sabetsu Suru*, Tokyo: Daiyamondosha, 1991, p. 130. Certainly there was room for improvement in the textbook field, as these excerpts from a 1977 junior high school English textbook make clear: 'Africa has a lot of natural resources. People in Africa are learning to use them' or 'African people are great musicians, too. When they were taken to America as slaves, they took their songs and dances with them. But they did not know how to play the piano or the guitar. There was no one to teach them. They had no money to buy such instruments. So they made instruments out of animal bones, sticks, and wooden boxes. Soon they mixed their music with the American music that they heard in the New World. This was the beginning of jazz'. *New Horizon English Course 3*, Tokyo Shoseki, 1977.

Minister in the Miyazawa cabinet (Nov. 1991–Aug. 1993) and served until illness forced him to resign those positions in 1993. Kajiyama went on to become secretary general of the LDP and the second-ranking figure in the Miyazawa cabinet, while Ishihara became one of the three new leaders of the LDP in mid-1993, along with Hashimoto Ryutaro and Kono Yohei. In short; making public statements with racist overtones has held none of these figures back in the Japanese political world.

Big business and racism

The negative images and perceptions of Blacks possessed by Japanese business leaders could be considered somewhat strange, as Japan's history of trade and commercial relations with Africa dates back to the late nineteenth century. However, these transactions with Africa were not carried out with Blacks Africans but with White colonial administrators, settler forces, companies from colonial powers and their local agents and middlemen, such as Indian traders in East Africa and Lebanese and Syrians in West Africa, who themselves generally held negative attitudes towards Black Africans.[26]

For Japanese businessmen, relations with Black people have generally been indirect and limited to their role as primary producers of items such as cotton or as actual or potential consumers of Japanese products. Since the 1960s this situation has gradually changed in Black Africa as Japanese businesses began to establish direct partnerships with African businessmen. In South Africa, however, Japan only began to establish contact with Black businesses in the early 1990s. Thus Japanese

[26] *Teikaihatsukoku Keizai Kyoryoku — Afurika Keizai Shisetsudan Hokoku*, Tokyo: Nihon Seisansei Honbu Kokusai Bu, 1967 (not for public sale), p. 94.

[27] Japanese attitudes to Blacks are clearly manifested in relations with the United States. Yabe Takeshi notes Japanese companies try to locate in White areas to avoid contact with Blacks and also avoid dealing with Black enterprises. Also see Kashiwagi Hiroshi, 'Zaibei Nikkei Kigyo no Koyo Sabetsu', *Asahi Journal*, 20 September, 1991, pp. 24-7. In an effort to cope with criticism of such discrimination, Keidanren formed the Council for Better Investment in the United States in 1988. In 1989, the name was changed to the Council for Better Corporate Citizenship and Sony's Morita Akio was named chairman, according to an internal Keidanren document dated July 1990.

businessmen's perception of Black people as lazy, stupid and a low-quality labour force have most probably been influenced, at least in part, by exchanges with the above-mentioned trading partners.[27]

Such perceptions of Black people in general and Black workers in particular are amply demonstrated by remarks made by members of the 1970 Kono Mission to Africa. In the published report on the mission's activities and observations, chairman Kono expressed surprise at the size of the continent and the fact that it was not all jungles; for he had observed many wide plateaus which he felt were suitable for development. Commenting on the people, Kono said:

> Ethiopia is an exception and the Presidents of Kenya, Tanzania and Zambia were very impressive, as were two or three cabinet members. However, most of the leaders displayed a lack of vigour and the common people seemed spiritless but docile in comparison to South-East Asians.[28]

Other economic mission members seemed to hold similar opinions. In the published account of an informal round table discussion among the members on the quality of the local workforce, Kono noted that he found the work habits of the natives were not so bad. Kawai, the president of Nippon Mining, agreed that the labourers worked quite hard, something he hadn't expected. Matsuo of Nippon Kokan K.K. countered that they were not good at the practical application of skills while Kawasaki, the president of Toyobo Company, noted that Black Africans were not yet qualified for middle-management level positions.[29]

While these widespread, negative perceptions may have been inherited initially from European colonialists and Japan's own colonial education system, they have been perpetuated in the Japanese business world and are reflected in the honorary White mentality of businesspeople and politicians alike.

The Springbok Club is an excellent example of the essence of the honorary White mentality in action in the Japanese business community. It demonstrates how many Japanese, while

---

looking down on Blacks and avoiding contact with them when striving to satisfy their desire to be accepted by the supposedly superior White group in South Africa, are able to find this dichotomy not problematic.

Established in Tokyo in October 1977 by a group of Japanese who had once worked in South Africa, it is what is called in Japanese an 'OB Kai' or 'old boys' club', where connections and friendships from the past can be nurtured and maintained. The club's regulations describe its objectives as follows:

> There is an old European saying that goes: 'Those who have drunk the water of Africa will definitely return to Africa.' In Japan it is still an unknown continent and South Africa is known only as the country of gold, diamonds and apartheid. Those of us who have lived in South Africa with our families for business or academic research, or travelled there for sport and tourism are still a minority and it is difficult to find those who really understand us when we talk of this country, blessed with abundant nature and natural resources. This club was created to provide an enjoyable opportunity to meet and speak with companions who can share our knowledge and experience of South Africa and a chance to deepen old friendships, make new friends and increase our knowledge.[30]

Membership is open to the those who have been stationed in South Africa, together with their family members aged eighteen or older, and those who have visited South Africa, provided they are recommended for membership by one member and one official of the club.[31]

The club's activities are listed in the regulations as: quarterly meetings, publishing a club newsletter, a directory of members, sports and hobby activities, participation in research conferences on South Africa, communication with the Nippon Club of South Africa, and a women's auxiliary that would get together with South African women living in Tokyo or visiting South Africans, and other appropriate activities.

[30] Supuringu Bokku Kurabu, *Supuringu Bokku Kurabu Kaisoku* (Zantac), Tokyo, 1977, p.1
[31] *Ibid.*

As the regulations reveal, the ultimate aim of the club is to maintain and promote friendly relations with South Africa through various personal exchange activities. The club's orientation is pro-Pretoria and its interest is in maintaining friendly relations with the White minority ruling class rather than the non-White population or Whites fighting apartheid. This orientation is symbolised by the club's first secretary-General, Makiura Toshio, who, as noted earlier, had links with SAA, SATA and the South Africa Foundation. The annual meeting of the club is regularly held at the South African consulate in Tokyo, and South African companies such as SAA, SATOUR and SAF Marine provide financial support for the group by advertising in the club newsletter.[32]

The Springbok Club began with just ninety members, but with the support of the Nippon Club of South Africa, government officials and the representatives of South African companies in Japan, it developed rapidly and by 1985 had 460 members.[33] The support the club receives from the Nippon Club of South Africa and the important network of connections it was designed to provide are evident in a 1978 address by the Nippon Club president:

> I am happy to report that last October the Springbok Club was formed in Tokyo and that Makiura Toshio, who once lived here, is secretary-general. The club will be reported on in more detail in another issue of the newsletter but I wanted to take this opportunity to mention it and encourage those of you who are returning home to join the club. It is being run by Nippon Club of South Africa old-timers and in future, I would like to keep in close communica-

[32] In 1989, almost a quarter of the club's income came from advertising paid for by these three companies. The 1989 budget report was published in the 1 December 1990, Springbok Club *Newsletter* and showed that of the club's ¥2,933,344 income ¥1,165,000 came from membership dues and ¥650,000 came from advertising by SAA (¥300,000), SATOUR (¥200,000) and SAF Marine (¥150,000). *Springbok Club Kaiho*, 13 (1 December 1990), p. 26.

[33] 'Government Officials Rapped over S. Africa Club', *Mainichi Daily News*, 17 February 1985. The 19 January 1978 edition of the *Springbok* reported the Springbok Club then had 168 members and urged returning businessmen to join.

tion with the club, with the future development of our own club in mind.[34]

The Springbok Club is not limited to the business community alone; it included twenty government officials among its members in 1983: fourteen Foreign Ministry employees (including eight in the diplomatic corps), three MITI officials and three JETRO employes.[35] While their numbers are not large, the presence of government officials definitely has a positive effect on the development of the club. For example, Kosugi Teruo, who once served as consul-general in Pretoria, joined the Springbok Club when he returned to Japan to serve as head of the Immigration Bureau in the Ministry of Justice in 1978.[36] He later went on to become ambassador to Kenya.

The Springbok Club suffered a serious setback in 1985 when the involvement in it of government officials was revealed by the Socialist Diet member Inoue Issei in a House of Representatives' Budget Committee session. Inoue criticised the government for allowing its membership in 'a movement which would eventually promote friendly relations with South Africa'.[37] The public airing of the issue led Miyake Wasuke, director-general of the Foreign Ministry's Middle East and African Affairs Bureau, to promise 'to make proper steps regarding diplomats who have been — or are now — in South Africa, and are still members of the club'.[38]

The incident publicised the existence of the club and served to force it underground, where it could continue its activities unhindered. The healthy state of the Springbok Club became apparent once again in June 1992, when the South African President F.W. de Klerk visited Tokyo. On the day of his

[34] *Springbok*, 70 (15 March 1978).
[35] The names of these officials were included in a list of Springbok Club members released by the JAAC on 1 February 1983.
[36] Moving from the post of consul-general in Pretoria to head of the Immigration Bureau was a route also followed by Kumagai Naohiro in 1987.
[37] 'Government Officials Rapped over S. Africa Club', *Mainichi Daily News* 17 February 1985.
[38] *Ibid*.

arrival (3 June), his first engagement was a two-hour meeting with members of the club.[39]

The racist behaviour of Japanese businesses, typified by the Springbok Club, is hardly surprising considering that the Japanese management system has in general given secondary importance to universal values, such as freedom, equality, social justice and respect for human dignity. This is reflected in the behaviour of Japanese companies in the United States but also within Japan itself. Generally, women workers in Japan serve as a safety-valve — easily expendable cheap labour exempted from the lifetime employment system and offered at best semi-skilled routine work. In addition, Japanese companies are extremely reluctant to hire people with physical impairments, *burakumin* and Korean residents born and raised in Japan, as full-time employees.[40]

Such racist and discriminatory behaviour has been challenged

---

[39] A copy of the itinerary provided to the Foreign Ministry Press Club dated 28 May 1992 shows that on Wednesday 3 June (the first day of De Klerk's four-day official visit), he was to reach Haneda airport at 10 a.m., meet with members of the Springbok Club at the Imperial Hotel from noon until 2 p.m., tour the Sony Media World from 2.30 to 3.30 p.m., meet with the prime minister at 6 p.m. and join him for an official banquet at 7 p.m. The next day he was to meet with LDP officials, the head of MITI and Keidanren officials. Since such an itinerary certainly cannot be worked out unilaterally, it also reflects the importance the Japanese government attaches to the Springbok Club and its functions.

[40] Although women made up 40.7 per cent of Japan's workforce in 1991, they were and still are concentrated in the manufacturing, distribution, restaurant and service sectors and have little chance for promotion. Japan Almanac 1993, Tokyo: Asahi Shimbun, 1992, pp. 80-2. Japan did introduce an Equal Employment Opportunity Law in 1986 but the law has no punitive provisions for violators. See Yayoi Uchiyama, 'Equal Employment Opportunity Law Disappoints Women', *Asahi Evening News*, 25 June 1991. In the tight job market of 1993, many companies stated outright that they were hiring no women that year. All the law allowed the Labour Ministry to do was to give such companies' guidance. See AERA, 10 August 1993, p. 68. In Arai Mitsuo, 'Most Companies Demonstrate Underwhelming Desire to Hire the Handicapped, *Daily Yomiuri*, 13 October 1992 it is noted most companies have failed to reach the goal of raising the number of their physically handicapped staff to 1.6 per cent of their total staff, as required by the Law to Promote Employment of the Disabled. The law was enacted in 1985 but the first punitive action against violators was not taken until 1991. Firms that failed to achieve the goal paid penalties totalling ¥25 billion in fiscal 1991.

by the minorities and various human rights groups, such as the anti-apartheid movement. The development of this latter movement provides an excellent example of the strength of racist attitudes in Japan and among Japanese.

The anti-apartheid movement in Japan

JAAC is the centre of anti-apartheid activity in Japan, but it is not a single, monolithic organisation. It is a federation of smaller regional groups that have sprung up in large metropolitan areas across the country. Most of these groups have fewer than a dozen members; the largest is JAAC Tokyo, with approximately thirty active members.

Each local group operates autonomously, organising its own activities and operating under its own name (JAAC Osaka or JAAC Shizuoka). However, it is JAAC Tokyo that generally represents the organisation internationally. Within the national organisation, JAAC Tokyo is almost always expected to play the role of nation-wide co-ordinator, although the local groups strongly retain their own independence and do not want JAAC Tokyo to go beyond its role as co-ordinator in any way that might compromise their local autonomy. JAAC Tokyo's central role has developed partly because Tokyo is the centre of govemment, business, education, culture and the media in Japan and partly for historical reasons, as JAAC's roots lie in Tokyo.[41]

JAAC's history. The groundwork for the formation of the group was laid at the 1963 Asia-Africa Peoples' Solidarity Conference held in Moshi (then Tanganyika). Japan's first anti-apartheid leader, the late critic and Africanist Noma Kanjiro, described the event this way:

> My first meeting with South Africans took place early in 1963 in Moshi at the foot of Mt Kilimanjaro in East Africa. It was the third Asia-Africa Peoples' Solidarity Conference, and the South African delegates asked for a special meeting

[41] For further research on this subject, see Jinno Akira, 'Current Situation of the Research on Apartheid in Japan', paper presented to the International Meeting (Cat. VI) of University Researchers to Elaborate a Five-Year Research Plan on Apartheid, Beijing, September 1986; and Morikawa Jun, 'Nihon ni Okeru Han Aparutoheito Undo no Kaiko to Tenbo,' in JAAC, *Nanbu Afurika Nenpo 1987-88* Tokyo, 1988, pp. 88-97.

with the Japanese delegation. The South African side was represented by seven men, including Oliver Tambo and Moses Kotane. The Japanese group included former Socialist Party Dietman Mineo Tanaka, his wife Sumiko, a member of the House of Councillors, myself and five others. The South African delegation charged that Japan, a non-White nation, ignored moves to cut off diplomatic relations with South Africa or to impose the economic sanctions suggested in the UN resolutions and was in fact the only non-White nation to have diplomatic relations with South Africa. The atmosphere was not tense but the criticism was severe, and we felt it was a challenge to Japan's progressive forces. I had heard of apartheid but was not well aware of how terrible it was. On behalf of the group, Tanaka said, that when we returned to Japan, we would make efforts to fulfill their expectations but it was an embarrassing moment for us.[42]

This external appeal for support led to the birth of the Japanese anti-apartheid movement in the spring of 1963. The South Africa Anti-Apartheid Planning Committee was set up under the auspices of the Asia-Africa Solidarity Committee of Japan, a broadly based amalgamation of groups, most of which were strongly influenced by the Japanese Socialist (JSP) and Communist (JCP) Parties. The committee's work led to the formation of the Japan Anti-Apartheid Committee in January 1964. It should be noted that although the English names of this group and JAAC are the same, this early group was a separate entity and the predecessor of the current JAAC.

This first anti-apartheid group immediately began a campaign of activities with slogans such as 'Oppose South Africa's Discriminatory Policies', 'Save South African Political Prisoners' and 'Boycott South African Products'. However, the Japanese anti-apartheid movement was soon faced with a serious internal crisis.

The deep rift between China and the Soviet Union caused Japanese left-wing organisations either to divide along pro-Soviet and pro-Chinese ideological lines or to go independent. Since the first Japan Anti-Apartheid Committee existed under the auspices of the Asia-Africa Solidarity Committee and by

[42] *Noma*, pp. 381-2.

extension, the JSP and JCP, it too got caught up in the strife and its activities were temporarily suspended.[43] Yet despite these political confrontations, Noma managed to extricate the anti-apartheid movement to create his own independent study group. This was a small independent 'circle', called the South African Problem Discussion Group, without rigid rules and without strong political or organisational backing — it met only once every one or two months. However, it published a mimeographed newsletter entitled *South Africa Tsushin* (South Africa News).[44]

Small as this circle was, it became the only group in Japan that was seriously and continously involved with the problem of apartheid, and was crucial in stimulating interest in the issue and establishing friendly ties with the ANC and West European anti-apartheid groups.

In May 1969, the Japanese anti-apartheid movement moved into its second stage of development when the Youth Section of JAAC was formed. That consisted mainly of students from the University of Tokyo and members of the Friends of Asia and Africa (Ajia-Afurika no Nakama) group. Gradually, the youth group began to gather support and encouraged the participation of other university study groups and other Japanese groups concerned with conditions in the Third World. Their goal was to support the activities of the South African Problem Discussion Group and to expand the overall activities of JAAC. At first, they concentrated on publishing a magazine called *Afurika o Manabu Zasshi A* (African Studies), but later revitalised activities that had slowed down due to Noma's declining health.

In 1970 a second anti-apartheid group called Comrade Africa was formed in Osaka to serve the Kansai area (the Kyoto-Osaka region). While this group gradually strengthened its ties with the Tokyo sister group, it also developed its own original projects, such as a study of the problem of the Kansai Electric Power Company's importation of Namibian uranium.[45] In the 1980s, this group campaigned with anti-nuclear groups

---

[43] Kusuhara Akira, *Jiritsu to Kyozon*, Tokyo: Aki Shobo, pp. 48-9.
[44] Noma, p. 384.
[45] JAAC Youth Section, *Afurika Kodo Iinkai News*, 20 (1977), pp. 123-6.

in the Kansai region to get the Osaka city government, the largest shareholder in Kansai Electric, to disinvest.

Nevertheless, the Japanese anti-apartheid movement was unable to develop momentum till the middle of the 1970s. Most local citizens' movements were more interested in domestic pollution problems or issues such as the Vietnam war and Korea. Further impetus for the movement did develop in the late 1970s, after Mozambique and Angola became independent in 1975, the Soweto uprising began in 1976 and international criticism of Japan's expanding trade with the Pretoria govenment intensified.

Japan's anti-apartheid movement was also given a big boost by the visit of Nelson Mandela to Japan from 27 October to 1 November 1990. The 'Welcome Mandela' rally held in Osaka on 28 October, organized by JAAC and the Anti-Apartheid Co-ordinating Committee (see below), attracted more than 20,000 participants, the largest crowd ever for an anti-apartheid activity in Japan.

Mandela was originally invited by the Japanese government in order to soften international criticism of Japan's South Africa policy, as well as to secure a place for Japan in the post-apartheid era, but the wide media coverage and the anti-apartheid events served to heighten the Japanese public's awareness of the apartheid problem. For JAAC, however, Mandela's visit produced mixed results. This arose from the gap that had developed between JAAC's expectations and Mandela's actions.

One of Mandela's main goals was to get a grant of $25 million from the Japanese government to cover the cost of repatriating exiled ANC members. With this in mind, Mandela tried to avoid offending the Japanese government by not mentioning issues of domestic discrimination, such as the Ainu, Korean residents and the aforementioned statement by the Japanese Justice Minster Kajiyama which likened prostitutes in Japan to Black Americans moving into White neighbourhoods and spoiling the atmosphere.[46] Mandela also maintained a certain distance from JAAC members.[47]

---

[46] T.P. Reid, 'Mandela rebukes Japan over lack of support for ANC', *International Herald Tribune*, 31 October 1990, p. 6.

Ironically, despite Mandela's careful avoidance of domestic discrimination issues and the red-carpet treatment given to him by the government (he was only the second non-government leader ever invited to address the Diet), Mandela's request for cash was flatly refused by Prime Minister Kaifu on the grounds that Japan 'does not usually give money to foreign political parties'.[48] Instead, he was offered a training programme for Black South Africans. It would invite ten to twenty individuals to Japan in the first year, at a cost to the Japanese government of approximately $77,000.[49]

Mandela vented his dissatisfaction with this response to his request at a press conference on 30 October at the Japan National Press Club in Tokyo. He called Japan's contribution 'insignificant' and noted that Japan's grants to the ANC had amounted to only $1.8 million.[50] In contrast, Mandela had received $5.8 million from India, $10 million from Indonesia, $15 million from Australia and $5 million from Malaysia.[51]

[47] Jocelyn Ford, 'Nelson Mandela's Money Drive Disappoints Staunch Supporters', *Asahi Evening News*, 2 November 1990, p. 3. 'But when Mandela departed Thursday after a six-day visit, he left some of his staunchest supporters with the impression that in Japan he had abandoned the moral high ground for the sake of the mighty yen. "In person, he was everything I had imagined — a true leader of the oppressed," said anti-apartheid activist Jinno Akira, one of the translators of Mandela's biography *Higher than Hope* by Fatima Meer. On stage, however, Jinno says that members of the audience told him the seventy-two-year-old deputy president of the ANC had disappointed them by his hard-sell appeals for a $25 million donation from the Japanese government. "For the public, he should have encouraged the people of Japan to offer not only financial support but also moral support," says Jinno, a member of the Kyoto Southern Africa Solidarity Committee. While many of his long-time supporters had hoped that he would draw attention to discrimination against minority groups in Japan and offer encouragement to political prisoners in Asia, Mandela steered clear of sensitive subjects that he apparently thought might offend Japan... He carefully avoided mention of economic sanctions in an address before the Diet and in a meeting with Prime Minister Toshiki Kaifu.'

[48] Charles Smith and Doug Tsuruoka, 'Mandela's Asian Tour Raises Cash and Backles', *Far Eastern Economic Review*, 15 November 1990, p. 13.

[49] *Ibid.*

[50] Kyodo News Service, 30 October 1990.

[51] *International Herald Tribune*, 31 October 1990, p. 6. For a detailed account of Mandela's visit to Japan, see *Posto Aparutoheito* (Post Apartheid), compiled by the Mandela Kangei Nihon Iinkai, Tokyo: Nihon Hyoronsha, 1992.

However, Mandela did not leave Japan empty-handed. He received a total of ¥ 43 million for the Nelson Mandela Freedom Fund but all of this came from Japanese labour unions, citizens and human rights groups.

It was clear that the Japanese government still considered De Klerk more important than Mandela. As noted earlier, De Klerk was invited to Japan in June 1992 and received state-guest treatment and an audience with the Emperor.

Structure of the JAAC. The JAAC is composed of ten feder-ated groups. Some are merely study groups or grassroots level groups organised by a single individual or a small group of individuals. A survey of the Tokyo membership conducted in 1988 shows that the group is predominately male, middle-aged and well educated. Most members are educators or journalists — a clear reflection of the dearth of broad-based national interest in the apartheid issue in Japan.

Although membership is small, with twenty core members in Tokyo and perhaps twenty more occasional members, the JAAC has a wide range of contacts with other citizens' groups involved in human rights, environmental issues and peace as well as churches and labour unions. These people are basi-cally sympathetic to the anti-apartheid cause and many of them support or attend activities sponsored by JAAC.

JAAC membership is of various political persuasions but over the years, the JAAC has had a co-operative relationship with the JSP (now called the Social Democratic Party), the only Japanese political party to take some positive interest in the problems of South Africa and Namibia, especially under the former party head Doi Takako (1986-91).[52]

In March 1974, the JAAC established contact with the UN Information Centre in Tokyo, which has actively disseminated information on the Southern African question, especially the

---

[52] On the eve of the fortieth anniversary of the Universal Declaration of Human Rights, Doi called for the Japanese government to impose economic sanctions on South Africa and to reject the honorary White Status which Pretoria has bestowed on Japanese as part of a ten-point concrete proposed programme to promote human rights. This plan also included proposals to assist migrant labourers in Japan, overseas students and former colonial subjects of Japan, equal employment opportunities for women and legislation on the use of government overseas economic aid. *Japan Times*, 10 December 1988.

problem of apartheid. The JAAC also expanded its network of connections by establishing contact with the Japan Christian Council and the Korean Christian Church in Japan.

JAAC Tokyo began receiving operating funds from the World Council of Churches Group to Fight Apartheid in 1975.[53] Noma Kanjiro died in that year, but his goal of creating a citizens' movement with a network of international connections was carried on by the new JAAC.

In May 1978 the first national JAAC conference was held in Shizuoka under the sponsorship of the Shizuoka JAAC. After that, the JAAC expanded its activities substantially. Local groups began to multiply (see Figure 6.1)[54] and an Anti-Apartheid Co-ordinating Committee, composed of Japanese human rights groups, Christian groups and other volunteer organisations, was formed in September 1986 to help support the activities of the JAAC. The co-operation of large, prestigious international organisations such as Amnesty International and the World Council of Churches also allowed the JAAC to increase its domestic influence and prestige. In 1987 JAAC Tokyo finally hired its first full-time employee.

Fig. 6.1. JAAC MEMBER GROUPS, 1988

	Established	*No. of active members*
JAAC Tokyo	1969	20
Solomn Mashangu Freedom College Support Group	1984	10
JAAC Osaka (Comrade Africa)	1970	2
JAAC Shizuoka	1977	3
JAAC Kyoto	1981	5
JAAC Nagoya	1985	10
JAAC Matsudo	1986	6
Japan Anti-Apartheid Women's Committee (Osaka)	1986	3
JAAC Hiroshima	1986	6
JAAC Kumamoto	1986	1

Source: Morikawa, *Minami Afurika to Nihon*, p. 210.

[53] See Jinno, 'Problems of Funding' section, p. 8.
[54] This chart was compiled with information obtained from the JAAC's Kusuhara Akira and numerous other members, who provided much valuable information for this study. It should be noted that Nelson Mandela's visit to Japan provided the impetus for the formation of almost a dozen new anti-apartheid groups, from Hokkaisdo in the north to Kyushu in the south of Japan.

Functions of the JAAC. Despite the small membership figures, the JAAC has been able to influence public opinion significantly by performing four important functions: education, personal exchange, research and pressure group activities.

In order to involve the general public in the anti-apartheid movement, the JAAC has concentrated on disseminating information in an attempt to educate the public and mobilise public opinion. The group's activities have included: organising seminars, meetings and events; producing slides, films and videos; printing postcards and posters; and publishing an annual JAAC report. This report also reflects part of the group's research function. This and other JAAC research publications have concentrated on examining the situation in South Africa as well as Japan's involvement in South Africa, such as its trade relations, direct investment and the sale of krugerrands in Japan. Most of the research publications originate with JAAC Tokyo. JAAC publications also serve to disseminate information in English on the situation inside Japan and appeal to international opinion.

Personal exchange and international networking functions encompass such activities as sending personnel to UN conferences on South Africa and Namibia and inviting African anti-apartheid organisations such as the ANC, the Pan African Congress (PAC) and the United Democratic Front (UDF) to Japan, as well as exchange with other anti-apartheid organisations in the Asia-Pacific region. In August 1988, the JAAC sponsored an Anti-Apartheid Asia Oceania Workshop in Tokyo with the support of the UN Special Committee Against Apartheid. Representatives from Australia, Japan, Hong Kong, Malaysia, New Zealand, the Philippines, South Korea, Taiwan and the United States, as well as a representative of the ANC, took part in the three-day conference that focused on the involvement of East Asian nations in the anti-apartheid movement.[55]

The JAAC also hosted receptions for visiting African dignitaries, such as Oliver Tambo and Nelson Mandela, separate from those organised and controlled by the government. Other networking activities have included extending financial and

[55] 'Asia-Pacific Region Targets Apartheid', *Japan Times*, 27 August 1988.

material support to the Solomon Mashangu Freedom College, a school for South African refugee children in Tanzania. In the early 1980s, the JAAC also sold *Africafe* coffee from Tanzania in Japan as a way of thanking Tanzania for its support of South African refugees.

Perhaps the JAAC's most significant role has been as a pressure group. They have held periodic demonstrations in front of the South African consulate and the Keidanren headquaters in Tokyo, requesting that the latter organisation comply with UN economic sanctions against South Africa. The JAAC also carried on a campaign to boycott South African products sold in Japanese supermarkets,[56] such as apple juice and tinned peaches. In 1987 and 1988, the group ran a series of opinion advertisements in South African newspapers and magazines, one of which included the signatures of ninety-nine opposition party members of the Japanese Diet (see Appendix).[57]

Another example of the JAAC's pressure group activities was its response to the formation of the JSAPFL in 1984. As noted above, the JAAC had sent an open letter to the new organisation and received a response in mid-July which included an outline of the group's activities and a membership list which included the names of forty-five LDP Diet members (see Appendix).[58] The JAAC responded by asking a So-

[56] 'Major Japanese Retail Chain Shops Selling S. African Goods', Asahi News Service, 16 June 1988. The article notes that Ito-Yokado, Japan's second largest retail chain, had announced it would be the first major retailer to stop selling South African goods in protest at the country's apartheid policy, although the company did refuse to reveal the value of South African goods sold at the store the previous year. The report said: 'The decision grew out of a March 22 workshop sponsored by anti-apartheid groups and attended by two Ito-Yokado employees assigned to work toward eliminating various types of discrimination within the company. The following day, the employees recommended to store managers that sales of South African goods be discontinued.' The article also noted: 'Seven-Eleven stores operated by a subsidiary of the company will continue to sell apple juice imported from South Africa.'

[57] Opinion ads appeared in the *New Nation*, 10 December 1987; the *Sunday Star*, 13 December 1987 and 10 April 1988 (including the signatures of ninety-nine Diet members); and the *Weekly Mail*, 15-21 July 1988.

[58] See JAAC, *Nanbu Afurika Nenpo 1985*, p. 34.

cialist Party member, to criticize the formation of such a league during proceedings in the Lower House of the Diet.[59] At the end of July, JAAC also sent an interim report on the group in English to the UN and anti-apartheid groups worldwide.[60]

On 26 October of that year, they were able to meet the *de facto* head of the league, Diet member Ishihara,[61] and followed this meeting up by having another Socialist Diet member, Inoue Issei bring up the question again in the Lower House Budget Committee on 16 February 1985.[62] At that time, Inoue asked probing questions concerning the details behind the formation of the group and its connection with the Springbok Club.[63] These activities created so much publicity for the JSAPFL that its public activities were in effect stifled, although it is possible that private connections continued.

It is difficult to evaluate the success of anti-apartheid activities in Japan. The JAAC faced many problems, including attracting new members, identifying funding sources and providing inspiring leadership capable of arousing the public. This difficulty largely arose from the fact that it was relatively unknown nationwide. This was partly due to organisational weakness, but the greatest problem was the general indifference of Japanese society to the issue.[64] This, along with the government's manipulative public relations practices and the media's general lack of a desire to go beyond the government press releases to dig more deeply into the issues,[65] made the job of organising concerted, effective action almost impossible. Considering the numerous problems faced, the JAAC made a remarkable contribution, and the importance of the role it played as a monitor of the

[59] *Ibid.*, pp. 39-40.
[60] *Ibid.*, p. 27.
[61] *Ibid.*, pp. 30-1.
[62] *Ibid.*, pp. 46-8.
[63] *Ibid.*, pp. 45-7.
[64] A symbolic example of this can be seen in the posture taken by the Japan Association for African Studies (Nihon Afurika Gakkai), an academic organisation established in April 1964. Although consisting of scholars of Africa, it never took a public or official stance on the issue of apartheid. However, on 23 May 1987 the general meeting of the Rekishi Gaku Kenkyukai, an association of historians, did adopt and announce an anti-apartheid declaration.

government's activities should not be underestimated. The JAAC was one of the most effective organs for mobilising anti-apartheid sentiment in Japan.

Since the transition to the post-apartheid era became apparent at the end of the 1980s, the JAAC and other Japanese civic groups have continued to call attention to the persistence of invisible apartheid. Further, they actively proceeded with support activities for victims of apartheid in South Africa.[66]

One of the most active of the non-governmental organisations involved is the Japan International Volunteer Centre (JVC) which in May 1992 became the first Japanese NGO to establish an office in South Africa. Among its activities, the JVC is engaged in rural development programmes in the Transkei in co-operation with the Ishinanba Community Development Centre. The JVC is also carrying out projects to help improve the standard of living in the Jeffsville Squatter Camp in Pretoria and provided the Jeffsville Squatters Development Association with support for the construction of a nursery and toilet installation in 1992.[67]

[65] The government's manipulation of the distinctive Japanese press club system is a key issue here. For more on how the press club system works, see Van Wolferen, pp. 93-101; Foreign Press Center Japan, *Japan's Mass Media*, Tokyo, 1990; and Kitamura Fumio, 'Internationalization and Press Clubs — Japan Should Open its Press Doors to Foreign Correspondents', *Daily Yomiuri*, 12 January 1993, p. 9. Needless to say, there were some Japanese journalists who wrote books critical of Japan's negative involvement in the apartheid issue. See Ito Masataka, *Nan-A Kyowakoku no Uchimaku*, Tokyo: Chuo Koronsha, 1971; Shinoda Yutaka, *Kumon Suru Afurika,* Tokyo: Iwanami Shoten, 1985; Idaka Hiroaki, *Minami Afurika no Uchigawa*, Tokyo: Simul, 1985; Jinichi Matsumoto, *Aparutoheito no Hakujintachi*, Tokyo: Suzusawa Shoten, 1989; and Ogawa Tadahiro's photo journalistic study of the liberation struggle in the Portuguese colonies, *No Pincha*, Tokyo: Taimatsu Sha, 1972. The journalist Saso Hiroo contributed greatly to the anti-apartheid movement in Japan through his direct participation and translation activities.

[66.] For example, the JAAC carried out a nationwide fund-raising campaign, beginning in May 1990, to provide financial assistance for the construction of facilities at the Weller Farm School, 30 km south of Johannesburg. With the support of other NGOs, the JAAC sponsored the exhibition of the works of South African photo journalist Victor Matom in the summer of 1993. The exhibit — The People of South Africa' — and his nationwide lecture tour of thirteen Japanese cities received widespread media coverage and attracted many participants nationwide. See JAAC, *Anchi Aparutoheito Nyusureta* (Anti-Apartheid Newsletter), 62 (September 1993), pp. 2-3.

The Buraku Liberation League of Japan established the International Movement Against All Forms of Discrimination and Racism (IMADR) Japan Committee in January 1988 and has carried out various anti-apartheid activities.[68] In the field of education, the People's Education Support Fund, Japan has provided support for purchasing school equipment and the school expenses of some elementary, junior and senior high school students in South Africa.[69]

Japanese NGO activities in South Africa have just recently begun and they are still on a relatively small scale. Their influence on Black society in general is still limited. However, considering that personal exchanges between Japan and Africa, especially in South Africa, have hitherto been limited mainly to diplomats and businessmen, the significance of these free and equal exchanges at the grassroots level, while still insufficient, should not be dismissed.

[67] JVC, JVC Annual Report 1992, Tokyo, 1993, pp. 22-5.
[68] The pamphlet 'Anti-Apartheid Activities by Buraku Liberation League and IMADR (29 June 1991) notes and group 'carried out activities as a leading member of the Campaign Committee on the International Day for the Elimination of Racial Discrimination', including fundraising for the purpose of assisting South African children and publication of a newsletter, Southern African Bulletin (in English).
[69] Brochure of the NGO Forum, Africa New-People Standin Up for Self Reliance, Tokyo, 2-3 October 1993, p. 10.

7

JAPAN AND AFRICA AT THE CROSSROADS

Previous chapters have looked at the interaction of the government, big business and the bureaucracy in the implementation of Japan's African diplomacy in the post-war years. This final chapter examines the current and future prospects of the international relationship — Japan and Africa at the crossroads.

On 5-6 October 1993, the Tokyo International Conference on African Development (TICAD) marked an epoch-making moment in the history of Japan's relations with Africa. Representatives from forty-eight African countries gathered in Tokyo for the conference. Its main themes were economic development and democratisation. Not all African nations were represented: Libya under the Gadafy regime had taken a posture of confrontation with the United States and Western Europe and the Islamicist regime in Sudan were not invited. Liberia and Somalia, being caught up in civil wars, were unable to send delegates. Belgium, Britain, Canada, Denmark, France, Germany, Italy, the Netherlands, Norway, Portugal, Sweden and the United States, together with the EC as a body, took part as well as eight international organisations: the African Development Bank, the UN Economic Commission for Africa, the World Bank, the IMF, the OAU, OECD, the UN Development Programme and the UN University (which is in Tokyo).[1]

According to accounts from participants, the main goal of the meeting was to show the international community's interest in African self-help efforts for economic reconstruction and to reaffirm its support for such measures.

In his keynote address to the conference on 5 October,

---

[1] List of participating delegations, Tokyo International Conference on African Development 5-6 October 1993. Observer status was granted to Australia, Austria, Brazil, China, Finland, Hungary, Indonesia, Ireland, Korea, Luxembourg, Malaysia, Romania, the Russian Federation, South Africa and Switzerland.

Japanese Prime Minister Hosokawa observed: 'We must not allow the needs of Africa to be ignored in any way because of development in other areas of the world', and added that the conference was intended to be a 'high-level forum for serious policy dialogues' that aims to 'cement a firm commitment and provide useful guidelines for African development'.[2] The *de facto* organiser of the conference, Suto Takaya, the Director-General of the Foreign Ministry's Middle Eastern and African Affairs Bureau, contributed an article to the *Japan Times* on the eve of the conference on the orientation of the discussions of economic development and the specific agenda. He noted:

> During this conference, designed to discuss how best to promote sustainable development of the African continent, African countries and their development partners will focus on six themes: political and economic reform; Asian experience and African development; economic development through private sector activities; emergency relief and development; regional co-operation and integration; and international co-operation.
>
> Under the theme of Asian experience and African development, the conference may be able to identify factors that have contributed to the economic growth of East and South-East Asia which might also be relevant to the African context.[3]

On 6 October, the conference closed with the adoption of the Tokyo Declaration on African Development 'Towards the 21st Century'. Outlining the six themes mentioned above, it proclaimed:

> We, the participants of the Tokyo International Conference on African Development (TICAD), consisting of African countries and Africa's development partners, declare with one voice our continued dedication to the development of Africa towards a new era of prosperity. We, therefore, solemnly adopt the present declaration, in the firm belief

[2] 'Hosokawa Pledges Support for Africa Reform', *Daily Yomiuri*, 6 October 1993.
[3] Suto Takaya, 'Tokyo Conference Aims to Lead Rally for Africa Development', *Japan Times*, 4 October 1992.

that it will serve to strengthen an emerging new partnership for sustainable development of Africa based on self-reliance of African countries and the support of Africa's development partners.[4]

Yet what were the real results of the conference? Who got what, and what benefits did they gain? For the African side the results of the conference had more symbolism than substance. While avoiding any large-scale pledge of aid, the donor countries emphasised the principle of self-help and prescribed the Structural Adjustment Programme (SAP).[5] The lessons to be learned from the rapid economic growth of East Asia and the ASEAN countries' experiences were also stressed, as was co-operation between those countries and Africa; in other words, South—South co-operation.

The basic posture of the northern, advanced, industrialised countries was reflected in the policy speech made on 6 October by Japanese Foreign Minister Hata Tsutomu with its restrained offer of aid: 'The economic structural adjustment programs will, in the short term, impose a heavy burden on their people. This adjustment policy, however, is a challenge they cannot avoid if they wish to strengthen the foundations for further economic development.'[6]

The report in the *Japan Times* noted:

> To help reform efforts pushed by economically struggling African nations, Hata said, Japan will provide them with non-project-type grant assistance of between $650 million and $700 million over three years, starting this year. In addition, Hata said, Tokyo will provide Sub-Saharan African nations with $250 million to $300 million in grant

[4] *Tokyo Declaration on African Development — Towards the 21st Century* Tokyo International Conference on African Development, 5-6 October 1993, p. 1. For the full text of the declaration, see Appendix P.

[5] For a critical view of SAP, see Bade Oninode (ed.), *The IMF, The World Bank and the African Debt*, vol.1: *The Economic Impact*, vol. 2: *The Social and Political Impact*, London: Zed Books, 1989, and the paper 'Africa and Orthodox Structural Adjustment Programmes: Perception, Policy and Politics', delivered by Adebayo Adedeji of the African Centre for Development and Strategic Studies, Nigeria to the symposium 'on Challenges of African Development: Structural Adjustment Policies and Implementation', UN University, Tokyo, 1 October 1993.

[6] *Japan Times*, 7 October 1993.

aid, intended to be used to increase water supplies, over the same period.[7]

While the African side made no major gains from the TICAD conference, the Japanese government on the other hand was able to obtain some considerable and direct diplomatic results. Japan was able to display, both on the domestic front and to the international community generally, its willingness and ability to play a major role as an external actor in African international relations. Although the Japanese government was hesitant to admit it publicly, the conference also contributed to the creation of a favourable climate for Japan's campaign to gain a permanent seat on the UN Security Council.[8] It strengthened the image of a country making a contribution to the world community; at the same time, the TICAD diplomatic show gave Japan an opportunity to secure the support of the African states which command fifty-two votes in the UN.

To those used to viewing Japan as a less visible actor in Africa whose diplomatic behaviour quietly followed the lead of the United States and Europe, its move in proposing the conference to the UN as well as hosting it may have conveyed a strong impression that its role had undergone a transformation. This was reinforced by Prime Minister Hosokawa's keynote address, emphasising the wish to build up friendly relations with Africa and further invoking the Tokyo Declaration and its call for a 'new partnership'.[9]

What needs to be determined, however, is if the change in

[7] *Ibid.*

[8] 'Tokyo proposed the present conference at a UN General Assembly meeting in 1991. Many other nations view Tokyo's sudden interest in Africa, with which it has only marginal trade relations, as an attempt to secure African support for its bid to become a permanent member of a reformed UN Security Council, though Tokyo flatly denies such allegations'. *Daily Yomiuri,* 6 October 1993. The newspaper also reported Japan's plans to chair 'three major international conferences aimed at providing financial support to developing countries' in the autumn of 1993. These included the first International Conference on Reconstruction of Cambodia, the Third Mongolia Assistance Group Meeting and the Tokyo International Conference on African Development. *Daily Yomiuri,* 9 September 1993.

[9] See the official text of Prime Minister Hosokawa's keynote address to the African Development Conference, Tokyo: 5 October 1993, p. 2.

the style of Japan's African diplomacy also signals a corresponding change in its substance as well and if so, to what extent? For if the basic framework of Japan's African diplomacy, as outlined above, is maintained, its expanded presence in Africa will not necessarily be seen as having a positive effect. To find an answer to these questions one must examine three aspects of Japan's African policy: its collaboration with the United States and West European countries; the 'key countries' approach; and the shallowness of the political philosophy guiding Japanese policy.

Co-operation with the United States and Europe

Japan's African diplomacy has been characterised by a tendency to follow the United States and Western Europe and there is every likelihood that this tendency will continue. In the unstable international environment brought on by the transition from the Cold War to the post-Cold War era, Japan will need to co-operate with the United States and West European countries to a greater degree than even in order to ensure solidarity with them and thus to secure the foundation of Japan's existence and prosperity. As the 1992 *Diplomatic Blue Book* pointed out.

> In multilateral co-operation, Japan, North America and Western Europe assume particularly-important responsibilities and roles. These countries share fundamental values such as freedom, democracy and market economies, which are also the guiding principles of the international community today. In addition, they account for more than 70 per cent of the world's gross national product (GNP). It is extremely important for Japan, the United States and the European countries to co-operate closely for securing world peace and prosperity based on these fundamental values, thereby extending beyond their bilateral relationships. Without their close co-operation, it would be difficult to effectively address the problems the world faces. The support efforts toward democratisation and market economies in the former Eastern bloc countries and in developing countries are good examples where Japan, the United States and Europe should be working together. Indeed, Japan, the

United States and Europe are undertaking multilateral co-operation from the perspective of achieving world peace and prosperity, as attested to by the Japanese participation in the international assistance to the geographically distant Central and Eastern European countries and by the European participation in the reconstruction of Cambodia in Asia. Against the background of their expanding roles and responsibilities, the policy co-ordination among Japan, the United States and Europe in such fora as the G-7 Summit is increasingly becoming important in both political and economic fields.[10]

Japan's organisation of the TICAD conference is also a product of that tripolar co-operation — or, in other words, a tripolar joint control operation. This joint co-operation was clearly reflected in the composition of TICAD participants,[11] 'the selection of the agenda and priorities, and in the content of the Tokyo Declaration. For example it seems likely that the major reason why Sudan was barred from the TICAD conference was Japan's desire to co-operate with the United States confrontational policy towards the Islamicist forces in Sudan. Consideration of the US and European position can also be seen in Japan's very modest offer of aid.

An economic co-operation policy of this kind is manifest in the speech made by Matsuura Koichiro, Director-General of the ministry of Foreign Affairs Economic Co-operation Bureau, to the Royal Institute of International Affairs in London on 18 July 1989:

There is . . . a worthwhile way to make our efforts more

---

[10] Ministry of Foreign Affairs, *Diplomatic Blue Book*, 1992, p. 15.

[11] 'The Sudanese Embassy in Tokyo issued a press release Wednesday complaining about the country's exclusion from the conference. "An unfair decision has been taken to single out the Sudan and to exclude its delegation from taking part in this event for political reasons that are of no relevance to this conference." Tokyo officials said Sudan was not allowed to participate because major western nations, including Japan, have suspended aid to the country due to its failure to improve its human rights situation. . . .' Washio Ako, 'Africa Talks Bar Some States', *Japan Times,* 8 October 1993. The article also reported a Foreign Ministry official as saying: 'Opposition to Sudan's participation was conspicuous among donor nations, especially the US and some European countries.'

productive and effective. . . Japan's experience as a donor country is limited compared with, say, that of Britain and the United States. We have achieved substantial progress in aid only over the past ten years or so. Japan is still on the learning curve in a number of matters.

In this regard it is agreeable to mention the frequent contacts and fruitful collaboration existing between Japan and Britain. I myself have had the privilege of a very close working relationship with Mr Chris Patten, the Minister for Overseas Development, and my colleagues also have been working closely with their British counterparts at various levels. Today, aid collaboration between Japan and the UK has become a very positive element in the overall bilateral relationship between our two countries.

Let me cite some example of joint activities. In Sri Lanka, Japan and the UK extended co-financing assistance to the Samanarawewa Hydroelectric Power Station Project, amounting to approximately $335 million. For Nigeria, Japan extended roughly $200 million in untied soft loans together with a British grant aid of $100 million as bridging finance for the Nigerian economy. In Mozambique, Japan will join British efforts on the Limpopo Railway Rehabilitation Project by supplying ballast wagons. In Zambia, Japan has supplied facilities and equipment for setting up the Veterinary Department of the University of Zambia and now Japan and Britain are extending their joint technical assistance to this Department. In Kenya and other countries, similar joint efforts are in the offing or will be considered in the future.[12]

It was noted earlier that Japan's presence in Africa is likely to expand greatly in the future; however, this expansion will not be pursued at the expense of the vital interests of London, Paris or Brussels, or the important but not so vital interests of the United States. Expansion in various regions of the continent will be pursued in co-operation with Western Europe and the United States.

However, it is potentially risky and even costly for the Japanese government and *zaikai* casually to follow the general

---

[12] Matsuura, pp. 380-1.

perceptions, judgements and policy proposals of the governing elites of the United States and Western Europe.[13] By doing so, Tokyo will possibly formulate and implement policies that contradict the actual needs and aspirations of the African people, thus recreating Japan's past policy mistakes, such as the pro-White Africa policy and the support of authoritarian regimes in Zaire, Malawi and Kenya. In addition to the immediate self-serving interests of Japan noted above, co-operation with the United States and Western Europe had been a major factor in these moves.

One expert offered this frank criticism of the West European orientation of Japan's Africa diplomacy:

. . . I would like to see Japan express its own viewpoint. Japan is not part of Western Europe. As one of the nations of Asia, it should ask itself: What does Africa mean to Japan? Japan's policy should be born of the answer to that question. . .

Japan will buy its resources from a country no matter what sort of harsh policy it carries out. For example, Zaire, a major producer of cobalt. While President Mobutu is cruel to his own people, for Japan he is an important figure. And behind him is the United States. This basic point should not be forgotten. When you think about Africa you should start from this point. It has been said that things have changed but I would like you to reconsider just how Japan's position has changed. While some scholars have cited change, in reality nothing has changed.[14]

Even after the TICAD Conference, this critical view that nothing has changed still seems to hold true.

[13] For Japanese decision-makers' perceptions of American and Soviet policies in Africa, see Hatano, pp. 13-14. For more on the United States policy in Africa, see Mohamed A. El-Khawas and Barry Cohen (eds), *The Kissinger Study of Southern Africa National Security Study Memorandum 39*, Westport, CT: Lawrence Hill, 1976; Chester A. Crocker, *South Africa's Defense Posture: Coping with Vulnerability*, Washington, DC: Center for Strategic and International Studies, Geogetown University, 1981; and Phyllis Johnson and David Martin (eds), *Destructive Engagement: Southern Africa at War*, Harare: Zimbabwe Publishing House, 1986.

[14] G.C. Mwangi, 'Afurika wa Tokunai', *Ritsumei Review* (November 1988), pp. 42-3.

The key countries approach

With the end of the Cold War era and the fact that it was no longer necessary to support anti-Communist regimes,[15] the themes of economic development and democratisation became the focus of the TICAD conference. Since Japan itself organised the conference, it might have been expected by some that the conference would veer from the key countries approach centring on the Anglophone countries, but such a change does not appear likely in the foreseeable future.

Perhaps the major reason for this is the very strong possibility that Japan will continue to co-operate with the United States strategy for African economic and social reconstruction by encouraging African governments to adopt and pursue the Structural Adjustment Programme (SAP) as well as following the aid plan outlined to the Keidanren CCA by the US State Department's Herman Cohen in 1989. This plan calls for assisting regional economic centres through the strengthening of aid to particular countries in Africa in the hope of developing the economies of surrounding countries as well. If Japan does pursue this approach, its support for certain countries such as South Africa, Nigeria, Kenya and Zimbabwe can be expected to expand, building on the existing close relationships.

In fact, this tendency can be seen in Japan's allocation of ODA to Sub-Saharan Africa in 1992. Only five countires (Zambia, Ghana, Ivory Coast, Tanzania and Cameroon) were given bilateral official development loans in 1992. The top ten

---

[15] Randall Robinson of the lobbying group TransAfrica discussed support for anti-Communist regimes in an interview with the *Los Angeles Times World Report* (reprinted in the 5 June 1993 issue of the *Daily Yomiuri*): 'Historically we have spent the bulk of American foreign assistance on those countries that we thought strategically important to us during the Cold War. These were the least democratic, the most autocratic, the most corrupt. . . basket cases economically and pits of repression. Somalia, Ethiopia, Kenya, Liberia, Zaire, Sudan were the countries over the last 30 years where we spent the vast majority of American assistance, because we didn't care whether they were democratic or not, as long as they satisfied the sole criterion for American support: they were anti-Soviet. . . . Only one of the leaders was elected — Daniel Arap Moi in Kenya — and just once. The rest were unelected and destructive of their societies, and we gave them the wherewithal to do it. . . . We've given many times more for tyranny in Africa than we have for democracy in Africa. . . .'

recipients of grants were Tanzania, Ethiopia, Mozambique, Zimbabwe, Madagascar, Senegal, Nigeria, Zambia, Kenya and Ivory Coast. In technical assistance, preferential treatment was given to Kenya, Tanzania, Zambia, Ghana, Senegal, Nigeria, Malawi, Niger, Zimbabwe and Ivory Coast.[16]

Based on Japan's earlier dual diplomacy and Cold War considerations, Tanzania and Malawi were consistently given key country status and the above data indicates that this attitude has not changed much even after the end of the Cold War. This stems in part from the belief in Tokyo that, as South Africa makes the transition to a multi-racial democratic society, it is considered important that the countries surrounding it also remain stable.[17]

Although it is not reflected in ODA figures, South Africa is also currently considered very important[18] from the perspective of the 'key country' concept. The Japanese government considers it necessary to create a concrete example of an aid success story in Africa.[19] As the largest 'steam locomotive' in Africa with its well-established infrastructure, South Africa offers the greatest possibility for success.

There is also the belief that the development and stability of South Africa will have a positive spillover effect on the rest of Southern Africa and on Black Africa in general. To realise this aid strategy, it is essential to offer economic support to strengthen South Africa. However, the Japanese aid policy towards South Africa faces several practical problems, primarily the method of support. Since Japan has classified South Africa as an advanced country, it is difficult to extend

---

[16] Ministry of Foreign Affairs, *Afurika Binran—Sahara Inan no Kuniguni*, 1993, p. 124.

[17] Information obtained during an interview with a Foreign Ministry official who wishes to remain anonymous.

[18] At the OAU Day Symposium on 'Japan-Africa: A New Economic Partnership for the Future' held 25 May 1994 at the Tokyo headquarters of the UN University, Shinomiya Nobutaka, Director of the First Africa Division of the Ministry of Foreign Affairs, noted: 'In the case of Nigeria and Kenya, some political instability exists. For Japan, South Africa is considered the most important nation.'

[19] Based on information obtained during an interview with a Foreign Ministry official.

ODA except for small-scale technical, medical and educational assistance.

Thus the most likely form of Japanese support for South Africa is *minkan keizaikyoroku* (private economic co-operation), such as trade, direct investment and technical co-operation. But here the government faces a second dilemma: the strong distrust and apprehension inside the *zaikai* towards the policy orientations of Black majority government and doubts about its ability to govern.[20] This has made the *zaikai* reluctant to expand trade and commerce relations to any substantial extent.[21]

The Japanese business community's concern was clearly expressed in the English-language summary of the 1992 Japanese Economic Mission to Southern Africa report. Fujimori Masamichi, the chairman of the CCA and head of the economic mission, said:

> Raising the Black's living standards is absolutely necessary for a complete end to apartheid and for social stability in South Africa. Most Japanese companies are understandably cautious about investments in South Africa because of its fluid political and social conditions. It is hoped, however, that Japanese companies will study as positively as possible what can be done to help bring stability to South Africa through investment or technical co-operation. As an industrialised country, Japan should keep this in mind. The important thing is to begin with small-scale aid to such

[20] The frank opinions of business leaders are revealed in the *Report of the Government Despatched Economic Mission to Southern Africa*, published by Keidanren in co-operation with the Foreign Ministry, December 1992 (in Japanese). Tajima Noriyoshi of Mitsubishi Heavy Industries said: 'I think it is necessary to realise the main causes of Black Africa's current economic stagnation lie with the Blacks themselves.' (p. 175) And Morishita Mitsuyuki, Bank of Tokyo: 'I think it can be said that a high level economy was created by the management ability of the elite White class, who fully utilised abundant mineral resources and the Black labour force. This is in contrast to some other Black African nations that also have abundant mineral resources and Black labour forces but where poor management has caused chaotic economic conditions.' (p. 183)

[21] In the same report, Imamura Akio, director of the Sumitomo Corp, said: 'Frankly speaking, from the perspective of private corporations, if the same amount of time and money is to be invested, we would rather look towards China and the Asian region.' (*ibid.*, p.40)

sectors as tourism, transport, mining, agro-business and consumer goods.[22]

The mission report also suggested:

Many Japanese companies are inclined to withhold investment in South Africa until real signs of political and social stability emerge in that country. Conversely, however, it may be necessary for us to take a certain amount of risks from the standpoint of helping South Africa to achieve political and social stability. In view of the tremendous impact South Africa's stability will have on the whole of the region, the Japanese government should throw support behind private-level efforts for the expansion of investment, trade, and technological and financial co-operation.[23]

At an informal meeting with the CCA in Tokyo on 24 January 1994 Sezaki Katsumi, the Japanese ambassador to South Africa, expressed his dissatisfaction with the passivity of the *zaikai's* position and their lack of sufficient involvement in the period of transition to a multi-racial democratic South Africa:

Japan has not expanded trade or investment in South Africa very much but the United States is extensively expanding and Europe is taking a positive approach. I am often asked by South Africa business and government leaders what Japan is thinking about South African and I answer that Japan has its hands full with the domestic recession at home. But a total of $350 million in ODA has been contributed to Black organisations in South Africa by various nations while Japan has given only $5 million of that — a sum which compares very unfavourably with that of other nations.[24]

In order to encourage and assist the *zaikai's* economic activities in South Africa, the Japanese government announced in June 1994 that it would extend $300 million ODA (about 80 per cent of it in yen loans) to South Africa and proposed to

[22] *Ibid.*, pp. 25-6.
[23] *Ibid.*, p. 19. For a full list of the requests and recommendations by the Japanese Economic Mission to Southern Africa, see Appendix N.
[24] *Keidanren Shuho*, 7 February 1994, pp. 2-3.

get around the fact that South Africa has been hesitant to be included on the Development Assistance Committee (DAC) list by considering the aid exceptional ODA. But even if the *zaikai* resumes large-scale economic co-operation activities and expands them in an attempt to contribute substantially to the expansion of the South African economy, such investment will not necessarily have a significant positive effect on the large gap that exists between the 'haves' and 'have nots' in South Africa.[25] For the short term at least, such activities of Japanese businesses will probably lead to further deterioration of the situation, since Japanese multi-national companies continue to work in partnership with the former White ruling class rather than with the much weaker non-White entrepreneurial class. In general, Japanese business leaders have yet to reassess their past actions and position as honorary Whites in South Africa. They have not come to terms with their strong distrust of the abilities of the Black business community.

Thus it is realistic to conclude that states other than the key countries, most of which fall into the LLDC (least less developed countries) category and are geographically in the Francophone area, will not find it easy to obtain preferential treatment from Tokyo, even if they make the utmost effort to work towards implementation of SAP and democratisation. This may appear pessimistic but given that the Japanese government has deemed it appropriate to allocate only about 10 per cent[26] of its total ODA to Sub-Saharan Africa, it seems unlikely to be proved wrong in the near future.

Political philosophy

The shallowness of the political philosophy that guides Japan's overall diplomacy is demonstrated by the willingness to subordinate anti-colonialism and anti-racism to economic expansionism and, in the past, to Cold War considerations. It can also be seen in the political leadership's inability to deal with the issue of responsibility for Japan's role in the Second World

---

[25] There is also a possibility that Japan's economic aid to the Republic of South Africa will further strengthen the economically dominant and subordinate relationships that exist between the Republic and other Southern African nations.

[26] Matusura *Koichiro*, p. 23.

War and the unwillingness to follow the spirit of the present peace Constitution. see Figure 59.

It has also been demonstrated by Japan's failure to undertake any serious assessment and restructuring of its past policy in Africa, a policy that was sustained by excessive elitism and secrecy. Although the Japanese government has begun to use the catchphrase 'New Partnership', the new policy principles and methodology necessary to guide this principle have yet to be set forth in concrete terms.

Such a lack of self-reflection on Japan's part was apparent in a Ministry of Foreign Affairs publication of September 1993, just before the TICAD conference. It describes the history and extent of Japan's relations with Africa as

. . . .the fruit of relentless efforts: Japan and Africa have not shared a very close relationship either historically or geographically in the past but nevertheless, exchange between the two sides has developed steadily and they have maintained close co-operative ties ever since the Asia Africa Conference, familiarly known as the Bandung Conference, held in Indonesia in 1955.

Needless to say, this development has been brought about by the relentless efforts of both Japan and Africa. Today at a time when Africa, Japan, and indeed the whole world are experiencing tremendous changes, Japan and Africa are being called on to make even greater efforts to bring about the further development of their firm and friendly relationship. For this purpose, it will be most important for them to further deepen their mutual understanding.[27]

Reading between the lines, the tone of the message clearly implied that Japan's relations with Africa have been those of equals and not exploitive. However, as this study has shown that viewpoint is a product of the Japanese government's diplomatic propaganda and wishful thinking.

So the question must be asked: why does the Japanese government not frankly admit the true nature of its African

[27] Ministry of Foreign Affairs, *Japan and Sub-Saharan Africa Hand in Hand Across the Globe,* Tokyo, September 1993, p. 2.

policy in the past and try to construct a new relationship with Africa? Since credibility is considered an important factor in the conduct of diplomacy, Japan should find it necessary to face its history and learn from it. However, Japan has yet to develop a political philosophy that allows it to face the history of its overall diplomacy and take responsibility for it.[28] That it took almost half a century for a Japanese prime minister to be able to make an official admission of his country's role as an aggressor in the second World War is a prime example of this characteristic.[29]

The future of Japan's African diplomacy can be built in part from an acknowledgement of what it has learned from its diplomacy in the Asia-Pacific region. Japan made a considerable contribution both to the US Cold War strategy as a junior partner of the United States along with its simultaneous success in achieving its own national interests. On the other hand, Japan has failed to gain any true friends in the region. This isolation stems from its arrogant behaviour patterns towards other Asian nations, based on the idea that 'might is right' and grounded in its superficial political philosophy.[30] Needless to say, this is incompatible with the tolerant 'forgive but never forget' posture adopted towards Japan by the Asian countries which had been its victims after the Second World War. Half a century later, Japan is still not seen as a truly credible partner in Asia.

An inadequate political philosophy is also observable in the way Japan's African diplomacy has been conducted. It has been

---

[28] For historical reflection on the shallowness of the political philosophy behind Japan's diplomacy, see Iriye, *Nihon no Gaiko*, pp. 171-6. Of course, it cannot be said that Japan learned no diplomatic lessons from the Second World War. However, they were primarily utilitarian lessons—for example, of becoming a merchant state rather than a military power or that it was better to co-operate with the Anglo-Saxon nations than seek confrontation with them.

[29] The Japanese government's stance on the past and the late Emperor Hirohito is seen in this description which appeared in the 1989 *Diplomatic Blue Book*, p. 9. 'The strong international representation at the Funeral Ceremonies was eloquent testimony to the world's great respect for both the Emperor himself and the Japanese Imperial Family as well as evidence of Japan's position in the world, the international interest in things Japanese, and the importance that the world places on Japan.'

[30] See Renato Constantino, *The Second Invasion — Japan in the Philippines*, Manila: 1979.

characterised by elitism and secrecy, despite promotion of the slogan '*kanmin ittai*' (government and people working together).[31] As we have seen in this study, while the government has appeared to encourage the people's participation, in reality, only the country's business elite have been allowed a truly participatory role. The public's role has been merely to provide the applause. Yet there are a few minor exceptions to this gloomy picture.

In order to supplement and lend credibility to its fragile African diplomacy, the government has *allowed* the general public a degree of participation in the implementation process of a policy into which they have had no input. Even so, it is necessary to view these efforts with reservations. The most noteworthy of them has been the establishment of Japan Overseas Co-operation Volunteers (JOCV) in 1965. Many were sent to Africa, and provided support and co-operation in the aid actitivities of NGOs in the late 1980s.

The JOCV's dual function

As the Secretary-General of the JOCV explained in 1985:

> The organisation follows the philosophy of assisting in manpower development, on the firm conviction that it is man who uses and controls machines and benefits by them. On this line of reasoning, all *kyo yokutai* members are instructed to live, speak and eat like anyone else in the communities they are sent to. Their mission is to work selflessly towards the construction of newly developing countries. The areas of service range from basket-weaving to computer operation. To date, members have helped in more than 130 kinds of jobs. In the early years of the JOCV, the majority of volunteers served in the primary industrial areas of agriculture, forestry and fisheries. But this has changed over the years. Today, these areas account for only 26 per cent of the JOCV's activities and the proportion is expected to decline further in the days ahead.[32]

The JOCV provides an official channel for young Japanese

---

[31] Miyake Wasuke (Director-General of the Ministry of Foreign Affairs Public Information Bureau), 'Nihon e no Tadashi i Rikai o Susumeru Tame ni', *Kokumin Gaiko*, 96 (March 1984), pp. 29-32.

[32] *Asahi Evening News*, 18 May 1985.

who wish to dedicate themselves to contributing to the development of developing countries. But there is another aspect to the programme: JOCV is also a useful instrument of support for Japan's Third World diplomacy and aid policy.

The JOCV's function as a diplomatic tool was outlined by former prime minister Kaifu Toshiki in a LDP booklet:

There are many reasons why Japan has come to be able to hold a position of honour in Asia, and I think I can proudly say today that one of the major reasons is the contribution of the LDP Youth Section. . . . Seventeen years ago when [former prime ministers] Takeshita, Uno and myself and others were leaders of the LDP Youth Section, it was the American world policy to send Peace Corps volunteers abroad, and it was agreed that there was no reason why Japan should not do the same. A national meeting of the LDP Youth Section gave birth to the JOCV. . . . it sends 400 volunteers abroad each year (5,000 have already returned) and today 1,200 are serving overseas. It is only natural that they are young members of the LDP Youth Section and support our policies. . . . Thanks to the sweat of the 5,000 young men and women who have served the JOCV, Japan is no longer considered the orphan of Asia and this is a strong reason why these policy efforts should be continued in future.[33]

These excerpts make it clear that the high ideals and energy of young volunteers who want to contribute to the development of the Third World are also being absorbed and mobilised at another level so as to realise specific Japanese national goals. Although Kaifu's claim that all volunteers were LDP supporters was no doubt exaggerated for rhetorical effect, it is clear that the activities of JOCV are directly controlled by the Foreign Ministry through JICA.[34]

[33] Kaifu Toshiki, *Sekai no Naka no Nippon*, To-in Kenshu Shiryo no. 12, Tokyo, 1983, pp. 20-2, 27.
[34] *Asahi Evening News*, 18 May 1985: 'The JOCV recruits volunteers from around the nation in spring and autumn every year. To qualify, they must be healthy men and women aged 20 to 35. Candidates who pass written tests are interviewed for further screening. All successful candidates undergo a three-month training session in Japan, at the end of which they are dispatched to various parts of the world. Their normal period of service is two years.'

Fig. 7.1. J.O.C. VOLUNTEERS IN AFRICA, 1965-92

	Botswana	*Burundi*	*Ethiopia*	*Ghana*	*Ivory Coast*	*Kenya*	*Liberia*	*Malawi*	*Niger*	*Rwanda*	*Senegal*	*Tanzania*	*Zambia*	*Zimbabwe*
1965						3								
1966						11						30		
1967						16								
1968						14						35		
1969						8						53	6	
1970						27						19	6	
1971						13		22				32	3	
1972			38			28		15				20	12	
1973			8			10	7					17	10	
1974			17			15		19				19	9	
1975						31		22				20	15	
1976			12			22		34				13	12	
1977			4	12		20		26				7	23	
1978				18		39		45				16	20	
1979			6	20		44	7	53				17	20	
1980			5	19		61		84			3	19	7	
1981			2	27		41	7	48			8	27	23	
1982			7	30		42	13	49			17	18	21	
1983			8	27		45	9	52	1		12	29	23	
1984			16	31		44	14	49	11		13	31	42	
1985			20	32		67	32	63	4		17	26	33	
1986			14	42		46	23	44	12	5	21	48	50	
1987			21	39		35	21	40	15	6	25	32	46	
1988			12	37		40	29	51	12	23	25	34	41	
1989			17	40		27	15	40	14	5	23	30	40	8
1990			8	34		17		26	17	3	21	28	35	9
1991			1	36	6	23		40	15	2	32	36	27	21
1992	5	6	10	37	3	31		41	18	8	16	32	32	25
Total	5	6	226	481	9	820	170	870	119	52	233	688	556	63

Source: Japan Overseas Cooperation Volunteers brochure, JICA, Tokyo, March 1994, p. 18.

Fig. 7.2. EXCHANGE OF NOTES BETWEEN JAPANESE
GOVERNMENT AND AFRICAN STATES ON SENDING OF
JAPAN OVERSEAS CO-OPERATION VOLUNTEERS

31 March 1966	Kenya
20 October 1966	Tanzania
10 April 1970	Zambia
21 December 1970	Uganda
2 July 1971	Malawi
9 November 1971	Ethiopia
17 February 1977	Ghana
21 August 1978	Liberia
18 April 1979	Senegal
17 May 1983	Niger
1 June 1985	Rwanda
11 July 1988	Zimbabwe
22 December 1989	Ivory Coast
3 March 1992	Botswana
23 March 1992	Burundi

Source: Kokusai Kyoryoku Jigyodan Seinen Kaigai Kyoryokutai Jimu Kyoku, Tokyo: Seinen Kaigai Kyoryoutai Jigyo Gaiyo, March 1994, p. 21; JICA, Tokyo.

Kyoryokutai JOCV activities in sub-Saharan Africa have been given as much or more importance than those in Asia. In 1965, the year after JOCV was established, volunteers were quickly dispatched to Kenya, and by 1985, 37 per cent of all volunteers were allocated to Africa.[35] As can be seen in Fig. 7.2, most of these people were dispatched to a small number of key countries. One country given special consideration was Malawi: as Fig. 7.1 shows, it was constantly given top priority in the allocation of volunteers between 1975 and 1985. The Japanese government has given no official explanation for this but the fact that Malawi was one of the few states in Black Africa that favour Pretoria was clearly a major factor. The Japanese government undoubtedly considered it important to contribute to the stability and development of the Banda regime, which established diplomatic relations with South Africa in 1967.

JOCV volunteers are sent out through a process by which the recipient country requests assistance and an exchange of notes is signed. In the case of Malawi, such a note was signed on 2 July 1971 and the first volunteer was dispatched the following month,[36] just before President Banda's official visit to

[35] *Ibid.*
[36] Seinen Kaigai Kyoryokutai OB Kai, *Seinen Kaigaikyoryokutai Heiwa Butai to Tojokoku Enjo*, Tokyo: Kyoikusha 1978, p. 45.

South Africa and Mozambique in August and September.[37] It appears likely that JOCV technical aid assistance to Malawi was an expression of goodwill from Tokyo in appreciation for its friendly diplomacy with South Africa. The sending of JOCV members to Malawi thereafter increased rapidly, despite the deepening crisis facing White minority rule as African national liberation movements advanced.

The genuine altruism of JOCV members' activities in Malawi and other African countries cannot be denied, but at the same time, although they certainly did not intend it, the volunteers' efforts have indirectly assisted the Japanese government's African policy objectives and played a role in softening criticism of the government's pro-Pretoria policy.

Japanese NGOs: a different breed?

The Foreign Ministry's support of and co-operation with NGOs has also provided the general public with a participatory role, albeit a limited one, in the implementation of the government's African policy. A Foreign Ministry English-language brochure explained economic co-operation with NGOs:

> Japanese non-governmental organisations have focused their operations mainly on Asia, but in recent years they have also increased their activities in such African nations as Mali and Zambia. The main features of co-operation by NGOs are that they make it possible to provide thorough assistance for small-scale projects that involve direct participations by ordinary citizens and that they can carry out assistance at the grassroots level. To support the activities and so on of the NGOs, the Japanese government since fiscal year 1989 has been positively implementing the Subsidy System for NGO Projects and the Small-Scale Grant Assistance.[38]

These positive claims deserve closer scrutiny. In actual fact, the government has established and developed co-operative relations with organisations such as the Africa Society of Japan,

[37] Ministry of Foreign Affairs Public Inforamtion Bureau, *Afurika Binran, 1980*, p. 96.
[38] Ministry of Foreign Affairs, *Japan and Sub-Saharan Africa — Hand in Hand across the Globe*, p. 8.

the CCA, SATA and the Sasakawa Africa Association (SAA). It strains credulity to classify such organisations as NGOs in the commonly accepted definition of the term but the Japanese government does regard them as such.[39] In an overview of Japanese aid, Takayanagi Akio remarked: 'NGOs distributed 0.8 per cent of Japan's ODA but most of these NGOs were not voluntary organisations but extra-governmental bodies and business groups.'[40] He continued:

> The Ministry of Foreign Affairs started a subsidy programme for projects of NGOs (in the sense of voluntary organisations) in 1989, which amounted to ¥236 m. in 1991 — 0.02 per cent of ODA. This was distributed to 47 projects by 24 NGOs. The programme is unpopular among NGOs for its very inflexible criteria and in particular for covering 'hardware' projects, such as buildings and facilities, not 'software' such as human resources and institutional development.
>
> NGOs are also critical of the fact that the programme is project-by-project based, [as well as] the lack of block grants, refusal to cover administrative costs and absence of funding for development education. There is also a government subsidy programme amounting to about ¥600 m for technical co-operation and sending volunteers for six NGOs — not all of which are voluntary organisations.[41]

Indeed, most voluntary NGOs with substantial aid activities did not begin work in Africa till the 1980s; thus their role should not be overestimated. Also, while the government supports the activities of NGOs, its relations with them are far

---

[39] 'The term "NGO" — while still not a household term — is appearing more and more frequently in the Japanese press and has become something of a fashionable term in Japan. It is also, however, increasingly being used inaccurately. For example, at the UNCED Conference, Keidanren, which in most countries would be called a business association, referred to itself as an NGO.' *Kokoro*, Newsletter of the Japanese NGO Center for International Cooperation, 6, 1 (March 1994), p. 1.
[40] Takayanagi Akio, 'Japan's Aid Performance' in ICVA & EUROSTEP, *The Reality of Aid — An Independent Review of International Aid*, London: Actionaid, 1993, p. 33.
[41] *Ibid.*, pp. 33-4.

from equal.[42] NGOs are expected to play the role of subcontractors of a sort within the framework of the government's own ODA policy.

Just how wide is the Japanese government's definition of an NGO and to what degree does a relationship exist between NGOs and ODA policy? An examination of the activities of the Sasakawa Africa Association and its founder, Sasakawa Ryoichi, provides important clues for answering such questions. In recent years the Association has played an important supplementary role in the implementation of Japan's African aid diplomacy. In fact, it was the SAA — along with the UN University, the Ministry of Foreign Affairs and the Japan Society for International Development — that jointly organised a symposium on the 'Challenges of African Development: Structural Adjustment Policies and Implementation', held at the Tokyo headquarters of the UN University on 1 October 1993. The event was considered an important prelude to the 1993 TICAD conference. To quote from its own brochure, the SAA is

. . . a non–profit, tax–exempt organisation, established on 11 March 1986 under Article 60 of the Civil Code of Switzerland for the purpose of increasing agricultural production in Africa.

The origins of SAA date back to 1984 — when famine ravaged 20 African countries. Sasakawa Ryoichi, chairman of the Sasakawa Foundation, was one of the first to contribute to emergency relief activities, but he also wanted to do something about the underlying cause of famine in Africa. He approached the agricultural scientist, Dr Norman E. Borlaug, who was awarded the 1970 Nobel Peace Prize for his work in sparking 'Green Revolution' in India and Pakistan during the 1960s. In 1985, Mr Sasakawa organised the

---

[42] For more on the development of NGOs in Japan, see Kita Yuji, 'Kaihatsu Kyoryoku ni Tazusawaru Nihon no NGO no Genjo to Kadai', *Tokai Seijigaku Kenkyu*, (1989), pp. 11-19; Hiroyuki Yumoto, 'Kokusai Kyoryoku to Volunteers', *Gendai no Esupuri*, April 1994, pp. 83-96; and Mine Yoichi, 'Kusanone Kaihatsu Kyoryoku no Tenbo to Nihon no NGO no Kadai' in Masahisa Kawabata and Sato Makoto (eds), Shinsei Minami Afurika to Nihon Tokyo: Keiso Shobo, 1994, pp. 213-33.

workshop in Geneva to discuss the possibility of establishing a similar process in Sub-Saharan Africa. Dr Borlaug said that, technically, enough research technology and information were available to double and triple food crop yields in most African regions, providing the appropriate agricultural policies and investments were made.

A product of this workshop was an agreement to start projects to transfer improved agricultural techniques to small-scale farmers, with Dr Borlaug providing technical leadership and Sasakawa Foundation providing funding. Based on this co-operation, the SAA was established in early 1986. They were joined by former US President Jimmy Carter, who offered his administrative structure — Global 2000 Inc. — to manage the projects and to work with the governments of African nations to form effective agricultural policies. The first agricultural development projects established in 1986 in Ghana and Sudan were the beginnings of Sasakawa–Global 2000 Projects.

Since 1991, the SAA has taken over the responsibility of administration and management of the projects which had previously been undertaken by Global 2000 Inc., with SAA's Tokyo office administrating the S-G 2000 projects in Ghana, Tanzania, Benin, Togo and Nigeria.[43]

The SSA is one of the many charitable projects funded by the Sasakawa Foundation and initiated by its head, the late Sasakawa Ryoichi, considered by many to be one of the world's most generous philanthropists. From the early 1970s, Sasakawa took some of the huge profits accrued through his motorboat racing empire and established numerous foundations under the umbrella of the larger Sasakawa Foundation.[44] Promoting himself as a kindly, white-haired, grandfatherly figure, he extolled the virtues of patriotism, filial piety and charitable works. This is the face of Sasakawa the philanthropist, the man many accused of seeking to erase his previous image

---

[43] English-language brochure of the Sasakawa Africa Asociation, February 1993, p. 1.
[44] Kaga Koei, 'Saigo no Don-Sasakawa Ichizoku no Anto', *Bungei Shunju* August 1993, p. 187. (Sasakawa Ryoichi died in July 1995. His organisation was renamed the Nippon Foundation in December 1995.)

and secure a Nobel Peace Prize for himself.[45]

This previous image is seen by many to be more godfatherly than grandfatherly; it is the face of the Japanese don of the right-wing and *yakuza* (gangster) worlds, the *'kuromaku'* (mover behind the scenes) who has 'bragged publicly that he was a drinking companion of Japan's leading godfather (the late) Yamaguchi-gumi head Kazuo Taoka'.[46]

Sasakawa's long and chequered career (much of it still not clearly documented) began as the leader of a fledgling right-wing party called Kokusui Taishuto in the 1930s. An ultranationalist whose activities during the war years are scantily documented, he was classified after the war as a Class A war criminal and sent to Sugamo prison.

After the war, Sasakawa used his special connections with Kishi[47] and other right-wing leaders to build a motor-boat gambling empire. In 1962, he set up the Japan Shipbuilding Industry Foundation which was able to secure government approval to manoeuvre 3.3 per cent of the motor-boat racing profits, which would otherwise have gone into government coffers, into his own private foundation to be used for the public interest or charitable purposes. It is currently estimated the Foundation takes in $6.6 billion a year.

The cordial relations that Sasakawa and his organisations enjoy with the Ministry of Foreign Affairs typifies 'Japan Inc'. and its back-scratching alliance between   government, the bureaucracy and big business (and right-wing organisations) which is even

[45] *Ibid.*, pp. 186–7. Kaga also notes that Sasakawa was an ardent admirer of Mussolini and met him in 1939 dressed in a formal black kimono bearing his family crest. (p. 184)

[46] David E. Kaplan and Alec Dubro, *YAKUZA: The Explosive Account of Japan's Criminal Underworld*, London: Futura Publications, 1988, p. 99.

[47] 'Kishi was held as a Class A war criminal by the Americans, but left Sugamo along with Kodama and others who were mysteriously released on December 23, 1948. Kishi then staged one of the world's greatest political comebacks. He was depurged in 1952 and immediately entered politics. By allying himself with key rightists within the government, and through a series of shrewd manuevers, Kishi soon moved to centerstage. He became secretary general of the LDP in 1955, and pushed on to become deputy prime minister under Yoshida's successor, Tanzan Ishibashi. But when Ishibashi was forced to resign after only three months for health reasons, Kishi went all the way. Backed by Kodama's money and influence, he staged an unstoppable run for prime minister... This mutual assistance among the Sugamo graduates would mark Japanese electoral politics for years to come.' (*ibid.*, p. 101)

built into the structure of the diplomatic system. Clearly, then, a Japanese-designated NGO can have very strong links with government and a less than selfless agenda.

Private organisations have clearly come to play a supplementary role in Japan's aid diplomacy towards Africa. While the government has set up close relationships with pro-establishment organisations like the CCA, the Africa Society, SATA and the SSA, it has also expanded co-operative relationships with groups that can be considered NGOs in the true sense of the word.

In order to implement what it considers an efficient and effective economic co-operation policy,[48] the government has deemed it necessary to bring the activities of these NGOs, many of them previously operating independently, within the framework of the country's African diplomacy. To do this the government has used the incentive[49] of enlarged financial assistance to such organisations. Many NGOs have responded positively to this approach since, compared to the pro-establishment organisations, most NGOs face a lack of both funds and personnel and are caught in the bind of trying to meet increased requests from the African side.[50]

The NGOs' co-operative overtures to the government accelerated after the birth of the coalition government in August 1993, but there has been little evidence of any change in Japan's African diplomacy since the emergence of the coalition (which

---

[48] Ministry of Foreign Affairs, Economic Co-operation Bureau (ed.), *Wagakuni no Seifu Kaihatsu Enjo*, vol. 1, p. 264.

[49] 'As the dollar amount of Japanese ODA skyrocketed, government officials have found themselves in the limelight, and Japanese ODA has come under closer scrutiny. With a budget of over US$ 9 billion, and a staff of around 1,600, the Ministry of Foreign Affairs found it prudent to turn its attention to the efforts and expertise of the NGOs at work in developing countries. The first Asian NGO Forum in March 1987 was significant in the fact that the Ministry of Foreign Affairs supported the cost of travel for the participants from abroad.. It seems that an NGO-government dialogue had begun. But is has been a slow-moving process. The central issue for JANIC and others has been the maintenance of independence and freedom from government intervention. At present, almost all official aid in grant form from the Japanese government "is tied". For example, if the government agrees to fund the building of a hospital in the Philippines, it comes with the condition that Japanese contractors are used in the construction. Up to this point, no government money has been given to NGOs for use entirely at their own discretion.' *Kokoro*, 1, 1 (1989), pp. 4-5.

in fact crumbled after Hosokawa Morihiro's resignation in the spring of 1994). Hosokawa's speech to the TICAD conference, which was composed by the Foreign Ministry, showed that there was no major change in the large role the bureaucracy plays in the formulation and implementation of Japan's African diplomacy.

The Hosokawa government's replacement by that of Hata Tsutomu in the spring of 1994 must surely have reassured the Foreign Ministry on this area as well, since the new Prime Minister, his Foreign Minister Kakizawa Koji and the Chief Cabinet Secretary Kumagai Hiroshi all share the distinction of having been founding members of the JSAPFL (see Appendix J).

In March 1994 the Japan Volunteer Center and other NGO groups formed the Africa-Japan Forum and stated its objectives:

Long-term objective

The long-term objective (purpose of forming a network) is to develop a mechanism and structure in which official funds can be directed to the activities of the local people, community-based organisations and NGOs. It means also that Africa-Japan Forum will submit concrete suggestions or recommendations making [sic] influence on the policy of Japanese government on aid to Africa. However, on those purpose [sic], it is essential, first of all, that Africa-Japan Forum has a broad network and has credibility to be able to use official funds. From that point of view, the following are given priority as main objectives:

Intermediate objectives

1. To create a forum on African development in Japan—

   (*a*) to establish, in Japan, a network on Africa regardless of

---

[50] 'One of the most crucial problems for Japanese NGOs is that of weak financial resources. On the one hand, it is difficult for NGOs to expect substantial donations from the general public. In contrast with countries like the United States, where the role of philanthropic activities is recognised and well supported by individuals, Japan has had very limited experience of private initiatives playing a principal role in the field of public welfare. By and large, it has been the government which has been the caretaker of public welfare. Private donations have functioned as something essential only during emergency relief occasions. It is also true that individuals have very little tax incentives to donate. 'The Current Situation of Japanese NGOS' *Kokoro*, 1, 2 (1989), p. 3.

each other's position, such as NGOs, researchers, academics, university professors, school teachers, foundations, all kinds of agencies, private companies, official development organisations, international organisations, people who are interested in African issues, etc.;

(*b*) to enhance activities of Japanese NGOs working on Africa;

(*c*) to promote Japanese society's better understanding on Africa regarding its society, culture, history and critical situation today.

2. To build a partnership between Africa and Japan

(*a*) to establish a network between NGOs in Africa and those in Japan.

(*b*) to enhance activities for better mutual understanding;

(*c*) to take practical actions to assist African NGOs and Japanese NGOs;

(*d*) to support South-to-South network.

3. To work with the international community on African development

(*a*) to keep co-operation [sic] and form networks in the international network on African development as the representative of Japan.[51]

Despite these goals and the intentions of the participants, the Japan-Africa Forum faces a major risk. In order to receive the government's approval for the NGO use of ODA funds, it may be forced to take an approach which accommodates the government and pro-establishment organisations. In other words, it may be forced to abandon its important role as a watchdog of government activities.

This is not to say that all NGO co-operative relationships with the government necessarily follow this kind of pattern. If NGOs overlook the various problematic aspects of Japan's past

[51] Published by the Secretariat of the Africa-Japan Forum, Tokyo; February, 1994, pp. 2-3.

and present diplomacy, especially its aid policy, they will undoubtedly continue to attract criticism.[52]

The leaders of NGOs, who feel that the expansion of co-
operation may lead to expanded contributions from the government, may be miscalculating the true value of the NGOs.
On the one hand, this thinking tends to underestimate the
importance of their role as a government watchdog[53] and their
function as organisations designed to educate and correct the
Japanese public's poor and distorted image of Africa, as well as
to set up grassroots-level personal exchanges. Secondly, such an
approach overestimates the importance of NGO aid activities
in Africa. For despite representing impressive individual efforts,
Japan's NGO aid contributions are really just a small drop in
the ocean.[54] A change in the direction of the NGOs could also
lead them to veer from their previously emphasised goals. Like
the relationship between Africa and Japan, Japanese NGOs are
also at an important crossroads.

[52] Unfortunately, the Africa-Japan Forum's programme of activities does not
appear to include a plan for monitoring and critiquing the problematic
activities of the Japanese government and *zaikai*. Also at the 2-3 October
1993 NGO Forum 'Africa Now,' which served as the opportunity for the
establishment of the Africa-Japan Forum and which was held immediately
before the TICAD conference, criticism of Japan's past South Africa policy
and of its economic support for authoritarian regimes in Black Africa was
carefully avoided.

[53] A good example of a Japanese NGO, other than the JAAC, performing
important watchdog activities can be seen in the case of the Narmada Dam
Project in India: 'A pair of Japanese NGOs, led by Professor Sumi Kazuo
of Yokohama University, were part of the movement which blocked the
continuation of the Narmada Dam Project in India. The project, which
had received approval for a US $450 million loan from the World Bank,
was due to receive an additional 2.85 billion yen (US $19 million) from
the Japanese government for hydro-electric power generating equipment.
Friends of the Earth Japan and the Japan Tropical Forest Action Network
(JATAN) held a symposium to bring public attention to the project which
would have flooded approximately 50,000 hectares of land and displaced
100,000 people. Three environmental activists came from India to gain
support for the movement against the dam project. . . . The decision to
discontinue the loan was one of the few times that aid officials reversed
a policy decision. Also significant was the fact that the government action
preceded the World Bank's decision to halt the loans, a series of events
which usually occur in reverse.' *Kokoro* (JANIC), 2, 2 (September 1990),
p. 3.

Finally, there is the question of the Japanese government's inability to come up with a new set of principles to guide its policy in Africa. Anti-Communism and economic expansionism had served as the guiding principles of its African diplomacy but the *raison d'être* for the former ceased when the Cold War ended, leaving only the latter.

Economic expansionism has been interpreted by the Japanese government as meaning that it is possible for Japan to make a contribution to the economic reconstruction of Africa through economic support. Japan asserts that this support would come through such avenues as the allocation of ODA and the investment and import expansion activities of private companies. However, the important issues that separate Japan and Africa are not restricted to co-operation in the economic field alone but also include such political questions as how to create equal and mutually beneficial relations. The guiding principle of economic expansionism alone is not enough, but what new political principles should be introduced?

Japan needs to set a new course based on the democratic values and principles of freedom, equality, social justice and respect for human dignity. First, democratisation must be present in African countries to support economic reconstruction. Secondly, Japan must adopt a more egalitarian way of thinking and behaving in Africa in order to change its basically racist policy into one that is impartial and confers mutual benefits.

Thirdly, it is necessary to control the problems of economic expansionism, such as human rights violations and environmental destruction carried out by Japanese multi-national corporations

---

[54] In a speech to the Interaction Annual Meeting, Ito Michio, Secretary-General of the Japan NGO Center for Interanational Cooperation (JANIC), outlined the activities of Japanese NGOs: 'Total expenditure for projects by 74 NGOs amounts to ¥ 4.5 billion, or approximately US $35 million. Of these 74 NGOs, project budgets range from US $11million (for the Japan Committee of UNICEF) to US $40,000 per organisation. By region he pointed out that twenty Japanese NGO groups are concerned with Africa (Ethiopia 4, Kenya, 3, Zaire 3, and Tanzania 3) but Africa, which includes some of the most needy regions of the world, receives minimal assistance, as only 4 or 5 of the 20 NGOS mentioned are faily active.' Ito Mishio, 'Strategic Issues for the 1990s Challenges to PVOs in an Interdependent World', speech at interaction Annual Meeting, Danvers, MA, May 1989.

in the name of economic development.[55] Fourthly, the democratic constitution introduced after the Second World War has the widespead support of the Japanese public and it is ideal for the conduct of grassroots-based diplomacy. Yet the possibility that the Japanese government will introduce democractic notions as the guiding principles of its African diplomacy is remote, since the government has yet to show any sign of wishing to reassess its past policies of dual diplomacy or *kanzai ittaishugi*. It will be up to the Japanese people themselves to find a way in future of monitoring and imposing democratic control on Japan's African diplomacy.

The Tokyo Declaration on African Development included the following statement:

> Convinced of the advent of a new international era, we, the African participants, reaffirm our commitment to pursue and further strengthen political and economic reforms, in particular democratisation, respect for human rights, good governance, human and social development and economic diversification and liberalisation. To achieve sustainable, broad-based economic growth, we, the participants of TICAD, believe that more open, accountable and participatory political systems are vital, including a stronger role for civil society.[56]

These laudable goals directed at the African countries are certainly no less relevant and applicable to Japan itself.

---

[55] The Tokyo Declaration cited two goals — economic development and democratisation — and suggested that Africa could learn from the experiences of East and South-East Asian nations. But the claim is hardly convincing when one considers that, generally, the rapid economic growth in these countries was carried out under authoritarian political systems that offered a favourable investment climate to multinational corporations and through the establishment of internationally competitive, export-oriented assembly industries. For a comprehensive analysis of Japanese multi-nationals in Asia, see Pacific-Asia Resource Center, Indonesian Study Group, *Indonesia no Nikei Takokuseki Kigyo*, Tokyo Ajia Taiheiyo Shiryo Centa (PARC), 1980. For a critical examination of the 'development from above' strategy and Japan's ODA policy, see Suzuki Yuji, *Tonan Asia no Kiki no Kozo*, Tokyo: Keiso Shobo, Tokyo: 1982.

[56] *Tokyo Declaration on African Development Towards the 21st Century*, Tokyo International Conference on African Development, 5-6 October 1993, p. 2.

There is an African proverb that says when two elephants fight, the grass cries. It is applicable not only to the African people seeking the road to peace and prosperity under the joint control of Japan, Europe and the United States pressing down upon them, but to all those who seek a just world order.

POSTSCRIPT

The main body of this book was completed in December 1993. Since then, one major event has had a profound influence on Japan's African diplomacy. That, of course, was the establishment of a government of national unity in the Republic of South Africa on 10 May 1994 under the leadership of Nelson Mandela. (For a detailed list of what the Japanese government considers to be its major post-TICAD initiatives in African diplomacy, see the 7 March Ministry of Foreign Affairs report, Appendix Q.)

Several of the problematic aspects of Japan's response to the new South Africa in 1994 and 1995 deserve mention here Japan's initial reaction to the new government was to take a 'wait and see' approach. For example, in a choice that did lead to some domestic criticism at home, it did not send one of its leading political figures to attend the ceremonies marking President Mandela's inauguration but instead chose to send the then Defence Minister Nakanishi Keisuke bearing the title of 'Ambassador on Special Mission'.

Part of the reason for the government's passive approach no doubt lay with its distrust of the ANC's ability to govern and its reconstruction policy for South Africa—the RDP. However, when the United States and Europe quickly accelerated their reentry into South Africa and Mandela's domestic and foreign policies showed he was prepared to follow a moderate course, these fears were soon alleviated. Japan was reassured by Mandela's plans:

(1) to solidify political stability by extending a policy of reconciliation to the former white ruling class;

(2) to pursue economic management emphasing enlargement of the economic pie by gaining the participation and cooperation of the former white ruling class rather than instigating a sweeping change of the colonial economic and social structure;

(3) gradually to dismantle the legacy of colonial rule and apartheid (Such as the redistribution of land from large white

landowners to black peasants); and
(4) internationally to apply a policy of reconciliation to countries that formerly cooperated with the Pretoria regime in order to acquire official development assistance, markets and the capital, machinery, equipment and technology of the multinational corporations of the world's leading economies the United States, Japan and the EU states.

Japan's first major offer of support to the Mandela government was an economic cooperation plan announced on 2 July 1994 just before the Naples Summit held on 8—10 July 1994. The most detailed description of the package yet released appeared in a Reuter report in the 9 October 1994 edition of Tokyo's *Asahi Evening News*: 'The package comprises $500 million in export-import loans at 4.24% interest to be repaid over ten years, $500 million in guarantees for Japanese investors coming to South Africa, a $250 million, 3% loan repayable over twenty-five years with a seven-year grace period and $50 million in grant aid. Of the entire package, $30 million is for projects for which only Japanese companies can tender, and the remainder untied.'

The problematic aspects of such a package will be mentioned later, but the intended public relations strategy behind this South African aid was revealed quite openly by the Deputy Minister for Foreign Affairs, Ueda Hideaki, of the Ministry's Economic Cooperation Bureau before the 25 July 1994 meeting of Keidanren's Committee on Sub-Saharan Africa when he noted: 'This [the aid package] was made public at the summit. The response was good and the timing was right, I think.'

The second overture of support to the Mandela government came during the economic mission to South Africa of the Keidanren Committee on Sub-Saharan Africa between 27 November and 1 December 1994. (Previous Keidanren missions to southern Africa and South Africa were dispatched in April 1991 and May 1992.) The forty-five member, high-powered economic mission of 1994 was led by the Committee's newly elected chairman, Kasahara Yukio, President of the Japan Energy Corporation. During its visit to South Africa, the mission announced cooperative support for the RDP in the 'kanzai ittai' tradition.

The press release the mission issued in Johannesburg on 1

December 1994 describes what efforts the Japanese economic community was ready to make:

> The South African economy accounts for nearly 40 percent of the economy of the sub-Saharan region as a whole, and Japanese business leaders are aware that it will play a very important role in the future economic development of the region. They also have high regard for the top priority that the Reconstruction and Development Programme has placed on economic development and on correcting the disparities that exist in the country, and they applaud the all-out effort to build a new country that is being made under President Mandela. Through expanded economic interaction, such as trade, investment and technical cooperation, Keidanren hopes to cooperate actively in the national reconstruction being promoted by the Mandela administration. Keidanren will endeavor to actively promote cooperation especially in the areas of education, human resource development and training in collaboration with its members and the government of Japan.

The third manifestation of support was of a political and diplomatic nature. It came in the form of a press release from the Ministry of Foreign Affairs Second Africa Division. Issued in Japanese only, the release, dated June 27, 1995 (the week before Mandela's third visit to Japan), is a frank admission of how the Ministry views South Africa. It covered four main points. First it professed support for new developments in Africa: 'Japan welcomes a "new wave" of post-Cold War African efforts for democratization, national reconciliation and sound nation building and wishes positively to support such moves. A representative example of this is the invitation to visit Japan extended to the South African President which demonstrates our position both domestically and internationally.' It should be noted that the press release's stated support for the so-called 'new wave' efforts are neither new — they have been trumpeted since 1960, the 'Year of Africa', nor convincing in the light of Japan's actions on colonial and apartheid issues and its support for dicatatorial regimes in Black Africa — reflected in Japan's statement of mere 'regret' at the execution of Ken Saro-Wiwa in November 1995 (see Appendix R).

The second point dealt with support for President Mandela:

'In order to move from its apartheid past and maintain a unified, multicultural nation and stable development, strong leadership based on President Mandela's charismatic appeal is indispensable. President Mandela is currently confronting difficult political problems such as establishment of a new constitution, rectification of the large disparity in the domestic economic and relations with the Inkatha Freedom Party, but our nation displays its support for the President's leadership.'

The third point was a show of support for the RDP, and the fourth point was affirmation that increased cooperation between the two countries on African development, United Nations reform, nuclear non-proliferation and other global problems is necessary to move the new partnership between Japan and Africa into the twenty-first century. The press release emphasised quite clearly that South Africa (accounting for 40% of the GDP in sub-Saharan Africa) held the principal position in economic development on the African continent and that stability and development in South Africa is indispensable for the development of not only southern Africa but Africa's development as a whole. Relations with South Africa are the linchpin of Japan's African diplomacy.'

It is important to look at these press release pronouncements in the context of the way Japan generally conducts its foreign policy: it is rare for the Japanese government to express public support of a specific leader or regime so explicitly. In its post-Cold War era African Diplomacy, Japan clearly views its relations with Africa's regional power, South Africa, as paramount.

As has been made clear in this book, Japan's African diplomacy, while paying considerable attention to the intentions and interests of certain key countries in black Africa, has historically given South Africa an especially high priority. However, it is important to note that this frank press release represents a public revelation of the government's intended shift from this somewhat 'multipolar' approach to an approach, centred on South Africa.

With such a statement of support behind him, President Mandela's 2-6 July 1995 state visit included meetings with top political, government and economic leaders and an audience with the Emperor (denied him on his previous visit) and his statements during his stay were limited to reflecting a political realism that emphasised increased cooperative bilateral relations and requests for direct investment.

But Japan's new South Africa-centred African diplomacy is not without its problematic aspects. The first is that while Japan is stressing the importance of direct investment and the fostering of black entrepreneurship as a means of contributing to South Africa's stability and development, reluctance on the part of the *zaikai* does not augur well for this approach as can be seen in the report of the Keidanren Economic Mission to the South Africa in December 1994, issued in January 1995. The following is an extract from the English-language summary:

> While it is expected there will be an increase in Japanese private-sector investments, especially in the mineral resources sector, the South African government representatives expressed their hope that Japanese investments will be made in high value-added and export-oriented sectors that would contribute to strengthening South Africa's economic international competitiveness. However, the mission fears that such Japanese investments would not take place in the immediate future.
>
> Furthermore, the South African government representatives expressed their hopes that Japanese investments would contribute to expanding employment opportunities and increasing the incomes of black South Africans, who account for more than 70% of the population. Specifically, the mission was urged to promote joint ventures projects with black South African entrepreneurs to encourage the development of small and medium enterprises. However, without the governmental assistance, Japanese corporations will face difficulties to meet such expectations.
>
> Recognizing that such investments are most desirable to support economic reconstruction and development efforts, which was initiated by President Nelson Mandela, the Keidanren mission believes that the Japan International Development Organization Ltd (JAIDO), established by Keidanren and the Japanese Government, may be a suitable actor to seek for ways and means for implementing these projects. For example, should support of the Japanese government be available, JAIDO may be able to cooperate with such institutions as the southern Africa Enterprise Develop-

ment Fund (SAEDF), newly established by the US government, in developing joint projects for South Africa.

The content of the Japanese government's $1.3 billion aid package for South Africa is also problematic. The lion's share of the package is comprised of loans and insurance while the outright grants make up a small percentage of the package and the trade insurance is designed to protect the economic penetration efforts of Japan's own corporations. MITI's International Trade Insurance Division section chief Masahiro Fujita clearly defined the true meaning of trade insurance at an informal meeting of Keidanren's Myanmar Research Group on 25 May 1995 when he noted: 'Trade insurance is different from the government's economic cooperation. It is a form of support for private business' (see Keidanren's *Keidanren Kurippu* (Clip), no. 11, 8 June 1995, p. 29).

Secondly, the new South Africa-centered approach conceals Japan's deeprooted pro-white orientation clearly demonstrated by Japan's decision to invite President F.W. de Klerk as a state guest in June 1992 even when it was already clear by then that the establishment of a black majority government was imminent. Behind the pro-White orientation is Japan's long and intimate relationship with the previous Pretoria government and the distance it maintained from non-white South African Society. It is also seen in the reality of the new South Africa, i.e that while the minority whites have lost their political monoply, they have maintained their dominant position in the economic, administrative and military spheres, and it is Japan's judgement that to maintain stability and development in South Africa and Southern Africa, it is not only necessary but most effective to make use of the strength—especially the economic strength— of the White minority. The Japanese government attempts to justify, in the name of political realism, strengthening relations with the white minority. But will this have the positive spill-over effects the government claims, or is it more likely, in the short-term and midterm at least, to increase the gap betwen the 'haves' and the 'have-nots' in South Africa?

There is also the question of whether the shift to a South Africa-centred approach, together with renewed close collaboration with the United States and Europe, will have a positive or negative effect on Japan's African diplomacy and African international relations in general. There is a very real possibility that Japan will use the goals of economic development and democratisation as a reason for supporting Pretoria and that this action will naturally contribute to the maintenance and expansion of a stratified regional order with South Africa's neighbours on the periphery. In terms of Africans relations in general, would the development of vertical international relations with African states under the umbrella of a new *Pax South-Africana* order be desirable?

And do African states wish for Japan's involvement in the promotion of such a process? For many of the countries of black Africa that have received only token interest and support from Tokyo since their independence, it is likely that the new direction willbe hard to accept. In the framework of Japan's Africa diplomacy, the shift to a South Africa-centred approach is likely to lead to even further bipolarisation in Japan's interest and support for Africa. It will leave many of the black African nations at the bottom of the priority ladder, allocating them to a position where their disappointment with Japan is likely to increase.

The emergence of such a state of affairs can only have a negative effect on Japan's overall African diplomacy. Japanese decision makers would do well to recall the sentiments and aspirations of the people of Black Africa reflected in the words of the Arusha Declaration:

> We have been oppressed a great deal, we have been exploited a great deal and we have been disregarded a great deal. It is our weakness that has led to our being oppressed, excploited and disregarded. Now we want a revolution - a revolution which brings to an end our weakness, so that we are never again exploited, oppressed or humiliated. (Julius K. Nyerere, *Freedom and Socialism*, Oxford University Press, 1968, p. 235)

It is time for the Japanese government, and Japanese society in general, to take these aspirations to heart and reflect on what course Japan should follow in Africa Japan should now make efforts to define its own vision of what its Africa diplomacy should be and develop a sense of proportion in the execution of that vision. The Japanese government's current South Africa-centred aid activities do not reflect a sense of proportion but the lack of it. Directing the lion's share of its aid to Africa's 'steam locomotive', South Africa, may have its merits, but Japan, as the world's number-one aid donor needs to consider Black Africa and other regions of the world as well. It is quite reasonable to suggest that it could double its current African aid allocation, which stands at around 10% and also pursue a much more active exchange of people, information and knowledge not limited to southern Africa. It could begin with a visit to Black Africa by the Japanese prime minister — an event that has yet to take place.

The tendency to minimise information on Africa while strengthening coverage of South Africa is very apparent in the Japanese mass media. It is a tendency that led the Gabon Ambassador, Vincent Boule, to ask Japanese newspapers and news organisations to 'devote more coverage to West Africa, especially positive aspects of life there' (*Asahi Evening News*, 2 July 1995).

In order to realise a more balanced approach to Africa, Japan must domestically activate debate and bring democratic control to its African diplomacy. However, the framework of Japan's new South Africa-centred policy which appeared suddenly and has been the subject of no public debate, not even in the Diet, suggests that the vision and sense of proportion that are so badly needed cannot be expected to emerge in the near future.

January 1996

APPENDIXES

A

CHRONOLOGY OF RELATIONS BETWEEN JAPAN AND SOUTH AFRICA, 1910-1993

1910   Ieppe Julius of Cape Town named Honorary Japanese Consul.

1912   Actual trade with South Africa begins.

1914   Japan's economic presence in South African market crystallises during the First World War.

1916   Japanese government sends first trade mission to South Africa.

1918   Japanese consulate opened in Cape Town.

1919   Japan supports South Africa's desire to integrate South West Africa at Paris Peace Conference.

1926   Kobe, Japan/Durban, South Africa sea route opened.

1930   Japanese begin to receive Honorary White status in South Africa.

1937   Sharp increase in South African wool imports to Japan; the two nations reach a pre-war peak in trade. Diplomatic relations established and Japanese embassy opened in Pretoria.

1941   December: Union of South Africa declares war against Japan.

1948   Trade with South Africa resumes.

1951   San Francisco Peace Treaty signed. US-Japan Security Treaty concluded.

1952   Japanese consulate opened in Pretoria.

1960   January: Revised US-Japan Security Treaty.

1961   Japan and South Africa agree to re-establish diplomatic relations. South Africa's Minister of Interior reaffirms Japan's Honorary White status before South African Parliament. JETRO office opened in Johannesburg. Nippon Club of South Africa established.

1962   South African consulate opens in Tokyo. Toyota sets up motor assembly factory in Durban.

1963   Postal agreement between Japan and South Africa signed.

1964   Japanese consulate re-opened in Cape Town. Japanese School of Johannesburg opened.

1968 Japan Airlines (JAL) opens Johannesburg office. Japanese government announces prohibition of direct investment in South Africa. Japan and South Africa sign Air and Sea Mutual Tax Exemption Agreement.

Japan's trade with South Africa increased drastically after the mid-1960s and criticism of Japan surfaced in the United Nations. From the late 1960s to early '70s, major Japanese trading companies opened branch offices in Johannesburg and Japanese automakers and electrical appliance manufacturers began to set up factories in South Africa.

1970 Japan's Kansai Electric Company concluded an agreement to import Namibian uranium. South African mission headed by Dr T.F. Muller, the chairman of ISCOR, visited Japan and asked for Japan's co-operation on Sishen-Saldanha Project.

1974 Japanese government announces restrictions on cultural, educational and sports exchanges with South Africa.

1975 SAA and SATOUR open offices in Tokyo. UN Council on Namibia mission visits Japan and asks Japanese government and *zaikai* for their co-operation.

1977 South Africa and Japan sign a fishery agreement. The Springbok Club (Japan-South Africa Kyokai) is established in Tokyo.

1978 Japan loses election for non-permanent seat on UN Security Council. Former Japanese Consul in South Africa, Kosugi Teruo, named head of Immigration Bureau of Japanese Justice Ministry.

1980 Sale of krugerrands begins in Japan.

1981 Full container ship service on Japan-South Africa sea routes begins.

1982 Japan becomes South Africa's largest export partner.

1983 Number of Japanese tourists annually visiting South Africa reaches 10,000 mark.

1984 Japan-South Africa Parliamentarians Friendship League formed and six members make official visit to South Africa. Japanese School in Johannesburg enlarged. Japanese government and business community organise African Famine Relief Campaign. South Africa Traders Association (SATA) established in Tokyo by twenty Japanese companies with interests in South Africa. Eight major trading companies play a central role.

1985 South Africa gives Japan favoured nation status. Japanese government announces ban on export of computers to South

African police and military and restrictions on the import of krugerrands.

1986 Japanese government barely wins election to a non-permanent membership on the UN Security Council. Head of Japanese Foreign Ministry's Second Africa Division dispatched to Zambia to meet with ANC. South African government officials visit Tokyo in succession: Tourism Minister (June), Finance Minister (August) and Foreign Minister Botha (September). As part of sanctions against South Africa, government refuses to import pig iron and steel products (except for advance orders under contact). Bishop Desmond Tutu visits Japan and appeals to Japanese public to take interest in apartheid problem in South Africa. Japan becomes South Africa's biggest trading partner.

1986 Japan imports almost half of Western World's production of gold (580 tonnes). Half is used for commemorative coins issued to mark sixtieth year of Emperor Hirohito's reign.

1987 Bank of Tokyo announces withdrawl from South Africa. Oliver Tambo of the ANC visits Japan as well as Rev. Allan Boesak. Japanese government pledges $400,000 for the start of an assistance programme for South African Blacks. Approval for ANC office in Tokyo granted. Japan is South Africa's biggest trading partner for second consecutive year. Former Japanese Consul in Pretoria, Kumagai, named head of Immigration Bureau of Japanese Justice Ministry. SAA flight originating in Taipei crashes near Mauritius with several Japanese on board; brings to light active fishery transactions between Japan and South Africa.

1988 UN General Assembly resolution criticises Japan for being largest trading partner of South Africa. US Black Congressional Caucus sends letter of protest to Prime Minister Takeshita over Japan's trade presence in South Africa. UN Special Committee on Apartheid chairman announces his regret over Japan's increase in trade with South Africa. MITI announces it is 'technically difficult' to create guidelines for restraint on trade with South Africa and that it does not feel the necessity to do so. Advertisement opposing apartheid is placed in South Africa's *Sunday Star* newspaper, signed by JAAC, Sohyo (General Council of Trade Unions of Japan), the Social Democratic Party of Japan, 25 organisations and 133 individuals, including Diet members from Japan's opposition parties. Tokyo ANC office is opened.

1989 SATA and *zaikai* begin fundraising campaign for establishment of the Japan-South Africa Fund to assist South African Blacks.

1990   27 November-1 December: Nelson Mandela visits Japan and appears at anti-apartheid events sponsored by JAAC and civic groups nationwide. His request for support for ANC is turned down by Japanese government.

1991   22-27 April: Keidanren economic mission visits South Africa. Upon return, Japanese government is asked to lift its economic sanction measures against South Africa.

June: Japan decides to lift restrictions on investment and finance in South Africa and to resume operations of commercial airliners between the two countries.

1992   June: South African President F.W. de Klerk visits Japan and treated as a state guest.

1993   October: Japanese goverment hosts TICAD conference in Tokyo. Civic groups organise NGO Forum 'Africa Now', held in Tokyo immediately preceding TICAD conference.

B

AFRICAN EMBASSIES IN TOKYO

Country	Established
Ethiopia	April 1958
Ghana	May 1960
Nigeria	October 1964
Congo (Zaire)	July 1967
Central African Republic	June 1968
Gabon	December 1968
Liberia	February 1969
Madagascar	March 1969
Ivory Coast	September 1969
Tanzania	February 1970
Guinea	December 1972
Zambia	August 1975
Senegal	September 1975
Kenya	January 1979
Rwanda	May 1979
Benin	April 1981
Djibouti	April 1981
Zimbabwe	March 1982
Somalia	October 1982
Cameroon	January 1988
Mauritania	July 1989

Source: Compiled by the author with data from Ministry of Foreign Affairs, *Afurika Binran—Sahara Inan no Kuniguni*, 1990.

C

NUMBER OF JAPANESE COMPANIES
ESTABLISHED IN AFRICA

	Total	Up to 1969	1970-9	After 1980
Morocco	5	–	4	–
Tunisia	1	–	–	1
Egypt	8	–	4	4
Sudan	3	1	1	–
Mauritania	2	–	1	–
Senegal	3	–	3	–
Sierra Leone	1	1	–	–
Liberia	128	1	66	34
Ivory Coast	5	–	4	1
Ghana	3	1	2	–
Burkina Faso	1	–	–	1
Nigeria	40	7	23	9
Niger	1	–	1	–
Cameroon	4	–	–	3
Gabon	2	–	2	–
Congo	1	–	–	1
Zaire	6	–	6	–
Ethiopia	3	2	1	–
Kenya	7	2	4	1
Uganda	2	2	–	–
Tanzania	7	6	1	–
Mozambique	1	–	1	–
Madagascar	4	1	1	1
Mauritius	2	–	2	–
Zimbabwe	1	–	–	1
Zambia	3	–	3	–
Swaziland	2	–	2	–
Total	246	24	132	57

Source: Keidanren Economic Co-operation Department internal document, *Waga Kuni to Afurika Chiiki to no Keizai Kankei*, Tokyo, 17 June 1986.

D

JAPANESE COMPANIES WITH OFFICES
IN SOUTH AFRICA

*List provided by Japanese Foreign Ministry in reply to request made
by Japanese Diet member*

C. Itoh & Co., Ltd
Nissho-Iwai Corp.
Toyo Menka Kaisha, Ltd
Nichmen Corp.
Chori Co. Ltd
Meiwa Trading Co., Ltd
Yamazen Co., Ltd
Toyoda Tsusho Kaisha, Ltd
Matsushita Electric Trading Co., Ltd
Mitsubishi Corp.
Mitsui & Co., Ltd
Sumitomo Corp.
Kanematsu-Gosho Ltd
Kinsho-Mataichi Corp.
Taiyo Bussan Co., Ltd
Sansei Trading Co., Ltd
Tokyo Shosha
Happy World SA Ltd
Toyota Motor Corp.
Toyo Kogyo Co., Ltd
Mitsubishi Motor Corp.
Hino Motor Ltd
Nissan Motor Co., Ltd
NGK Spark Plug Co., Ltd
Sanyo Kokusaku Pulp Co., Ltd
Nippon Yusen Kaisha
Mitsui OSK Lines Ltd
Nippon Kaiji Kyokai
Hanshin Air Cargo Service
Taiyo Fishery Co., Ltd
Federation of Japan Tuna Fisheries Co-operative Associations
Nippon Suisan Kaisha, Ltd
Bank of Tokyo (Reportedly retired)
T. Kakiuchi & Co., Ltd
The Kyodo News Service

List compiled with information from Nippon Club of South Africa.

Ajinomoto Interamerica
African Adventures
Japanese Resturant Fuji
Japan External Trade Organisation
Marumi-ya (Pty) Ltd
Sanko Kisen (USA) SA (Pty) Ltd
Sanyo Electric Trading Co., Ltd

Companies with offices in South Africa listed in the 1986 edition of Kaigai Shinshitsu Kigyo Soran (Directory of Japanese Companies Overseas), Tokyo: Toyo Keizaisha

Fuji Electric Co., Ltd
Furuno Electric Co., Ltd
Toyoda Machine Works Ltd
Nissan Diesal Motor Co., Ltd
Isuzu Motors Ltd
Hitachi Construction Machinery Co., Ltd
Mori Seiki Co., Ltd
Okuma Machinery Works Ltd
Washino Machine Co., Ltd
Fanuc Ltd
Ikegai Corp.
Shibusawa Tekkosho
Komatsu Ltd
Hitachi Seiki Ltd
Tanabe Kakoki Co., Ltd
Tsubakimoto Chain Co.
Marubeni Corp. Maekawa Mfg. Co., Ltd
Hitachi Ltd
Sharp Corp.
Toshiba Corp.
Sony Corp.
Nippon Seiko KK
NTN Toyo Bearing Co., Ltd
Janome Sewing Machine Co., Ltd
Koyo Seiko Co., Ltd
Nippon Kokan K.K.
Sumitomo Electric Industries Ltd
Bridgestone Corp.

Appendixes

Information obtained from other JAAC sources

Fuji Photo Film Co., Ltd
Konica Corp.
Hanshin Electric Railway Co., Ltd
Daihatsu Motor Co., Ltd

Source: Information compiled by the JAAC, 1986.

E

KEIDANREN COMMITTEES

(Special Committee for) Promotion of Political Reform
Corporate Ethics
General Economic Policy
Administrative Reform
International Co-ordination of Economic Policies
Fiscal and Monetary Policies
International Finance
Taxation
International Taxation
Statistics
Industrial Affairs
Competition Policy
Energy
Environment and Safety
Natural Resources
Information and Telecommunication Policy
Quality of Life and Consumer Affairs
Distribution
Transportation
Private Initiative
Housing and Land Development
Concentration Problems in Tokyo
Agricultual Policy
Industrial Technology
Oceanic Resources
Life Science
Corporate Finance
Economic Legislation
Corporate Management and Disclosure
Foreign Relations
Foreign Trade
Economic Co-operation
Trade in Services
International Industrial Co-operation
Foreign Affiliated Corporations
Promotion of GIF
Public Affairs
Corporate Philanthropy

Promotion of Inter-Cultural Understanding
Visual Communications for Industry and Culture
Economic Research
Ad Hoc Committee on the Japan-US Structural Talks
BIAC (Business and Industry Advisory Committee to the OECD)
 Japan

Bilateral relations committees

Japan-Canada Economic Committee
Committee on Japan-EC Relations
Committee on Japan-EFTA Relations
Japan-Greece Economic Committee
Committee on Co-operation with Eastern Europe
Committee on Co-operation with Asia
Japan-Mexico Economic Committee
Japan-Brazil Economic Committee
Japan-Venezuela Economic Committee
Japan-Colombia Economic Committee
Committee on the Middle East
Japan-Algeria Business Cooperation Committee
Japan-Tunisia Business Cooperation Committee
Japan-Turkey Economic Committee
Japan-Iran Economic Cooperation Committee
Committee on Co-operation with Africa (name changed to Committee on Sub-Saharan Africa, May 1994)
Defence Production Committee
Space Activities Promotion Council
Committee on International Co-operation Projects

Bilateral relations committees organised by Keidanren and other economic organisations

Japan-Thailand Trade and Economic Committee
Japan-Indonesia Economic Committee
East Asia Businessmen's Conference, Japanese Committee
Japan-Hong Kong Business Co-operation Committee
Japan-Soviet Business Co-operation Committee

Source: Keidanren (ed.), *Keidanren 1991*, Tokyo: June 1991, pp. 5-12 (English).

Role of Committee on International Co-operation Projects

The committee will determine whether particular projects proposed by individual companies and international organisations are qualified as Keidanren projects. After the decision by the committee, JAIDO will make pump-priming investments in joint-venture projects with developing countries up to about 10% of the total equity participation by Japanese side. The committee's secretariat is located in the Keidanren headquarters.

The concept of the whole system is illustrated in the chart.

F. ORGANISATION OF KEIDANREN INTERNATIONAL CO-OPERATION PROJECT PROMOTION SYSTEM

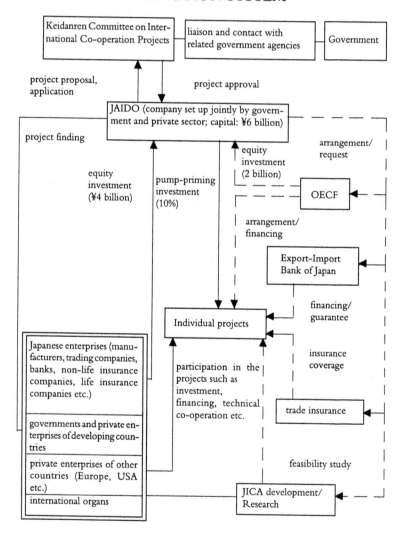

Source: *Keidanren Review*, no. 116 (April 1989).

G. DIRECT OVERSEAS INVESTMENT BY INDUSTRY AND REGION, END 1982 (CUMULATIVE) (unit: US $1m.)

	North America		Latin America		Asia		Middle East	
	No. cases	Amount	No. cases	Amount	No. cases	Amount	No. cases	Amount
Manufacturing industry								
Foods	311	367	96	154	335	176	1	0
Textiles	115	217	142	372	635	1,002	3	4
Lumber-pulp	73	426	38	189	252	162	—	—
Chemicals	151	384	112	521	637	990	21	1,009
Iron, non-ferrous	100	435	83	1,037	510	1,487	10	59
Machinery	294	417	111	296	545	367	6	10
Electrical machinery	301	1,141	105	273	859	643	5	12
Transport machines	59	614	42	488	180	350	5	4
Others	313	250	98	103	990	623	16	39
Total	1,717	4,250	827	3,435	4,943	5,800	67	1,137
Non-manufacturing industry								
Agriculture/forestry	136	233	173	163	321	235	3	2
Fisheries	62	85	80	83	140	83	5	1
Mining	210	776	134	1,404	164	5,383	9	39
Construction	151	166	62	142	260	128	45	28
Commerce	4,188	5,332	478	651	1,664	652	48	12
Finance/insurance	124	1,546	92	470	182	360	15	50
Services	696	627	126	237	472	1,115	12	4

[continued overleaf]

	North America		Latin America		Asia		Middle East	
	No. cases	Amount	No. cases	Amount	No. cases	Amount	No. cases	Amount
Shipping	46	25	447	1,140	52	78	3	2
Real estate	138	426	12	10	14	39	—	—
Others	856	1,182	850	1,060	505	500	31	85
Total	6,607	10,398	2,454	5,359	3,774	8,573	171	223
Establishment/expansion of branch offices	265	92	47	35	465	142	35	1,117
Real estate	2,005	485	99	23	169	37	1	2
Grand total	10,594	15,225	3,427	8,852	9,344	14,552	274	2,479

	Europe		Africa		Oceania		Total	
	No. cases	Amount	No. cases	Amount	No. cases	Amount	No. cases	Amount
Manufacturing industry								
Foods	32	44	29	8	42	57	846	806
Textiles	81	156	50	39	8	6	1,034	1,795
Lumber-pulp	1	0	1	0	75	122	440	899
Chemicals	68	158	8	16	18	99	1,015	3,176
Iron,-non-ferrous	295	171	25	82	84	338	1,107	3,608
Machinery	99	145	—	—	21	30	1,076	1,265
Electrical machinery	87	226	7	5	11	21	1,375	2,322
Transport machines	15	115	5	8	12	242	318	1,822
Others	102	166	8	6	25	70	1,552	1,258
Total	780	1,181	133	154	296	985	8,763	16,952

Non-manufacturing industry								
Agriculture/forestry	2	0	12	7	164	84	811	723
Fisheries	4	2	72	57	101	46	464	358
Mining	9	859	126	556	187	1,274	839	10,291
Construction	16	40	13	19	13	12	560	536
Commerce	1,364	1,455	21	5	353	376	8,116	8,482
Finance/insurance	173	1,288	13	3	31	85	630	3,802
Services	94	125	53	520	77	90	1,530	2,717
Shipping	7	1	97	396	6	6	658	1,649
Real estate	9	37	1	—	14	9	187	521
Others	221	947	351	777	155	385	2,969	4,937
Total	1,899	4,755	758	2,340	1,101	2,367	16,744	34,016
Establishment/expansion of branch offices	164	171	11	1	11	10	998	1,568
Real estate	180	38	21	2	70	7	2,538	595
Grand total	3,023	6,146	923	2,507	1,478	3,370	29,063	53,131

Source: Foreign Press Centre, Japan, *Direct Overseas Investment Registered during Fiscal 1982*, Tokyo: Ministry of Finance, May 1983, p. 5.

H. NUMBER OF A.O.T.S. REGULAR TRAINING PROGRAMME TRAINEES, 1959-90

ASIA (34,717)

Country	No.	Country	No.	Country	No.	Country	No.
Afghanistan	37	Bangladesh	401	Bhutan	12	Brunei	59
Cambodia	67	China (PRC)	4,914	China (Taiwan)[a]	1,122	Hong Kong	737
India	1,878	Indonesia	5,791	Korea, South	4,312	Laos	45
Macao	12	Malaysia	4,181	Maldives	20	Mongolia	21
Myanmar	250	Nepal	86	Pakistan	929	Philippines	1502
Singapore	2,178	Sri Lanka	679	Thailand	4,555	Vietnam	654
Others	275						

MIDDLE EAST (2,093)

Country	No.	Country	No.	Country	No.	Country	No.
Bahrain	81	Iran	430	Iraq	351	Israel	2
Jordan	37	Kuwait	177	Lebanon	31	Oman	78
Qatar	74	Saudi Arabia	432	Syria	63	UAE	139
Yemen	198						

AFRICA (2,399)

Country	No.	Country	No.	Country	No.	Country	No.
Algeria	130	Angola	12	Benin	3	Burkina Faso	3
Cameroon	6	Burundi	19	Canary Is.	8	Central African R.	5
Congo	2	Comoros	4	Djibouti	6	Egypt	436
Gabon	125	Ethiopia	3	Gambia	1	Ghana	159
Ivory Coast	12	Guinea	18	Kenya	173	Liberia	38
Madagascar	99	Libya	20	Malawi	28	Mali	5
Mauritius	10	Mauritania	47	Morocco	17	Mozambique	6
Nigeria	17	Niger	437	Reunion	5	Rwanda	15
Seychelles	22	Senegal	4	Sierra Leone	7	Somalia	14
Tanzania	99	Sudan	167	Togo	17	Tunisia	12
Uganda	40	Zaire	21	Zambia	63	Zimbabwe	39
Others	25						

LATIN AMERICA (3,800)

Antigua	8	Argentina	325	Bahamas	8	Barbados	8
Belize	1	Bermuda	6	Bolivia	75	Brazil	1,530
Cayman Is.	4	Chile	98	Colombia	144	Costa Rica	71
Cuba	174	Dominica	3	Dominican Rep.	29	Ecuador	72
El Salvador	109	French Guiana	1	Grenada	7	Guadeloupe	2
Guatemala	75	Guyana	10	Haiti	9	Honduras	56
Jamaica	21	Martinique	3	Mexico	357	Montserrat	3
Neth. Antilles	20	Nicaragua	12	Panama	56	Paraguay	61
Peru	238	Puerto Rico	9	St Christopher & Nevis	7	St Lucia	10
St Vincent	5	Suriname	4	Trinidad & Tobago	61	Uruguay	13
Venezuela	95						

OCEANIA (384)

Cook Is.	2	Fiji	42	French Polynesia	3	Kiribati	6
Marshall Is.	13	Micronesia	18	Nauru	2	New Caledonia	5
Northern Marianas	20	Palau	5	Papua New Guinea	174	Solomon Is.	8
Tonga	4	Vanuatu	12	Western Samoa	12	Others	58

EUROPE (448)

Cyprus	33	Greece	63	Hungary	69	Malta	13
Poland	76	Portugal	9	Spain[b]	13	Turkey	61
Yugoslavia	10	Others	101				

Total 43,841

(a) up to 1972. (b) up to 1984.

Source: Association for Overseas Technical Scholarship, Guide to AOTS, Tokyo, Foreign Press Centre, 1991, p. 4.

J

MEMBERS OF THE JAPAN-SOUTH AFRICA PARLIAMENTARIANS FRIENDSHIP LEAGUE (JSAPFL), 14 July 1984

Chairman: Nikaido Susumu (Vice President of LDP)

Vice Chairman: Hasegawa Takashi (former Transport Minister)

Secretary-General: Ishihara Shintaro (former Director-General of Environment Agency)

Secretariat: Shiina Motoo

Members from the Lower House of the Diet (all LDP members)

Aizawa Hideyuki
Aichi Kazuo
Aino Koichiro
Ishibashi Kazuya
Uekusa Yoshiteru
Uemura Senichiro
Etoh Takami
Obuchi Keizo
Ohomura Joji
Kakizawa Koji
Kosaka Tokusaburo
(former Transport Minister)
Kondo Motoji
Sakurai Shin
Shiga Setsu
Shiojima Dai
(former Construction Minister)
Takahashi Tatsuo
Takeshita Noboru
(Finance Minister)

Nikai Toshihiro
Tomono Taketo
Nakagawa Shoichi
Nakagawa Hidenao
Hata Tsutomu
Harada Shozo
Hiranuma Takeo
Fujimoto Takao
Hori Kosuke
Muto Kabun
Morita Hajime
Yamazaki Heihachiro
Yamashita Tokuo
Yosano Kaoru
Sato Takashi
Ozawa Tatsuo
Tosuka Shinya
Kumagai Hiroshi
Kitagawa Masayasu

Members from the Upper House of the Diet (all LDP members)

Ishii Ichiji
Sato Eisaku
Moriyama Mayumi (**Parliamentary Vice Minister for Foreign Affairs**)

Ishimoto Shigeru
Hayashi Hiroko

Source: This list was obtained directly from the JSAPFL by the JAAC.

K

RESPONSES TO JUSTICE MINISTER KAJIYAMA'S STATEMENT

October 12, 1990

Mr Kabun Muto,
Member of the Diet, Japan,
Minister of International Trade & Industry,
1-3-1 Kasumigaseki,
Chiyoda-Ku,
Tokyo, Japan

Your Excellency:

I have learned, with great regret, of the derogatory remarks made by your colleague, Justice Minister Kajiyama, on Friday, September 21, 1990.

The Minister, after observing a night-time raid by police and immigration authorities on foreign women for alleged prostitution in the Shinjuku district of Japan, the Minister stated, 'it is like in America, when neighbourhoods become mixed because blacks move in and whites are forced out . . . . they ruin the neighbourhood in the same way.' I find these remarks unbecoming of a public figure—they are racist and unacceptable.

As a Member of Provincial Parliament in Ontario, Canada, I hereby lend my strong support to the African Diplomatic group in Japan. I also support the Congressional Black Caucus' request for the immediate resignation of Minister Kajiyama.

Sincerely,

ALVIN CURLING,
M.P.P. Scarborough North

CONGRESSIONAL BLACK CAUCUS ASSAILS JAPANESE RACIAL INSENSITIVITY

October 22, 1990

Dear Colleague:

I write at the request of the members of the Congressional Black Caucus to convey our outrage and utter dismay at the continued failure of Japanese officials to comprehend the serious ramifications of the recent statements made by Justice Minister Kajiyama.

We are incensed that modifications to H. Con. Res. 378 have been perceived in high governmental circles in Japan as indicative of a lack of resolve within the United States Congress and a weakening of our position. Under no circumstances is the heat off nor have efforts at damage control been successful. We bring to your attention continued demands throughout Japanese society for the Justice Minister's resignation and ask that you join us in supporting a strengthened resolution when it is brought to the House floor. The Congressional Black Caucus will continue to demand the resignation of Justice Minister Kajiyama and we shall pursue these issues until every vestige of racism is removed.

Sincerely

RONALD V. DELLUMS
Chairman

Source: Russell, *Nihonjin no Kokujinkan*, pp. 228-9.

L

AFRICAN DIPLOMATIC GROUP RESPONSE TO JUSTICE MINISTER KAJIYAMA'S STATEMENT

His Excellency
Mr Taro Nakayama
Minister of Foreign Affairs
Tokyo

Your Excellency:

The African Diplomatic Group in Tokyo has learned with shock and surprise, the declaration made by a leading personality of the Liberal Democratic Party who is also a member of the Japanese Government: Mr Seiroku Kajiyama, Minister of Justice.

'It is like a bad currency driving out a good currency. . . It is like in America when neighbourhoods become mixed because blacks move in, and whites are forced out.' Mr Kajiyama made this declaration to journalists after visiting on September 21st 1990, a district in Tokyo mainly populated by Japanese prostitutes.

Noting the wanton contempt carried by this remark, the African Diplomatic Group objects to it and strongly protests against it.

This declaration of Mr Kajiyama was made at a time when the African Diplomatic Group is actively engaged into the preparations for the visit to Japan, of Mr Nelson Mandela, Vice President of ANC.

This man who has lost twenty seven precious years of his life in the prisons of South Africa, feels better than anyone the evil effects of racism. Receiving Mr Mandela with insulting remarks aimed at his race seems to be highly inappropriate.

This affirmations of Mr Kajiyama, are such that the honorability of any black, be it, diplomat or not is badly undermined. Consequently, for the sake of maintaining the good relations they are trying foster with their neighbourhoods in the framework of mutual respect, it is necessary that further to the apologies of Mr Kajiyama, an adequate action be taken by the Japanese Govenment so that similar anti-black declarations would be avoided in the future.

The African Diplomatic Group requests that steps be taken by the Government so that the proof is made that while these declarations have been made repeatedly made, they do not reflect the real stance of the Japanese Government.

It is to be reminded that although African Diplomats had morally suffered from it, the African Diplomatic Group, showing its confidence to the Government, had refrained in the past from making any reaction, when the same kind of unwelcome remarks were made by former Prime Minister Yasuhiro Nakasone and former Finance Minster Michio Watanabe.

With my best regards I remain sincerely yours,

On behalf of the African Diplomatic Group
KENA BIRABE UISSE
Ambassador of Senegal

Source: Russell, *Nihonjin no Kokujinkan*, pp. 230-1.

M

JAAC ADVERTISEMENT IN *WEEKLY MAIL*, JOHANNESBURG, 15-21 JULY 1988

(*see opposite*)

Source: *Weekly Mail*, 15-21 July 1988, p.18.

JAPAN ANTI-APARTHEID COMMITTEE

Together with a South African anti-apartheid movement, African embassies, churches, trade unions and human rights organisations, we shall all gather on 16th July in Tokyo to celebrate Nelson Mandela's 70th birthday. We offer our support to brave Winnie Mandela and their daughters.

We long for Mandela's freedom and for the freedom of all political prisoners — especially the children. And we abhor the fact that the freedom of all our friends in South Africa has been severely restricted by the extension of the State of Emergency.

But at least our friendship is being strengthened as we persuade more major Japanese supermarkets no longer to stock South African goods.

We request our friends — the people in South Africa — to write to us with your ideas about how we can support you. And please let us have any special information about trade between Japan and South Africa and about the activities of Japanese companies in South Africa.

■ Contact address: Japan Anti-Apartheid Committee, 306, Ebisu 4-5-23, Shibuya-ku, Tokyo, Japan.

This message has been brought to you by the following groups and individuals (surnames placed first):

Southern African Committee of Group of African Heads of Missions in Japan

Japanese Private Sector Trade Union Confederation (JPTUC-RENGO);
General Council of Trade Unions of Japan (SOHYO);
All Japan Prefectural and Municipal Workers' Union (JICHIRO);
Japan Teachers' Union (NIKKYOSO);
Japan Telecommunications Workers' Union (ZENDENTSU);
National Trade Union of Metal and Engineering Workers (ZENKOKU KINZOKU)
National Union of General Workers, Sohyo (ZENKOKU-IPPAN);
National Christian Council in Japan;
International Movement against all forms of Discrimination and Racism (IMADR);
Kyoto Southern Africa Solidarity Committee;
Japan Anti-Apartheid Committee, Sapporo;
Sakamoto Junior High School Anti-Apartheid Committee.

Yasutake Toshiko; Tsukochi Fusako; Kono Masayoshi; Sakamoto Tamiko; Marumoto Akinori; Tomomura Toshitaka; Sudo Kunio; Anmou Chizuru; Tanaka Yuichi; Kawamura Tomomi; Oonita Kuniko; Inoue Masatoshi; Miyazaki Shogo; Hori Shingo; Koide Teruyuki; Satake Akemi; Oneual Karuko; Nakamura Yasuhiro; Sunakawa Masumi; Sunano Yukitoshi; Ryu Hideomi; Harada Masarumi; Kurihara Kiyoko; Nakayama Mineko; Matsunaga 'Koichi; Matsumura Yuichiro; Nishida Naomi; Ootsuka Mitsunobu; Nishimoto Saichiro; Ida Masaaki; Yamaguchi Seigo; Hayashida Keiko; Hayashida Hiroko; Boita Nobuyuki; Gobingindi Kholateu; Mine Yoichi; Sugizaki Haruyuki; Ikeda Reigo; Isoda Tetsuji; Sais Bingo; Hashizume Setsuko; Kuriwa Takumi; Suzuki Masao; Shimizu Tatsuya; Miyamoto Masaoki; Kurunose Keiko; Tanaka Toshikaru; Matsushima Setsuko; Matsushima Karuko; Matsushima Teiko; Watanabe Minoru; Kuroeawa Hiromi; Tsuda Yukihiro; Yamashita Yukio; Tsuda Risako; Ohnishi Motoki; Kenmieshi Toshiya; Hongyo Kiyoko; Tsutsui Masako; Yamashita Noriko; Kawabata Sachiko; Yasui Kazuko; Ohtomo Yoko; Imai Mutsuko; Awazu Noriko; Nogiri Yukiko; Horikawa Tamiko;

Fukushima Makoto; Ohno Kaori; Kanbe Noriko; Honda Tsugiko; Shimizu Miyako; Toshida Reiko; Ellen Ebeta; Takahashi Atsuko; Yamamoto Hideko; Hibari; Nakamura Mamoru; Toshitani Takako; Kamei Masato; Kawaguchi Shigeo; Imoto Toshiaki; Arakawa Tomoko; Okada Shoji; Aratake Kiyoe; Takagi Mariko; Akatsuka Mayako; Higashi Ridaaki; Shitaya Fusomichi; Nishida Keiko; Hamoto Hiroko; Orihara Hiroko; Moriyama Sachiko; Shiota Takaaki; Sawamura Mieko; Shimoda Nobuko; Shimoyama Reiko; Kashima Shiruko; Toshikawa Hiroko; Tsuji Tomoyuki; Okagami Kyoko; Tokota Masashi; Abe Kyoko; Abe Shinko; Suzuki Rideyuki; Suzuki Tomo; Mizeguchi Tohe; Nishibe Akio; Muneta Tazuko; Ito Kyoko; Watanabe Taigen; Mizutsuya Shigeo; Mizutsuya Kazuko; Mizutsuya Chuta; Mizutsuya Shinpei; Kobayashi Makio; Sato Mitsuaki; Kobayakawa Yuiko; Osanai Ai; Igarashi Toshio; Nakajima Kunihiro; Toji Hiroshi; Matsuhara Aki; Igarashi Tomoko; Yutani Ebuji; Kaneya Yutaka; Terai Toui; Terai Takako; Ikeda Susumu; Ikeda Shinji; Imai Maki; Namota Ryoichi; Ebihara Tomoharu; Terasawa Yuki; ......and others.

265

N

REQUESTS AND RECOMMENDATIONS FROM THE JAPANESE ECONOMIC MISSION TO SOUTHERN AFRICA, 9 JULY 1992

The Japanese Economic Mission to Southern Africa requests or recommends

1. Keidanren, as part of its activities
(1) to hold a seminar on political and economic conditions in southern Africa next year in order to help private Japanese companies deepen understanding of the region,
(2) to explore opportunities for export promotion-type investment in southern Africa through the Japan Intenational Development Organization, Ltd. (JAIDO), and
(3) to urge Japanese companies to accept more trainees from southern African countries in supporting the activities of the Japan International Training Cooperation Organization (JITCO),

2. private Japanese companies
(1) to try to position trade with or investment in southern Africa positively in their corporate strategies, and
(2) to expand economic cooperation with southern Africa in such fields as human resource development and nurturing of black businesses from the viewpoint of contributing to economic prosperity in southern Africa and of assisting the blacks of South Africa,

3. the Japanese Government
(1) to help expand private-level economic cooperation through
    (i)   increased ODA including yen credit to the southern African states, excluding South Africa,
    (ii) increased Export-Import Bank finance to South Africa,
    (iii) flexible application of the trade insurance scheme and cut in premiums,
    (iv) conclusion of bilateral investment protection agreements and double taxation prevention treaties,
    (v)   early conclusion of an aviation agreement with South Africa and support for opening a direct flight service,
    (vi) cooperation in accepting investment promotion missions from southern African states,
(2) to supply food to the drought victims and expand aid for food production, and

(3) to help facilitate democratization talks in South Africa and expand economic aid to the black populations,

4. the Four Southern African States visited by the mission

(1) to further promote political democracy and free economy,

(2) to keep step with the IMF and World Bank policies,

(3) to maintain public order,

(4) further to improve investment environment,

(5) to formulate long-term economic plans and select priority industrial sectors in line with policies toward an open economy,

(6) to promote human resource development, including the training of engineers, managers, etc., and

(7) to step up cooperation and joint projects among the southern African states.

Source: Keidanren Keizai Kyoryoku Bu, Gaimusho, Chukinto Afurika Kyoku, Afurika Dai Ni Ka, *Seifu Haken Nanbu Afurika Keizai Mission Hokokusho*, Tokyo, December 1992.

P

TOKYO DECLARATION ON AFRICAN DEVELOPMENT 'TOWARDS THE 21ST CENTURY'

We, the participants of the Tokyo International Conference on African Development (TICAD), consisting of African countries and Africa's development partners, declare with one voice our continued dedication to the development of Africa towards a new era of prosperity. We, therefore, solemnly adopt the present Declaration, in the firm belief that it will serve to strengthen an emerging new partnership for sustainable development of Africa based on self-reliance of African countries and the support of Africa's development partners.

Background

1. Africa's economic and social crises of the 1980s highlighted the development challenges faced by this Continent. To address these challenges, many African countries have embarked on far-reaching political and economic reforms. We, the participants of TICAD, are encouraged by signs in recent years of both positive macro-economic performance and political development resulting from those reforms. In so doing, we nevertheless recognize the continued fragility and vulnerability of Africa's political and economic structures and situations that inhibit the achievement of sustainable development. TICAD intends to give further impetus to these reforms, taking into account the United Nations New Agenda for the Development of Africa in the 1990s (UN-NADAF)
2. With the end of the Cold War, African countries and the international community now have an opportunity to share a broader common understanding of the need for dynamic development cooperation. The development of the Continent has emerged as an imperative in our search for a better future.
3. While special consideration should be given to obstacles confronting Africa, we are determined to strengthen our collective forward-looking efforts for the development of the Continent. This has been the spirit in which we have conducted our deliberations on the issues central to sustainable development in Africa.
4. These issues include the on-going process of simultaneous political and economic reforms, the necessity of increased private sector participation in domestic economic activity, the promotion of regional cooperation and integration, and the detrimental effects of humanitarian emergencies on

Africa's socio-economic development. We recognize that the Asian experience of economic development and the catalytic role of international
cooperation offer hope and provide a challenge for African economic
transformation.

Political and Economic Reforms

5. Convinced of the advent of a new international era, we, the African
participants, reaffirm our commitment to pursue and further strengthen
political and economic reforms, in particular democratization, respect for
human rights, good governance, human and social development and
economic diversification and liberalization. To achieve sustainable, broad-
based economic growth, we, the participants of TICAD, believe that more
open, accountable and participatory political systems are vital, including a
stronger role for civil society. We recognize that political, economic and
social reforms must be initiated and carried out by African countries
themselves; based on their visions, values and individual socio-economic
background. Africa's development partners should therefore support African initiatives in these areas.
6. We, the participants of TICAD, recognize that simultaneous implementation of political and economic reforms, while conductive to development, may often entail painful transition processes. The interaction between political and economic reforms, which over time
should be mutually reinforcing, is a complicated process which
requires support to bring about progress. We, Africa's development
partners, reaffirm our commitment to providing priority support to
countries undertaking effective and efficient political and economic
reforms. We, the participants of TICAD, also reaffirm our commitment to enhancing constructive dialogue to facilitate the reform
processes.
7. We, the African participants, reaffirm our commitment to improving
the quality of governance, in particular, transparency and accountability in
public administration. We recognize that criteria for public expenditure
should aim at enhancing overall socio-economic development and reducing non-productive expenditures. The building of human and institutional
capacities for sustainable development is essential for all of these objectives.
We commit ourselves to creating the enabling environment for training,
retaining and effective utilization of human resources and improving
institutional capacities. We, Africa's development partners, will enhance
our support for African capacity building including improved technical
assistance.
8. We, the participants of TICAD, reaffirm that structural adjustment
programmes should take more actively into consideration the specific
conditions and requirements of individual countries. We reiterate that

political and economic reforms should ultimately lead to the allevia-
tion of poverty and enhanced welfare of the entire population. To
that effect, structural adjustment programmes should contain, more
than in the past, measures to improve the access of the poor in
particular to income earning opportunities and to effective social
services, while seeking to shield them as far as possible from adverse
social consequences. Increased priority should be given to investment
in human capital through nutrition, health and education programmes,
especially to improve the situation of women and children. Addi-
tionally, noting that the overall economic development in Africa has
not kept pace with Africa's rapid population growth, we recognize
the importance of sound population policies and call upon African
Governments and the international community to address this issue
within the socio-economic development process.

Economic Development through Activities of the Private Sector

9. The private sector is vital as an engine for sustainable development. We, the participants of TICAD, agree that though foreign aid
has an impact on development, its role is only supplementary in
magnitude and catalytic in nature. We recognize that a workable and
practical cooperation between government and the private sector is
a key factor for development. A climate of trust between these two
actors should be encouraged and interaction promoted. We realize
that political and economic stability is a prerequisite to commitments
for long-term investments.
10. We, the African participants, are determined to continue policies which foster a greater role for the private sector and which
encourage entrepreneurship. While stepping up deregulation measures,
we will provide and maintain, in cooperation with our development
partners, physical infrastructure and viable administrative, legal and
financial institutions. We consider in general the informal sector as
a source of vitality for African economies which deserves support in
order to further mobilize entrepreneurial capacity, generate employment, and to facilitate the transition into the formal economy.
11. We, the participants of TICAD, are convinced that further improvements in financial systems and practices are needed to stimulate
domestic savings and investment, and to prevent and reverse capital
flight.
12. In support of these efforts, we, Africa's development partners, shall
continue to provide assistance in order to improve the enabling environment which requires economic reforms and privatization, the
building of human and institutional capacities, and the development
of financial intermediation. We recognize the importance of appro-

priate insurance and guarantee schemes to protect private enterprises investing in Africa from political and economic risks.

13. We, the African participants, affirm the central importance of international trade to our future development prospect. We, Africa's development partners, will work to facilitate market access for African products globally and to assist in up-grading and diversifying African exports. We, the participants of TICAD, support the vital role of private associations such as the African Business Round-Table and confirm the usefulness of investment- and trade-promotion initiatives within Africa and between Africa and the rest of the world.

Regional Cooperation and Integration

14. We, the African participants, reaffirm our vision and aspiration for ultimate regional integration and cooperation goals as embodied in the Abuja Treaty establishing the African Economic Community. We, the participants of TICAD, realize that although these goals have been, since the early years of independence, a logical development strategy for African countries, most of which have small national markets, greater efforts must now be made in promoting intra-regional trade and investment.

15. We, the African participants, will ensure that our commitments to regional schemes are fully incorporated in our national development plans, policies and programmes.

16. We, Africa's development partners, welcome and support the renewed commitment to regional cooperation and integration as has been recently demonstrated by African countries. These regional arrangements should continue to be consistent with the multilateral open trading system, and contribute to trade expansion. We will continue to extend our support to African countries' efforts aimed at reducing obstacles to integration through measures such as reduction of trade and investment barriers and policy harmonization, and to viable regional endeavours particularly in the area of infrastructure development and capacity building. We, the participants of TICAD, believe that regional integration should also be pursued by encouraging private sector initiatives, adopting consistent and gradual approaches for broadening exchanges and rationalizing existing schemes.

Emergency Relief and Development

17. We, the participants of TICAD, note with great concern that over the last two decades, and particularly in recent years, that a large number of African countries have suffered and are still suffering from natural and man-made disasters. The international community has responded generously to

these situations since the early crises in the 1970s.

18. These disasters have constrained development in many African countries, destroyed the very basis for development, increased the number of refugees, and diverted human and financial resources that otherwise could have served development purposes.

19. We, the participants of TICAD, realize that man-made disasters are the result of a complex interplay of political, economic and social factors. In this context, lack of democratization and respect for human rights and the rights of minorities are among the root causes of these disasters.

20. We, the participants of TICAD, accept that responsibility for disaster prevention and management rests primarily with Africans themselves. We, the African participants, are therefore determined to devote our efforts to addressing the root causes of these disasters. We also confirm the critical role of regional cooperation as demonstrated in the past. We, the participants of TICAD, underscore the need to establish effective mechanisms for prevention, preparedness and management of man-made and natural disasters in general, and to strengthen food security schemes in particular. We, therefore, welcome the decision of the Organization of African Unity to establish the Mechanism for Conflict Prevention, Management and Resolution and pledge our support to strengthen the effective functioning of this mechanism. We also reaffirm our willingness to assist victims of disasters, and urge the removal of all hindrances to effective distribution of relief supplies.

21. We, African's development partners, having recognized that there is a continuum between emergency relief and development, will ensure that the humanitarian assistance for the affected communities will continue to be provided for resettlement, rehabilitation and reconstruction.

Asian Experience and African Development

22. Over the past 30 years, in contrast to Africa, the countries of East and South-East Asia have achieved high rates of growth in per capita income. We, the participants of TICAD, are mindful that in view of the differing international and internal conditions no one model of development can be simply transferred from one region to another. Nevertheless, we acknowledge some relevance of the Asian experience for African development. The very diversity of successful Asian countries gives hope that lessons can be drawn for African development.

23. We, the participants of TICAD, have noted that as demonstrated by the successful examples of the Asian development experience, the

backdrop of development success ties in the combinations of a strong commitment by the leadership and the people to economic prosperity, appropriate long-term development strategies and functional government administration to pursue these strategies coherently.

24. We have also noted that the policy factors which contributed to the remarkable performance of East and South-East Asia have included (1) the rational application of macro-economic policies and maintenance of political stability, (2) the promotion of agricultural production through technological research and innovations as a solid basis for socio-economic development, (3) long-term investment in education and human resource development as priority of development strategy, (4) market-friendly and export-led policies to advance and adapt modes of production in order to increase opportunities for trade and economic growth, (5) measures to stimulate domestic savings and capital formation by developing financial intermediation and by expansion of banking services at the community level, (6) policy emphasis on the private sector as an engine of growth and development, and (7) early implementation of land reform.

25. We, the participants of TICAD, recognize that development achievements in East and South-East Asia have enhanced opportunities for South—South cooperation with Africa. We welcome the interest shown by some Asian and African countries in promoting this cooperation.

International Cooperation

26. We, the participants of TICAD, have concluded that the current situation in Africa calls for increased solidarity among us to act in full partnership to address this situation. This new partnership should be based on Africa's objective to achieve self-reliance on the one hand and responsive support by Africa's development partners on the other.

27. We, the participants of TICAD, agree that stability and security are prerequisites to sustainable development, and that it is essential to make efficient use of scarce resources and to minimize military and other unproductive expenditures.

28. We, the participants of TICAD, realize that development calls for full participation by the people at all levels, who should be galvanized toward action as agents for progress. In this regard, we acknowledge the dynamic and diversified role fo African women in various sectors of the economy and recommend that special measures be taken to promote their rights and roles in order to enhance gender equity and to remove all legal, social and cultural barriers for advancement of women. Furthermore, we recognize the need to

enhance cooperative efforts wth local NGOs and other institutions of civil society which play constructive roles for African development.
29. We, Africa's development partners, will make all efforts to enhance development assistance to Africa, despite current global economic difficulties. This assistance will be increasingly oriented toward the priorities set by African countries. In making commitments to continued and enhanced cooperation, we will take into account the expectation of our constituencies that resources be spent where they are most efficiently utilized for the greatest development impact.
30. As African countries are at various stages of development, and have different cultural and historical backgrounds, we, Africa's development partners, may take differentiated approaches as we plan and implement our development cooperation, with due regard to aid coordination.
31. We, Africa's development partners, will apply a comprehensive approach covering aid, trade, debt strategy and investments. We, the participants of TICAD, reaffirm that debt and debt service still pose serious difficulties to many African countries. We emphasize the necessity to urgently address the debt issue within the overall context of debt relief and flows of new financial resources for development. We confirm the validity of the international debt strategy and invite the Paris Club to continue reviewing the question of debt relief for the poorest highly-indebted countries, especially with regard to earlier reductions in the stock of debt on a case by case basis. We urge creditor countries to take into account the difficulties that heavily indebted African countries are now facing.
32. We, the participants of TICAD, reiterate the importance of a successful conclusion to the Uruguay Round of GATT negotiations and will make all efforts to remove trade barriers and other trade practices that prevent the expansion of African exports including exports to other African countries. We underscore the importance of primary commodities for many African countries' export earnings and the need for diversification to reduce the volatility of these earnings.
33. We, the participants of TICAD, confirm that United Nations Conference on Environment and Development (UNCED) agreements should be steadfastly implemented with a special emphasis on balanced relationships among agriculture, population and environment policies, particularly drought and desertification.
34. We also recognize that many of the gains made in Africa are threatened by the HIV/AIDS pandemic and related diseases which are already of a disastrous proportion in some countries. There is a need for a much stronger response by Africa and its development partners, for preventing and controlling these diseases including caring facilities as well as measures addressing its socio-economic impacts.

Follow-up

35. We, the participants of TICAD, pledge to take, in our respective spheres of responsibility, measures aimed at advancing the spirit of this Declaration through effective policies and actions. We have entrusted the three co-organizers of TICAD with evaluating and reviewing progress made towards the implementation of this Declaration. Ultimately, we intend to hold a conference of a similar magnitude and membership at the latest before the turn of the century.

By virtue of the deliberations, guidance and consensus of the conference we believe that prospects for significant development of Africa have been greatly enhanced.

Source: Tokyo International Conference on African Development (TICAD), Tokyo, 1993.

Q

POST-TICAD (TOKYO INTERNATIONAL CONFERENCE ON AFRICAN DEVELOPMENT) INITIATIVES BY THE JAPANESE GOVERNMENT

1. Support for Democratization

(1) *Peace Process in Mozambique*
Background:
- Since the comprehensive peace agreement signed on October 1992, peace process in Mozambique made steady progress. General elections were successfully conducted from 27 to 28, October 1994.
Japan's Assistance:
- Dispatch of 53 government officials to ONUMOZ (UN Operation in Mozambique).
- Audio-visual equipment worth 130 million yen (1.3 million US dollars) to help education voters.
- Dispatch of 15 election observers.
- Announcement of assistance measures in December 1994 in order to support the new government for social stability and nation building.

(2) *South Africa*
Background:
- From April 26 to 29, 1994, South Africa held its first non-racial general elections.
- These general elections marked a period to the history of Apartheid, which lasted for more than 340 years.
- Economic development and correction of economic and social imbalance are the major challenges for South Africa's new administration.
Japan's Support for the elections:
- 40 election observers from both public and private sectors in Japan.
- 7 vehicles to UNOMSA (UN Operation in South Africa).
Japan's Aid Package for South Africa (July 1994)
- 1.3 billion for the next two years (ODA: $300 million, Export-Import Bank loan: $500 million, and the credit line for trade insurance and overseas investment insurance: $500 million).

276

(3) *Somalia*
Background:
- Although a reconciliation agreement was reached among conflicting clans on March 1994, Somalia is still in unstable conditions.
- Self efforts by Somali people for conciliation have become all the more necessary since UNOSOM II (UN Operation in Somalia II) was withdrawn in March 1995.
Japan's Assistance:
- 10 million dollars for reconstruction of judicial and police system in Somalia.

(4) *Other Election Support*
Dispatch of election observers since the TICAD.
- Uganda (three observers in March 1994)
- Malawi (three observers in May 1994)
- Ethiopia (two observers in June 1994)
- Namibia (three observers in December 1994)
Financial assistance since the TICAD
- Guinea (300 million yen in December 1993)
- Uganda (170 million yen in March 1994)
- Malawi (110 million yen in May 1994)

(5) *Seminar on Democratization*
Purpose: to encourage the democratization of South Africa.
Participants: 10 keypersons of the South African government who are directly involved in its democratization process.
Date: October 11 to 28, 1994.
Program: Lectures and seminars on issues related to democracy.
Another seminar was held from January 18 to February 3, 1995, with participants from 10 Southern African countries.

2. Support for Economic Reforms

(1) *SPA-3 (Special Program of Assistance for Low-Income Debt-Distressed Countries in sub-Saharan Africa)*
Background:
- SPA is a program initiated by the World Bank to support structural adjustment efforts by low-income heavily indebted countries in sub-Saharan Africa.
Japan's Contribution:
- 1.1 billion dollars (800 million dollar loan under co-financing with IDA and 300 million dollar non-project type grant aid.)

- This assistance will be disbursed to Sub-Sahara African countries during three years of the SPA-3 Program (1994–96).

Recipients of Japan's Non-Project Type Grant Aid since the TICAD:

- Ghana (2 billion yen, January 1994)
- Senegal (2.5 billion yen, January 1994)
- Rwanda (300 million yen, January 1994)
- Mali (500 million yen, February 1994)
- Zambia (3.5 billion yen, March 1994)
- Niger (1 billion yen, March 1994)
- Benin (500 million yen, March 1994)
- Central Africa (300 million yen, March 1994)
- Côte d'Ivoire (2 billion yen, November 1994)
- Guinea (1 billion yen, November 1994)

(2) *ESAF-II (Enhanced Structural Adjustment Facility-II)*
Background:
- ESAF was a loan program for low income IMF member countries undertaking economic reform programs to strengthen their balance of payments and improve their growth prospects.
- ESAF, though planned to end by November 1993, was extended until February 1994.
- ESAF-II was established on February 23, 1994.
Japan's Contribution to ESAF-II:
- SDR 2.15 billion (320 billion yen: 43% of the total SDR 5 billion) for loan contributions.
- SDR 250 million (37 billion yen: 16.7% of the total SDR 1.5 billion) to subsidize the rate of interest.
- Japan's share is the largest in the donor countries.
- SDR 2.15 billion committed by the Export-Import Bank of Japan.

3. Support for Human Resources Development

(1) *African Youth Invitation Program*
Background:
- On the occasion of the TICAD, GOJ announced a program to invite 100 young people from African countries every year.
Purposes:
-Training young Africans who will be core of nation building efforts in future.

\- Deepening mutual understandings between Japan and
African countries.

FY 1993:
\- 50 women involved in education stayed in Japan from
February 20 to March 21, 1994.

FY 1994:
\- 100 government officials and teachers stayed in Japan
from September 29 to October 25, 1994.

(2) *Symposium on Education in Africa* (November 18, 1994, Tokyo)
\- Examined past and present efforts on human resources
development in Africa.
\- Discussed self-efforts by African countries and appropriate
measures to support them by donors.

(3) *Asia-Africa Forum*
Background:
\- `Asian Experiences and African Development' was one of
the major topics in the TICAD.
\- The Tokyo Declaration adopted in the TICAD urged to
promote South-South cooperation.
Sponsors: Japan, Indonesia, UN, UNDP, GCA
Host Country: Indonesia
Date: December 12 to 17, 1994
Purposes:
\- Sharing development experiences between Asian and
African countries.
\- Promoting development cooperation between Asian and
African countries.
Themes:
\- Theme 1: Promoting Sustainable Development in Africa:
Sharing Experience
Theme 2-1: Human Resource and Institutional Development
\- Theme 2-2: Enhancing Productivity in the Agricultural
Sector
\- Theme 2-3: Financing Development
\- Theme 3: Modalities of Development Cooperation Between
Asia and Africa
'Conclusions and Recommendations' were adopted with
consensus in the Forum.

(4) *JICA-CIDA Co-sponsored Seminar*
Sponsors: JICA (Japan International Cooperation Agency),CIDA
(Canadian International Development Agency)
Host country: Japan
Date: March 22 and 23, 1995

Participants: NGOs from 11 countries in Southern Africa.
Purposes:
- Exchanging the results of researches on effective support to the South African region by JICA and CIDA.
- Exchanging views on appropriate measures to support the region, including joint support by Japan and Canada.

4. Environment Related Assistance

(1) *Underground Water Development and Water Supply Project*
Japan's Basic Stance:
- Japan recognizes that supply of sufficient and good quality water is exteremely important for people in Africa.
Concrete Measures:
- Japan has conducted researches on underground water development in Sub-Sahara African countries.
- Japan intends to double its current amount of grant aid for underground water development and water supply projects to 250-300 million dollars. This assistance will be disbursed between FY 1993 and FY 1995.
Recipients of this Assistance since the TICAD
(Grant Aid Projects)
Zimbabwe (777 million yen, January 1994)
Mauritania (903 million yen, January 1994)
Namibia (713 million yen, January 1994)
Mali (921 million yen, January 1994)
Senegal (598 million yen, February 1994)
Zambia (749 million yen, April 1994)
Central Africa (813 million yen, April 1994)
(Development Researches)
Ethiopia
Tanzania
Madagascar

(2) *Other Environment-Related Assistance*
(Development Researches)
Kenya (Waste Control Project of Nairobi City)

5. Enhancing Policy Consultations and Exchanges of High Ranking Officials

(1) Parliamentary Vice Minister for Foreign Affairs Mr Azuma visited southern African countries from January 5 to 18, 1994.
(2) State Minister for Defense Mr Tamazawa visited Kenya,

Zaire, Rwanda, Mozambique and South Africa from September
22 to 25, 1994.

(3) Parliamentary Vice Minister for Foreign Affairs Mr Yanagisawa
visited Zaire and Kenya from October 14 to 18, 1994.

(4) Parliamentary Vice Minister for Defense Mr Watase visited
Zaire, Kenya, Mozambique and South Africa from November
22 to 26, 1994.

(5) President of Uganda Mr Museveni visited Japan (September
1994).

(6) President of Benin Mr Soglo visited Japan (February 1994).

(7) Foreign Minister of Burkina Faso Mr Sanon visited Japan (March
1994).

(8) Foreign Minister of South Africa Mr Nzo visited Japan
(January 1995).

(9) Interior Minister of Congo Mr Mberi visited Japan (October
1994).

(10) Finance Minister of Kenya Mr Mudavadi visited Japan (August 1994).

(11) Comprehensive Research Mission on Economic Cooperation - Kenya in February 1994.

(12) Policy consultation Missions
    - Mozambique and Southern African Development Com-
      munity (April 1994)
    - Senegal (November 1993)
    - Tanzania (April 1994)
    - Namibia, Lesotho, and Swaziland (April 1994)
    - South Africa (June 1994)
    - Ethiopia and Eritrea (September 1994)
    - Kenya and Uganda (February 1995)

(13) Loan Project Finding Mission (March 1995: South Africa,
    Zimbabwe, Namibia, Swaziland)

(14) Japan-Africa Seminar on Tourism (March 29, 1994, Tokyo)
    - Participants included officials of the tourism bureaus of
      Tanzania, Mauritius, Kenya, South Africa, and Zimbabawe.
    - Reports and discussions on attraction, tasks and prospect
      of African tourism.

March 7, 1995

R

THE EXECUTIONS IN NIGERIA, NOVEMBER 1995

Statement by the Press Secretary/Director-General
for Press and Public Relations of the Foreign Ministry
on the Execution of the Human Rights
Activists and Others in Nigeria

1. Japan considers it inhumane and undemocratic conduct that the Government of Nigeria passed a death sentence, through doubtful legal procedures, on nine human rights activists, including Mr Ken Saro-Wiwa, confirmed the sentence hurriedly, and carried out the executions on November 10, despite repeated appeals made by the international community. It expresses its regret on such a situation.

2. Japan hopes again on this occasion that guaranteed human rights and democratization will be speedily established in Nigeria.

Foreign Press Centre, Japan (MEA-1)
November 13, 1995

SELECT BIBLIOGRAPHY

SOURCES IN ENGLISH

Andrews, E.M., *A History of Australian Foreign Policy*. 2nd edn. Melbourne: Longman Cheshire, 1988.

Asahi News Service.

Association for Overseas Technical Scholarship, *Guide to AOTS* 1991.

Barber, James and John Barratt, *South Africa's Foreign Policy — The Search for Status and Security 1945—1988*. Cambridge University Press, 1990.

Bryant, William E., *Japanese Private Economic Diplomacy — An Analysis of Business-Government Linkages*. New York: Praeger, 1975.

Constantino, Renato, *The Second Invasion — Japan in the Philippines*. Manila, 1979.

Crocker, Chester A., *South Africa's Defense Posture: Coping with Vulnerability*. Washington, DC: Center for Strategic and International Studies, Georgetown University, 1981.

Economic Planning Agency, *Economic Survey of Japan 1989-1990*. 1990.

El-Khawas, Mohamed, and Barry Cohen (eds), *The Kissinger Study of Southern Africa,* National Security Study Memorandum 39, Westport, CT: Lawrence Hill, 1976.

First, Ruth, Jonathan Steele and Christabel Gurney, *The South African Connection. Western Investment in Apartheid*. London: Temple Smith, 1972.

Foreign Press Center, Japan, *Japan's Mass Media*, 1990.

Fukui Haruhiko. 'Bureaucratic Power in Japan' in Peter Drysdale and Hironobu Kitaoji (eds), *Japan and Australian*. Canberra: Australia National University Press, 1981.

Grundy, Kenneth W., *The Militarization of South African Politics*. Bloomington: Indiana University Press 1986.

Houghton, D. Hobart, *The South African Economy*, Cape Town: Oxford University Press 1967.

Johnson, Chalmers, 'The Re-employment of Retired Government Bureaucrats in Japanese Big Business', *Asian Survey*, 14, 11 (November 1974).

——, *MITI and the Japanese Miracle: The Growth of Industrial Policy, 1929-1975*, Tokyo: Charles E. Tuttle, 1986.

Johnson, Phyllis, and David Martin (eds), *Destructive Engagement: Southern Africa At War*, Harare: Zimbabwe Publishing House, 1986.

Kaplan, David, and Alec Dubro, *YAKUZA: The Explosive Account of Japan's Criminal Underworld*, London: Futura, 1988.

Keizai Joho Center, Japan Institute for Social and Economic Affairs, *Japan 1990: An International Comparison*, 1989, 1991.

Kitazawa Yoko, *From Tokyo to Johannesburg — A Study of Japan's Growing Economic Links with the Republic of South Africa*. New York: Interfaith Center for Corporate Responsibility, 1975.

Kitazawa Yoko, 'Japan's Namibian Connection: Illegal Japanese Uranium Deals Violate UN Resolution', *AMPO Japan-Asia Quarterly Review*, 12, 3 (1980).

Kotani Toru, 'Rising Sun over Africa?', *Africa Report*, November-December 1985.

Kuper, Hilda, 'Strangers in Plural Societies: Asians in South Africa and Uganda', in *Pluralism in Africa*, Berkeley: University of California Press, 1969.

Kusuhara Akira. 'The Attitude of the Japanese Government on the Recognition of Guinea Bissau', *Africa: News and Reports*, 17 (February 1974).

Lanning, Greg, with M. Mueller, *Africa Undermined: Mining Companies and the Underdevelopment of Africa*, London: Penguin, 1979.

League of Nations, *Official Journal*, November 1926.

Legum, Colin, and John Drysdale (eds), *Africa Contemporary Record Annual Survey and Documents, 1968-69*. Vol. 1. London: Africa Research, 1969.

Leonard, Richard, 'BASF's Strategic Role in South Africa', report prepared for the Oil, Chemical and Atomic Workers' International Union, October 1986.

Morikawa, Jun, 'The Anatomy of Japan's South Africa Policy', *Journal of Modern African Studies*, 22, 1 (March 1984).

——, 'The Myth and Reality of Japan's Relations with Colonial Africa 1885—1960,' *Journal of African Studies* (UCLA), 12, 1 (Spring 1985).

Morrison, Godfrey, 'Japan's Year in Africa', *Africa Contemporary Record Annual Survey and Documents, 1972-73*. London, 1973.

Moss, Joanna, and John Ravenhill, *Emerging Japanese Economic Influence in Africa — Implications for the United States*. Berkeley: Institute of International Studies, 1985.

New Horizon English Course 3. Tokyo: Shoseki, 1977.

Nakamura Takefusa, *The Postwar Japanese Economy—Its Development and Structure* (Jacqueline Kaminski), University of Tokyo Press, 1981.

Onimode, Bade, *The IMF, the World Bank and the African Debt*, 2 vols, London: Zed Books, 1989.

Organisation of the Government of Japan, Institute of Administrative Management, 1992.

Power, Paul F., 'Gandhi in South Africa', *Journal of Modern African Studies*, 7, 3, (1969).

Rix, Alan, *Japan's Economic Aid Policy-Making and Politics*, London: Croom Helm, 1980.

Roth, Martin, 'Japan and Africa', *Africa Economic Digest* 3, 49 (December 1982).

South Africa, Official Yearbook of the Republic of South Africa. Pretoria.

South African Institute of Race Relations, *Survey of Race Relations in South Africa*, Johannesburg (published annually).

Tokyo International Conference on African Development, October 1993.

US Department of State, Papers relating to the Foreign Relations of the United States, *The Paris Peace Conference 1919*, Vol. 3 House Document No. 874, Washington, DC: 1943.

Van Wolferen, Karel, *The Enigma of Japanese Power*, London: Macmillan, 1989.

Yanaga Chitoshi, *Big Business in Japanese Politics*, New Haven, CT: Yale University Press, 1968.

Young, Alexander, *The Sogo Shosha — Japan's Multinational Trading Companies*, Charles E. Tuttle, 1979.

UNITED NATIONS PUBLICATIONS

Council for Namibia, Report on the Activities of Foreign Economic Interests, April 1987.

Friedman, Julian R., 'Basic Facts on the Republic of South Africa and the Policy of Apartheid', *Notes and Documents 20/74*. UN Unit on Apartheid, Dept of Political and Security Affairs (August 1974).

Institute for Namibia, *Namibia: Perspectives for National Reconstruction and Development*, Lusaka, 1986.

Khalifa, Ahmed M., *Assistance to Racist Regimes in Southern Africa: Impact on the Enjoyment of Human Rights*, New York, September 1979.

UN Information Center, *Aparutoheito — Nihon ni Totte no Imi* (The Meaning of Apartheid for Japan), May 1983.

Unit on Apartheid, Dept of Political and Security Councl Affairs, *Notes and Documents,* January 1972.

SOURCES IN JAPANESE*

Africa Society of Japan, *Gyomu Hokoku*.

APIC. *Kokusai Kyoroku Tokubetsu Joho*. 11 (January 1985).

* The place of publication is Tokyo unless otherwise stated.

Asahi Shimbunsha (ed.), *Enjo Tojokoku Nippon*, 1985.

Chiyoura Masamichi, 'Nihon Kigyo no Tai Afurika Toshi Katsudo', *Dokkyo Daigaku Keizai Gaku Kenkyu*. 23 (October 1979).

Darwish, Khalil T., 'Keizai Enjo to Nihon no Afurika Seisaku', *Kokusai Mondai*. May 1987.

Engineering Consulting Firms Assn., Japan, *Keizai Kyoryoku Enjo ni Okeru Kigyo to Kokka no Arikata*, 1990.

Fukuda Kiku, *Kokuren to NGO*, Sanseido, 1988.

Fukunaga Eiji (ed.), *Nihon Kigyo no Taiken-teki Afurika*, Yuhikaku, Publishing, 1986.

Fujita Midori, 'Edo Jidai ni Okeru Nihonjin no Afurika Kan', *Nihon Chuto Gakkai Nenpo*, 2 (1987).

Gaimusho. Kyoikusha, 1979.

Gakko Yoran 1987.

Hatano Yoshio. 'Afurika to Nihon — Enyo Kyoroyoku no Mondaiten', *Gekkan Afurika*. 23, 5 (May 1983).

Hayashi Koji (ed.), *Minami Afurika — Aparutoheito Taisei no Yukue*, Institute of Developing Economies, 1987.

Heiwa Keizai Keikaku Kaigi Okusen Hakusho Iinkai (ed.) *Kokumin no Dokusen Hakusho*. 6, Ochanomizu Shobo, 1982.

—, *Kokumin no Dokusen Hakusho*. 8 Ochanomizu Shobo, 1984.

Hiroaki Idaka, *Minami Afurika no Uchigawa*, Sinul, 1985.

Hosoya Chihiro and Watanuki Joji (eds.), *Taigai Seisaku Kettei Katei no Nichibei Hikaku*, University of Tokyo Press, 1977.

Ikei Maseru, 'Pari Heiwa Kaigi to Jinshu Sabetsu Mondai' in Nihon Kokusai Seiji Gakka: (ed.). *Kokusai Seiji Nihon Gaiko Shi Kenkyu— Dai Ichiji Sekkai Taisen*. Yuhikaku, 1963.

Iriye Akira, *Nihon no Gaiko — Meiji Ishin Kara Genzai made*, Chuo Koronsha, 1966.

—, *Shin Nihon no Gaiko*, Ghuo Koronsha, 1991.

Ishikawa, Yozo, *Watashiro no Afurika Monogataro*, Banseisha, 1984.

Ishikawajima-Harima Heavy Industries (IHI). *IHI Jukogyo Shashi-Gijutsu Seihin Hen*. 1992.

Itagaki Yuzo. 'Paresuchina Mondai to Nihon', in Kojima Shinji et al. (eds) *Ima Ajia o Kangaeru*. Sanseido, 1985.

Ito, Masataka. *Nan-A Kyowakoku no Uchimaku*. Chuo Koronsha, 1971.

JAAC, Minami Afurika Mondai Kenkyujo. *Nanbu Afurika Nenpo*. Published annually.

Japan International Volunteer Center. *JVC Annual Report 1992*. 1993.

Japan Overseas Development Corporation. JODC.

Kaifu Toshiki. Sekai: no Naka no Nippon. LDP Kenshu Shiryo No. 12. 1983.

Katsumata, Makoto, *Gendai Afurika Nyuomon*, Iwanami Shoten, 1991.

Kawabata, Masahisa, *Afurika Kiki no Kozo*, Sekai Shishosha, 1987.

Kawata, Tadashi, *Sho Nihon Shugi no Susume*, Daiyamondo Sha, 1972.

Kita Yuji. 'Kaihatsu Kyoryoku ni Tazusawaru Nihon no NGO no Genjo to Kadai'. *Tokai Daigaku Seijigaku Kenkyu*. 5 (1989).

Kitagawa Katsuhiko. 'Senzenki Nihon no Ryoji Hokokuni Mirareru Afurika Keizai Jijo Chosa no Kenkyu', *Kenkyu Ronshu Dai 50 60*. *Kansai Gaikokugo Daigaku*. 50 (July 1989).

—, 'Nihon Minami Afurika Kankei Shi', in Kawabata Masahisa and Sasaki Ken (eds) *Nanbu Afurika: Post Aparutoheito to Nihon*. Keiso Shobo, 1992.

Kitamura Hiroshi, Murata Ryohei and Okazaki Hisahiko, *Nichibei Kankei o Totsumeru*, Sekai no Ugoki Sha, 1983.

Kitazawa Yoko. *Watashi no Naka no Afurika, Han Aparutoheito no Tabi*. Shakai Shisosha, 1979.

—, *Kuroi Afurika*. Seibun Bukkusu, 1981.

—, 'Namibia Uranno Mitsuyo o Yameyo', *Sekai Kara*. (August 1983).

Kono Fumihiko, 'Afurika Shokoku o Rekiho Shite', *Kokusai Jihyo* 65 (September 1970).

Kurata Masahiko, *Rinjin toshite no Ajia Nihon*, Kirisuto kyodan, 1993.

Kusuhara Akira, *Jiritsu to Kyozon*. Aki Shobo, 1976.

—, *Afurika No Ue to Apartoheito*. Aki Shobo, 1984.

—, 'Nihon sei — Zaikai to Aparotoheito Taisei no Fukai Yochaku Nan A to Nihon o Tsunagu Kage no Fixer', *Nanbu Afurika Nempo*, JAAC, 1987.

—, 'Apartoheito to Aijia—Nihon, Taiwan, Kankoku wa Do Kawatsute iru Ka', *Sekai*. (January 1988).

Labor Federation of Government Related Organizations, *Amakudari Hakusho*. 1986.

Liberal Democratic Party, Policy Affairs Research Council, Special Committee on External Economic Co-operation (ed.), *Waga To no Keizai Kyoroku Seisaku ni Tsuite*, 1982.

Maeda Tetsuo. 'Nihon no Gunsan Fukugotai', *Gunshuku Mondai Shiryo*, 131 (October 1991).

Maema Takanori. *Jetto Enjin ni Toritsukareta Otoko*. Kodansha, 1992.

Mainichi Shimbun. *Kokusai Enjo Bijinesu — ODA wa do Tsukawarete Iru Ka?* Aki Shobo, 1990.

Matsumoto Jinichi, *Aparutoheito no Hakujin Tachi*. Suzusawa Shoten, 1989.

Matsuura Koichiro, *Enjo Gaiko no Saizansen de Kangaeta Koto*, APIC, 1990.

Miyamoto, Masaoki, *Bungaku kara Mita Afurika*, Daisan Shokan, 1989.

Mine Yoichi, 'Kusanone Kaihatsu Kyoryoku no Tenbo to Nihon no NGO no Kadai' in Kawabata Masahisa and Sato Makoto (eds.), *Shinsei Minami Afurika to Nihon*, Keiso Shobo, 1994.

—, 'Kokujin no Chi o Suu Genpatsu', *Buraku Kaiho*. (June 1989).

Miyake Wasuke. 'Nihon e no Tadashii Riikai o Susuneru Tame ni', *Kokumin Gaiko*. 96 (March 1984).

Monose Hiroshi, *Kokusai Kankei Gaku*, University of Tokyo Press, 1993.

Morikawa Jun, *Minami Afurika to Nihon*, Dobunkan, 1988.

Morita Akio and Ishihara Shintaro, *No to Ieru Nihon*. Kobunsha, 1989.

Murai Toshinori, *Ebi to Nihonjin*, Iwanami Shoten, 1988.

Mwangi, G.C. 'Afurika Wa Tokunai', *Ritsumei Review*, 88 (November 1988).

Nakamura Takafusa and Ito Takashi (eds), *Kindai Nihon Kenkyu Nymon*, University of Tokyo Press, 1977.

Nan-A Nipponjin-Kai, *Nan—A Nipponjinkai Kaisoku* (revised edn), 1979.

Nihon Gomu Seihin Yushutsu Kumiai, *Minami Afurika Rempo*, Chosa Kenkyu 8 (1937).

Nihon Keizai Shimbunsha. *Jiminto Seichokai*, Nihon Keizai Shimbunsha.

Nanbu Afurika Nenpo, Nanbu Afurika Mondai Kenkujo, 1985, p. 35.

Nishikawa, Jun, *Dai San Sekai to Heiwa*, Waseda University Press, 1987.

Nishino Terutaro, 'Meiji ki ni Okero Nihonjin no Afurika Kan', (Japanese Views of Africa in the Early Meiji Period), *Toyo Bunka Kenkyusho Kiyo* 33 (March 1964).

—, Ryo Taisen Kan ni okeru Afurika Keizai Chosa (1, 2)', *Afurika Kenkyu* 1:1 (December 1963; 1:2 (March 1964).

Noma Kanjiro, *Sabetsu to Hangyaku no Genten: Aparutoheito no Kuni*, Rironsha, 1969.

Okakura Takashi and Kitagawa Katsuhiko (a), *Nihon Afurika Koryushi* Dobunkan, 1993.

Ogawa Tadahiro, No Pincha 1972.

Oyama Ujiro. 'Nan-A yushoku jin haiseki to Nihonjin Nyokoku Mondai', *Gaiko jiho*. 56-4, 623 (1930).

Pacific-Asia Resource Center, *Aparutoheito e no Nihon no Katan*. October 1975.

—, Indonesia Study Group. *Indonesia no Nikkei Takokuseki Kigyo*. 1980.

Puranto Yushitsu Nenkan. Jukagaku Kogyo Tsushinsu, 1980.

Russell, John G., *Nihonjin no Kokujinkan — Mondai wa Chibikuro Sanbo Dake Dewanai*, Shin Hyoron, 1991.

Saito Takashi. *Senkanki Kokusai seiji Shi*. 1979.

Sakamoto, Yoshikazu (ed.), *Boryoku to Heiwa*, Asahi Shimbunsha, 1983.

Sasaki Ken, *Nihongata Takokuseki Kigyo*, Yuhi Kaku, 1986.

Sato Shintaro. 'Inin Tochi to Nihon' in *Nihon Gaiko Shi*, vol. 14,

Kajima Kenkyusho, 1972.

Seinen Kaigai Kyorokutai OB Kai, *Seinen Kaigaikyoryokutai Heiwa Butai to Tojokoku Enjo*, Kyoikusha, 1978.

Sekai (ed.), *Gunjika Sareru Nihon*, Iwanami Shoten, 1984.

—, *Gunji Taikoku Nihon*, Iwanami Shoten, 1987.

Shadan Hojin Afurika Kyokai (ed.), *Gyomu Itokoku 90-91*, 1991.

Shinoda Yutaka, *Kumon Suru Afurika*. Iwanami Shoten, 1985.

Shiraishi Kenji, *Zanjibaru no Joshigun*. Tokisha, 1971.

Shugiin Jimukyoku, *Shugin Iinkaigi Roku 13, Yosan 2, Bunkakai, 1984-85* (25 March 1985).

Suzuki Yuji, *Tonan Asia no Kiki no Kozo*, Keiso Shobo, 1982.

Tada Minoru, *Nichibei Ampo Joyaku*, Mikasa Shobo, 1982.

Takahashi Hiroshi, *Shocho Tenno*, Iwanami Shoten, 1987.

Takayanagi Akio, 'Japan's Aid Performance' in ICVA and EURO-STEP. *The Reality of Aid — An Independent Review of International Aid*, London: Actionaid, 1993.

Ueno Takao, 'Nihon to no — Kankei Mada Toi Afurika', *Shinko Afurika*, 92, 2 (December 1962).

Unno Yoshio. 'Dainiji Itaria-Ethiopia Senso to Nihon', *Niigata Dait Hosei Riron*, 16,2 (January 1984).

Wagatsuma Hiroshi and Yoneyama Toshinao, *Henken no Kozo — Nihonjin no Jinshukan*, Kyokai, 1967.

Warner, Peggy and Seno Sadao. *Tokusho Senkotei Senshi*, Jiji Tsushinsha, 1985.

Watanabe Akio *et al.*, *Koza Kokusai Seiji — Nihon no Gaiko*, vol. 4. University of Tokyo Press, 1989.

Yabe Takeshi. *Nihon Kigyo Wa Sabetsu Suru*. Daiyamondosha, 1991.

Yagi, Nagato, 'Minami Afurika no okeru Hai nichi no Shinso', *Gaiko Jijo*, 56-1, 620 (1930).

Yajima Mitsuhiro. *Hai Kochira Ishihara Shintaro Jimusho Desu*. Nihon Bungeisha, 1991.

Yamamoto Tsuyoshi, *Nihon no Keizai Enjo*, Shakai Shisosha, 1988.

Yoshida Kenji, *Nan-A Rempo Shi*, Funzanbo, 1944.

Yoshida Masao, 'Nihon no Afurika Enjo' in Hayashi Koji (ed.), *Afurika Enjo to Chiiki Jiritsu*, Institute of Developing Economies, 1988.

Yoshida Nagao, 'Afurika Shokoku no Doko to Nihon', *Kokusai Mondai*, 54. (September 1964).

Yoshihara Koichiro, *Nihon no Heiki Sangyo*. Shakai Shisosha, 1988.

Yoshimura Akira, *Shinkai no Shisha*, Bungei Shunjusha, 1990.

Yumoto Hiroyuki, 'Kokusai Kyoryoku to Volunteers' in *Gendai no Esupur* (April 1994).

290   *Select Bibliography*

JAPANESE GOVERNMENT PUBLICATIONS

Pre-Second World War Government publications
'Afurika Keizai Jijo Tembo', Japanese Ministry of Foreign Affairs, Commerce Bureau, Second Section. 1932.
Gaimusho. *1919 Pari Kowakaigi Keika ni Kan Suru Chosho*. 3 (15 March 1919).
Noshomusho, Shokokyoku. 'Minami Afurika Boeki Jijo', *Shoko Isan*. 48 (1917).

Ministry of Foreign Affairs publications
Diplomatic Blue Book — *Japan's Diplomatic Activities*. Published annually in English.
Economic Co-operation Bureau (ed.). *Wagakuni no Seifu Kaihatsu Enjo*. APIC. Published annually.
Gaiko Seisho — *Waga Gaiko no Kinkyo*. Published annually. Replaced *Waga Gaiko no Kinkyo* from 1987.
Gaimu Hodokan (ed.). *Keizai Kyoroku Q A*, Sekai no Ugokisha, 1989.
Gaimusho Kohyoshu. A collection of official materials released to the general public by the Foreign Minsitry at intervals.
Japan and Africa South of the Sahara — *Expanding and Deepening Relations*, 1979.
Japan and Sub-Saharan Africa — *Hand in Hand across the Globe*, September 1993.
Middle Eastern and African Affairs Bureau, *Afurika Binran* — *Sahara Inan no Kuniguni*, 1980, 1986, 1990, 1993.
Middle Eastern and African Affairs Bureau, Economic Co-operation Bureau, *Keizai Kyoroku Kunibetsu Shiryo. Senegal, Niger, Mali*, 1980.
—, *Keizai Kyoryoku Kunibetsu Shiryo. Tanzani*. 1980.
—, *Keizai Kyoryoku Kunibetsu Shiryo, Zaire, Djibouti*. 1982.
Middle Eastern and African Affairs Bureau, Second Africa Division, *Malawi Kyowakoku Gaiyo*. 1980.
Nihon Gaiko Hyakunen Shoshi. Yamada Shoin, 1959.
Public Information Bureau. *Nihon to Afurika - Sahara Inan no Kuniguni*. 1982.
—, *Sekai no Ugoki*. (November 1982).
—, *Afurika* — *Sahara no Muko no Sekai*. 1984.
The Developing Countries and Japan. 1979.
Waga Gaiko no Kinkyo, published annually, replaced in 1987 by *Gaiko Seisho* — *Waga gaiko no Kinkyo*.
Warera no Sekai 219 (May 1984).
Zai Puretoria Nihonkoku Soryojikan (ed.), *Minami Afurika Kyowakoku, Lesoto Ookoku, Botsuwana Kyowakoku, Suwajirando Ookoku, Nansei Afurika. Nihon Kokusai Mondai Kenkyusho*, 1973.

Zaikai-related publications

Akaruku Nobiyuku Afurika, report on the official government Africa Economic Mission, June 1972 (not for public sale).

CCA, *Afurika Iinkai Seisaku Iinkai Meibo*, internal document, 11 December 1985.

CCA (ed.), *Seifu Haken Afurika Keizai Mission Hokokusho*, December 1988.

Hirake Yuku Burakku Afurika, 1970 (not for public sale).

JETRO, *Kaigai Shijo Hakusho-Toshi*, published annually.

Africa Business Guide, 1979.

The Role of Trading Companies in International Commerce, revised edn, 1982.

Keidanren, *Keidanren Ho Afurika Shisetsudan Hokoku*, December 1980.

Keidanren, International Economic Affairs Department, *Keidanren Nan A Keizai Shakai Shisatsu Mission Hokokusho*, June 1991.

Keidanren 1981 (in English).

Keidanren Review on Japanese Economy. 67 (1981).

Keidanren Economic Co-operation Department, *Keidanren Afurika Iinkai ni Tsuite Shiryo Ichiran*, internal document, 17 June 1986.

Newsletters

JETRO.

Keidanren Shuho.

Nippon Club of South Africa, *Springbok*, monthly.

Nan-A Nipponjin kai (ed.). *Springbok — Minami Afurika Nihonjinkai Gekkan Shimbun Hyaku Go Kinen Soshuhen*. 1981.

Springbok Club Kaiho.

MITI publications

Tsusho Hakusho: Kakuron; *Tsusho Hakusho Soron*, published annually.

MITI Sangyo Kozo Shingikai (ed.), *Keizai Anzen Hosho no Kakuritsu o Mezashite*, 16 August 1982.

UNPUBLISHED SOURCES

Ampiah, Kweku, 'British Commercial Policies Against Japanese Expansionism in East and West Africa', paper presented to the African Studies Association Conference, Atlanta, GA, November 1989.

Adedeji Adebayo, 'Africa and Orthodox Structural Adjustment Programmes: Perception, Policy and Politics', paper presented at symposium on 'Challenges of African Development: Structural Adjustment Policies and Implementations', UN University, Tokyo, October 1993.

Bradshaw, Richard A., 'Japan and European Colonialism in Africa 1800-1937', unpublished. Ph.D. diss., University of Ohio, Athens, 1992.

Furukawa Tetsushi, 'Japanese-Ethiopian Relations in the 1920-30s: The Rise and Fall of "Sentimental" Relations', paper presented at the 34th Annual Meeting of the African Studies Association, St. Louis, MO, November 1991.

Ito Michio, speech at 'Strategic Issues for the 1990s: Challenges to PVOs in an Interdependent World', Interactive Annual Meeting. Danvers, MA, May 1989.

Morikawa Jun, 'Japan's African Diplomacy and the Hirohito Factor: A Case Study of Japan's Post-WWII Court Diplomacy', paper presented at US African Studies Association Annual Meeting, Seattle, November 1992.

Spring, Martin C., 'Japan, China and the Politics and Economics of the Far East', address, University of the Witwaterstand, Johannesburg, 25 October 1967.

Woods, Geoffrey Roger, 'Taiwanese Investment in the Homelands of South Africa', unpubl. Ph.D. diss., Ohio University, Athens, 1991.

NEWSPAPERS AND JOURNALS

AERA (Tokyo)
Africa-Japan (Tokyo)
Asahi Evening News (Tokyo)
Asahi Journal (Tokyo)
Asahi Shimbun (Tokyo)
Bungei Shunju (Tokyo)
Daily Yomiuri (Tokyo)
Far Eastern Economic Review (Hong Kong)
Financial Mail (Johannesburg)
Gekkan Afurika (Africa Monthly) (Tokyo)
International Herald Tribune (Paris)
Israel Monthly (Japan-Israel Friendship Association, Tokyo)
Japan Times
Japan Times Weekly (Tokyo)
Japan Quarterly (Tokyo)
Journal of Japanese Trade and Industry (Tokyo)
Keidanren Review (Tokyo)
Mainichi Daily News (Tokyo)
Mainichi Shimbun (Tokyo)
Newsweek (New York)
New York Times (New York)

Nihon Keizai Shimbun
PHP Intersect (Tokyo)
Yomiuri Shimbun (Tokyo)
Rand Daily Mail (Johannesburg)
Sekai (Tokyo)
South Africa Digest (Pretoria)
Sunday Star (Johannesburg)
Sunday Times (Johannesburg)
Weekly Mail (Johannesburg)

INDEX